Second Edition

Rugby
STEPS TO SUCCESS

Tony Biscombe
Peter Drewett

HUMAN KINETICS

Contents

Foreword

Rugby has been a big part of my life. In my playing career, which lasted 15 years, I was lucky enough to play top-class rugby against the best nations in the world. I earned 32 caps for Scotland (9 as captain) and 8 for the British and Irish Lions during the 1974 and 1977 tours. These experiences continued to fuel my enthusiasm for the game and drove me on to coach the British and Irish Lions, Scotland, Northampton and the London Wasps.

When coaching my players, I try to share my passion and appreciation of rugby. It is not simply about a group of talented individuals; rather, it is a wonderfully strategic game that requires exceptional discipline, competitiveness, skill, spatial awareness, tactical understanding and strategic execution by a cohesive unit of players aiming to outperform the opposition.

For a team to work as the ultimate unit, it must contain individuals who are able to execute the fundamental techniques of rugby to a high standard. Each player must be able to use these techniques within the mini-units that make up the team. Finally, every player must be familiar with key team tactics and strategies for defence and attack.

Anybody coming to *Rugby: Steps to Success* will find everything needed to gain an excellent understanding of how to execute and develop the fundamental skills of rugby and to then apply them in game situations.

The characteristic of *Rugby: Steps to Success* that most impressed me was how it introduces each technique and tactical concept. The practices and drills that follow offer players the opportunity to fully exploit their potential with achievable targets, which can then lead to more challenging ones. The scoring system is a great way for players to check their progress and gauge whether they are ready to further develop their rugby skills by moving to the next step.

I have known the authors for many years, and I have always been impressed by their level of rugby knowledge and their ability to communicate their ideas to the players they are coaching. *Rugby: Steps to Success* superbly reflects their coaching philosophy and delivery. Any player will benefit from the coaching advice of Tony Biscombe and Peter Drewett.

I look forward to seeing the stars of tomorrow playing great rugby using many of the techniques and tactics described in *Rugby: Steps to Success*.

Ian McGeechan, OBE

Climbing the Steps to Rugby Success

What attracts us to the game of Rugby Union? Why do we have lifelong club members who go from playing to coaching or administration, and all for no reward? What excites people about the game at all levels? The answer is simple—rugby is a game for all shapes, sizes, abilities, ambitions, fitness levels and backgrounds. It is a game for life. The strict disciplines the game engenders and those specific rules that are required to play it successfully have a carry-over into everyday life. The Laws of the game and those of society are there to be obeyed, administered and respected. Without such discipline, there would be no game.

There have been three great occasions in the history of Rugby Football. The first was the split in 1895 when players who needed time off work to play rugby on a Saturday were at a financial disadvantage because it was a 'no work, no pay' society. The outcome was the game of Rugby League, which was originally played semiprofessionally to compensate those who needed to take time off to play. Both sports have lived, sometimes uneasily, side by side in a few countries around the world since then. League has enjoyed a resurgence of interest following the creation of the Super League in England in 1996. Although initially solely played in the north of England, it is currently nurturing professional teams in Wales, London and France. The dominant force in the game is still Australia, but New Zealand and Great Britain are close seconds, and New Zealand's defeat of Australia in the Rugby League World Cup of 2008 is indicative of the narrowing of the gap in performance.

The second great occasion for Rugby Union was the formation of a Rugby World Cup (RWC) in 1987. This competition has grown into a truly worldwide occasion. The effect of the global TV coverage of the RWC should not be underestimated; 86 nations from five continents contested the 2007 RWC, and 191 qualification games prior to the finals in France took just over two and a half years to complete.

The colour, pace and excitement of rugby during these tournaments attracts many new players in clubs, schools and institutions and is an ideal tool for those involved in the promotion of and recruitment to the game. Currently, more than three million people worldwide play Rugby Union, and more are doing so every day.

Globally, the television audience and attendances at games are also increasing. The Rugby World Cup is now the world's third-largest sporting event, and the 2007 tournament in France broke all previous attendance and broadcast records with just over 2.25 million spectators and a cumulative worldwide television audience of 4.2 billion. In England alone, 17 million viewers watched the final, which was the most-watched event in the whole of 2007. The growing global appeal of the game is indicated by enhanced coverage of the Rugby World Cup in the existing markets of Spain, Portugal, Italy and the Asian continent as well as the emerging countries of India, Russia, Canada and the United States.

Finally, the game went professional in Europe in 1995, thus ending accusations of shamateurism aimed at many clubs and players. The eventual formation of the Premiership League in England, the Leagues for the Scottish and Welsh district teams and an enhanced Super 14 and Tri Nations moved the game rapidly forward with access to a global television audience of billions.

This surge in attendance and awareness is also reflected in other major cup and league competitions around the world; the Heineken Cup in Europe, the Currie Cup in South Africa, the Top 14 in France and the Air New Zealand Cup are just some examples of major competitions that enjoy bumper crowds and global television audiences. These, in turn, have generated massive increases in the numbers of players, coaches and referees. It is this huge foundation group of players that the professional game is built upon. Comparatively few players can earn a living playing the game, but at both the amateur and professional levels, the learning, teaching and coaching processes remain the same; only the intensity, attitude, fitness level and skill level of the players differ.

The modern game demands players who are not only bigger, faster and stronger than those of the past, but also play with vision and understanding and have excellent decision-making skills. These skills, which test both players and coaches alike, have often been neglected in the early learning environment of previous generations of players. *Rugby: Steps to Success* reflects current practices in preparing rugby players for the demands of the modern game, a game for life.

The staircase to success in Rugby Union branches off in many directions, leading to a variety of achievement levels. It is up to you to choose the direction in which you wish to continue to climb.

On the first few steps up the staircase, you will learn the skills important for all players and how to practise them so that you improve. You should familiarise yourself with these first sections before you begin to specialise and climb any staircase of technical skills.

Follow the same sequence on each step of the staircase. Start by practising with no pressure and gradually increase until your technique, performed against full opposition, becomes a skill. At the same time you must be aware of and follow the information given to you on essential protective and safety equipment and how to prepare your body to play a contact sport.

Here is the learning sequence for success:

1. Read the explanations of what the step covers, why the step is important and how to execute the step's focus, which might be a basic skill, concept, tactic or combination of all three.

2. Check your technique against the photographs, which show exactly how to position your body to execute each basic skill successfully. There are three general parts to each skill description: preparation (getting into the right position), execution (performing the skill that is the focus of the step) and follow-through (finishing correctly).

3. Look over the common errors that might occur and recommendations for how to correct them.

4. Read the instructions, the Success Check items for each drill, and the drill scoring. Practise accordingly and record your scores and note any improvement. Drills are arranged in an easy-to-difficult progression. This sequence of drills is designed specifically to help you achieve continued success. Pace yourself by adjusting the drills to either increase or decrease their difficulty, depending on your skill level.

5. At the end of each step, have a qualified observer, such as your teacher, coach or training partner, evaluate your basic skill technique. This provides a qualitative, subjective evaluation. By focusing on correct technique, you can enhance your performance. Ask your observer to suggest improvements.

When learning a new skill, check the numbered photographs at the beginning of each step. You might ask a teammate or coach to observe your early attempts at the skill and check your positioning, foot position or body movement, for example, against the photographs and explanations of the technique. Some of the advanced technical skills require a very experienced observer to help you achieve success in these early stages. As you progress up the staircase, you will find that achieving success becomes easier because you have been constantly refining your skills.

As with most staircases, the rugby steps to success are climbed many times in a lifetime. The time you spend revisiting the first few steps will never be wasted in Rugby Union. Even the most successful international rugby players climb the steps of basic skills three or four times each week. These skills are the foundation on which all else is built, and you must climb the staircase regularly to improve.

By planning your journey up the staircase carefully, you will learn new skills that you can take to the game of Rugby Union. The most successful teams are often those that involve all 15 players in a journey up a staircase of success, which ultimately leads to open, exciting, skilful and successful Rugby Union.

Acknowledgments

Many people have influenced the content of this book. Our roles in the Performance Department of the Rugby Football Union (RFU), especially between 1997 and 2008, allowed us to work side by side with some of the best coaches, medical staff and administrators in the world. In particular, the influence on us of Sir Clive Woodward, Andy Robinson and Phil Larder from 1997 to 2005 honed our specific knowledge of the game and taught us how to achieve success through elite practice and performance.

It would have been impossible to give complete attention to any writing without full support from our families, and in this regard we are indebted to Larraine and Jenny and our respective children for their continued interest in this project.

The Sport of Rugby Union

In the early years of rugby in the 19th century, the game was played primarily by the great public schools, who played it for recreation. Many schools had their own sets of rules, but in nearly every case the ball was both handled and kicked, and only the method of scoring changed from place to place.

By 1845 the game was already very well established, and the first set of 'Laws of Football' was produced at Rugby School in England. In those days, the game was far less complicated than it is today. It had many differences from the modern game but also some similarities, and a number of modern terms already existed—for example, *offside, knock on, try* and *touch.*

In those days, no player was allowed to play until he had been awarded his cap, and this is thought to have been the precedent for the awarding of caps at the international level. The length of the match varied, but a match could have been played for a number of afternoons over an extended period of time, with over 50 players on unequal sides. Eventually, numbers were reduced to 20 a side, and ultimately to 15.

The rugby game played now was developed largely from the actions of a schoolboy named William Webb Ellis. He died in 1872, the year after the formation of the Rugby Football Union (RFU) and the adoption of the Laws of Rugby School. He is buried in Menton, France, and local rugby enthusiasts care for his grave. Little could Webb Ellis have known that his actions would ultimately create an organised worldwide game enjoyed by thousands of players and watched by huge numbers of spectators at live matches and on television. A stone has been erected at Rugby School to honour Webb Ellis; it reads: 'This stone commemorates the exploit of William Webb Ellis, who, with a fine disregard for the rules of football as played in his time, first took the ball in his arms and ran with it, thus originating the distinctive feature of the rugby game. AD 1823'. The Rugby World Cup (RWC) trophy has been named the Webb Ellis Trophy in recognition of the schoolboy from Rugby School.

The original rugby ball was a pig's bladder inside a leather casing. When inflated, the bladder formed an oval shape. Nowadays, ball manufacturers using modern materials reproduce this shape, and many improvements to the technology of the ball have been introduced. The tiny pimples on the surface for better handling, the aerodynamics of the shape for better flight and the ball casing material for better weatherproofing are just some of the advances that science has brought to the game.

Rugby has become a way of life for many people throughout the world. The Rugby World Cup competition every four years has given rugby an even greater international identity, and the number of people playing the game continues to increase. The International Rugby Board (IRB) has appointed a number of officials to oversee the funding and development of rugby in emerging nations. According to the International Rugby Board, men and women of all ages play Rugby Union in over 100 countries spanning six continents, and most of those have an IRB rugby team.

Most unions offer women's rugby, encouraging women and girls to take up the game. Indeed, women's rugby is one of the fastest growing sports in many countries. Every four years, usually in the year preceding the Rugby World Cup, 12 teams contest the Women's Rugby World Cup.

As the world governing body, the IRB controls the Rugby World Cup, the Women's Rugby World Cup, Rugby World Cup Sevens, IRB Sevens World Series, Junior World Championship, Junior World Trophy, Nations Cup and the Pacific Nations Cup. It lobbies the member countries for votes to decide where all of these events shall be held, except in the case of the Sevens World Series. For that competition, the IRB contracts with several national unions to hold individual events.

The success of the Rugby World Cup has attracted new audiences to Rugby Union around the world. The number of spectators and participants has multiplied annually. Many innovations have been adopted to make the game accessible to all. For example, spectators at Rugby Union matches are entertained not only by the play on the field but by prematch and half-time events as well.

LAWS OF RUGBY UNION

The Laws of the game of rugby football state: 'The objective of the game is that two teams of fifteen players each, observing fair play according to the Laws and a sporting spirit, should by carrying, passing, kicking and grounding the ball score as many points as possible, the team scoring the greater number of points to be the winner of the match'. Although this describes the game in a nutshell, there are many Laws, and it will take time for you to learn all of them. The Laws of rugby are amended and developed by the International Rugby Board (IRB). The IRB constantly reviews and, when necessary, changes Laws to help players enjoy a safer and more exciting game. These Laws are to be found in the Book of Laws produced by the International Rugby Board and the rugby unions of each playing member of the international community.

Before a game starts, the team captains meet to toss a coin, and the visiting captain calls. The winner of the toss can choose to kick off or to receive kick-off and defend a particular goal line for the first half. Captains often choose a particular end because of weather conditions; for example, the wind or bright sun might give a team an advantage. The game starts with a kick-off (drop kick) at the centre of the half-way line, and the ball must reach the opponents' 10-metre line.

The players on the side that gains possession must attempt to work the ball down to their opponents' goal line by running, passing the ball laterally or backwards or kicking the ball. If one team manages to carry the ball over the goal line and place it down, a try, currently worth 5 points, is scored. That team then has the opportunity to kick a goal, currently worth 2 points, in line from where the try was scored. The game restarts back at the half-way line with a drop kick.

If the ball goes over the sidelines (touch lines), the game is restarted with a line-out (refer to steps 8 and 9). For handling infringements, a scrum (refer to step 8) brings the ball into play, and for offences against an opponent, the referee may award either a free kick or a penalty. Points may be scored from penalties by kicking the ball over the crossbar of the posts, currently worth 3 points. Anyone in position on the field may also drop kick the ball over the crossbar to score 3 points. Usually, the game is played outdoors on grass, although it may be played on clay or sand if it is not dangerous. Figure 1 shows the markings and dimensions of the playing area for the 15-per-side adult game.

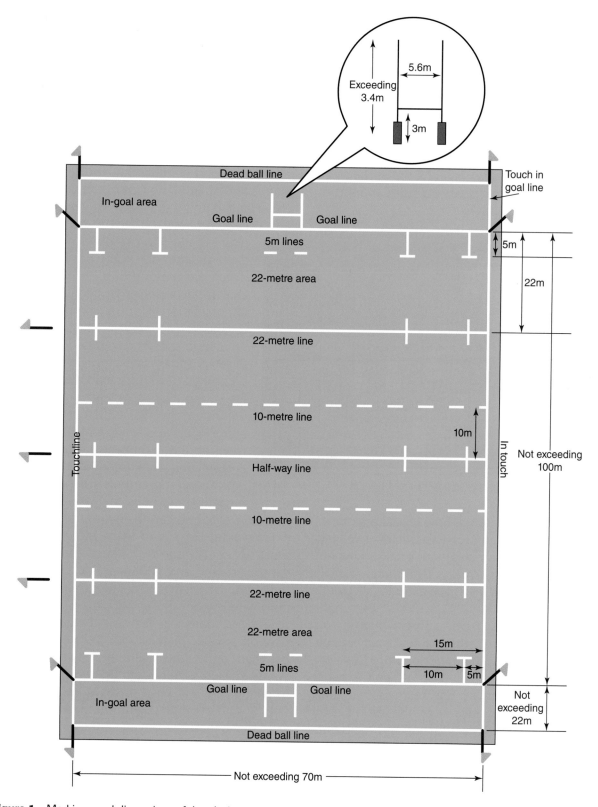

Figure 1 Markings and dimensions of the playing area for the 15-per-side game.

Once the ball is in play, each player has a part to play. Everyone should be a good ball handler, tackler and runner. Although most positions have a specialist role when the game is restarted, the best teams contain individuals who have excellent overall skills.

The IRB recommends names and shirt numbers for each player position. Different countries, however, have a variety of names for playing positions (see glossary). Figure 2 shows the numbers and playing positions of a team at a scrum situation.

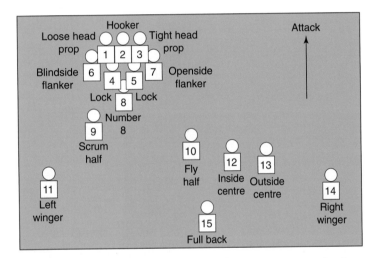

Figure 2   Numbers and playing positions of a team at a scrum situation.

At senior and international levels, a game of rugby lasts for 80 minutes. It is split into two playing periods of 40 minutes, with a half-time interval of 5 or, more normally, 10 minutes. During the interval players rest, have a drink, talk tactics and change ends.

One of the best rugby Laws, which makes rugby different from other games, is advantage, which can override a number of other Laws but not those that cover foul play. 'When the result of an infringement by one team is that their opponents gain an advantage, the referee shall not whistle immediately for the infringement.' The purpose of the advantage Law is to make play more continuous as a result of fewer stoppages for transgressions. You should encourage your team to 'play to the whistle' despite infringements by your opponents, because this often results in your team scoring. The advantage can be tactical (a good attacking opportunity) or territorial (a gain in ground).

When rugby first began to be played, captains acted as referees and made decisions during the game. There has always been a great emphasis on fair play in rugby. Perhaps that is why you can travel the world and always receive a fine welcome in any rugby club. You will make a lot of lifelong friends playing rugby. You are now part of the ever-increasing rugby family.

Rugby is a game for the whole family. It is played by people of both sexes and all ages, sizes, shapes and abilities. Tournaments and matches are arranged for 6-year-olds to veterans, with certain Law variations to help everyone play safely. For example, noncontact, two-handed touch rugby or tag rugby (in which the removal of a ribbon signals a tackle) can be played by people of all ages for recreational fun or competitively in organised leagues.

It has long been recognised that a complicated game such as rugby needed to be broken down into manageable pieces for young players to learn. Many major unions have worked hard to introduce the game safely and at a level and pace commensurate with the physical development and abilities of children. Coach and player education programmes around the world recognise the need for young players to learn in a safe and caring environment.

For young players to learn effectively, they must experience the techniques and skills in a controlled way and with repetition. For many, this is impossible in a 15-a-side game that can be dominated by one or two big players. It has been recognised that those learning the game should play on smaller pitches with reduced numbers per team and with players their own age. Also, young players should learn the techniques prior to taking the field for a game, even a modified one. Some unions regulate the ratio of practice sessions to matches played to encourage regular training and preparation time.

Young players should learn the game in a progressive way and at a pace that suits their age group. Tackling and contact are removed from the game for the youngest players, who are encouraged to run and play with the ball without fear of injury. The size of the pitch and number of players per team are modified. Most countries now have

Substitutes and Replacements

Due to the contact nature of rugby, it is common for at least one player to leave the field as a precaution after receiving a soft tissue injury or after becoming very tired by his exertions during the match. The Laws allow a team to make up to seven substitutions in the game. However, once substituted a player may not return to the field unless he is a front-row player who is taking the place of an injured front-row player.

Players who are bleeding may be replaced temporarily and may return once any blood has been removed, any contaminated playing kit exchanged and the blood flow stopped.

The IRB nominates certain shirt numbers for specific positions and by Law each team must have suitably trained players on the substitutes' bench to play at prop and hooker. Certain age groups also recommend eight substitutes or replacements so that a full front row can be included on the team bench. Substitute regulations vary depending on the age group and also the country in which the game is being played. For example, in 2009 the RFU required a full replacement front row on the substitutes' bench, increasing the number of substitutes from seven to eight.

Apart from the front-row players, the composition of the rest of the substitutes' bench is at the discretion of the team coach. The coach decides on a four-to-three or five-to-two split between forwards and backs. Normally the positions and shirt numbers are as follows: 16 hooker, 17 prop, 18 prop or lock, 19 lock or back row, 20 back row, 21 scrum half, and 22 back (normally a fly half, centre or full back or a utility player). In a four-to-three split, the scrum half wears 20 and the two extra backs wear 21 and 22.

If sufficient front-row players are lost to injury during the game, so that the team cannot field a fully fit and trained front row, then noncontested scrums come into play. This means anyone can go into the front row. No pushing is allowed, and the team putting the ball into the scrum must win it.

Substitutions can be made for a variety of other reasons. For example, a team might have different kinds of players on the bench compared to those on the field, players who might be able to change the nature of the attack or defence to the team's advantage. This is known as an *impact bench*. Often these players are used when the team needs to change its tactics.

rules and regulations governing the game from under 6 or under 7 upwards.

For example, in New Zealand players at the under 7 level play on a full-sized pitch between the 10-metre line and the goal line. Each team has seven players. Two-handed touch is used instead of tackling. Games are played to a maximum of 20 minutes in one direction and then, after halftime, 20 minutes in the other direction. In England, young players are introduced to the game through tag rugby. Pitches are about 60 by 30 metres plus 5 metres for in-goal areas. Games are played for 10 minutes each way. In most countries, young players use smaller rugby balls.

As players progress through the levels, the game modifications change. For example, young players in England, New Zealand and Australia move from noncontact rugby through mini rugby to midi rugby by their early teens. Contact is controlled and gradually introduced to players and then into games. The number of players on a team is gradually increased, playing areas increase in size and the intensity develops as tournaments and matches become more important.

Rugby-playing countries have developed their own kinds of noncontact rugby. In England, they play tag rugby. Players in New Zealand have Rippa rugby; in Australia, they play Walla rugby. These games are suitable for introducing the game and also for girls and boys to play with and against each other. In early developmental stages, boys and girls play together. However, once tackling and contact become the norm, mixed-sex rugby is discouraged beyond a certain age, which varies from country to country.

Experience has taught the major rugby-playing nations that going straight from a 7-, 8-, or 9-a-side game to a 15-a-side game requires a steep learning curve. Although young players may have experienced simple scrums and reduced-number line-outs, this is scant preparation for the 15-a-side game. Consequently, many countries transition players to a 12-a-side game in which more realistic units can be introduced. The strategies and tactics used in a 15-a-side game are more easily learned with 12 players on each side and full contact. This midway point—midi rugby—is an ideal transitional vehicle in the lives of young players. Players taught this way often find it easier to step into 15-a-side rugby because they understand how to play the game effectively and have already learned its integral parts.

A Game for All

The rise of sport for players with disabilities has had a profound worldwide effect on the major sports. The magnificent spectacle of the Para Olympics has made people realise that sports shouldn't exclude anyone.

In recent years, the rise in popularity of wheelchair rugby has been phenomenal, providing opportunities for those in wheelchairs to take part in a contact sport. Most rugby unions take some responsibility for wheelchair rugby, and addresses and contact information can be found at the union's Web site.

Likewise, players with learning disabilities also can take part in modified games and can be encouraged to play to at least tag rugby level. With careful coaching, some players may be able to play the full game. For players with severe learning disabilities that affect their spatial awareness, exercising and practising with groups of similar abilities and using different-shaped and -coloured balls can provide a great deal of enjoyment. A sympathetic and stimulating environment such as modified rugby can be a wonderful tool for those who care for these individuals and are looking for new learning situations and experiences.

PLAY PREPARATION AND RECOVERY

You may try to avoid contact as much as possible while you are playing, but nevertheless, at times you will collide with members of the opposition, members of your own team or the ground. Under no circumstances, therefore, should you take the field physically underprepared for these collisions.

Players in their late teenage years might consider using a weight-training schedule to gradually build up the strength and power required to play against bigger and older players. However, players in their early teenage years should exercise using only their own body weight as resistance.

Initially, an overall strengthening programme will be quite sufficient. However, different playing positions make different strength demands. For example, the strength required of a prop is not the same as that of a winger. To build up further strength in your body, you should take part in body-weight circuits. On occasions you may wish to use a partner's body weight as the resistance, but your own is often quite sufficient. You might also consider wrestling for the ball against a partner or working with a heavy tackle bag that you repeatedly drive into, lift and throw to the ground. All these actions are very similar to those you perform in the game. As you move towards the senior game, you will begin to develop weight-training protocols for specific areas of the body. These will help protect you from injury and help you cope with the forces generated using the various techniques of the game. Your coach or fitness coach will help formulate these for you as you go through the age group teams in your club.

Because of the rough-and-tumble nature of the game, on occasion each of the joints of your body will come under extreme force and will be moved through a wide range of movement even if you do not want it to be. Therefore, you should follow a daily flexibility regime that stretches muscles and extends the range of your joints. However, before any exercise, including rugby practice, you must follow a warm-up and stretching routine to help prepare your body for exercise.

Warm-Up

Warm-up is exactly what the name suggests: increasing the body's temperature to prepare it for vigorous exercise. Wear warm clothing at first. Begin by jogging for a short period of time to raise your body temperature, go into your routine of stretches and finish with a second jog to raise your temperature even further. If you feel any tightness in your muscles, stretch again after the second jog. Remember your sequence of stretches and follow it during warm-up.

Remember these golden rules when stretching.

It is better to stretch after you have raised the temperature of your body. This is not achieved by sitting next to a radiator, but by exercising gently for a short period of time. Under no circumstances should you bounce up and down in your stretch position. This kind of ballistic stretching can cause injury.

Apply all stretches firmly and gradually to the point of full stretch. Hold the fully stretched position for approximately 10 to 20 seconds. After 10 seconds you should find that the stretched muscles begin to automatically relax and any tension begins to disappear. At this point, begin to increase the range of movement in the area you are stretching. As you release the stretch, it often helps to shake the muscle gently to release any residual tension.

You should always follow a systematic stretching routine. Work from one end of the body to the other in sequence: for example, from ankles up to neck, or down the other way, or from the large abdominal muscles outwards.

Cool-Down

After playing or training, it is a good idea to go through a number of cool-down stretches to help avoid stiffness in the muscles. Follow the same sequence as in your warm-up stretches.

It is widely accepted that sitting in a bath of ice and water after heavy exercise will speed up your recovery time. Your coach may require you to do this initially, but it should become part of your recovery regime. Drinking water or a sport drink immediately after the match to rehydrate and replenish your carbohydrate stocks is also strongly recommended. A banana is an ideal after-match or after-training snack, as bananas are packed with easily accessible carbohydrates. All of this will help you recover more quickly from strenuous activity.

Check to see if you have any lumps, bumps or grazes. Small lumps and bumps can be reduced easily by the application of ice, wrapped in a thin towel or inside a plastic bag. Clean any grazes or small cuts with an antiseptic, and apply dressings as required. Any severe swelling or pain in and around joints should be checked by the medical team. Make sure that any superficial injuries are seen and dealt with before you go into your ice bath.

Always bathe or shower after your recovery routines, not only for cleanliness, but also to invigorate you and help you relax and recover.

To avoid stiffness the next day and to fully recover from a game, perform some gentle exercise such as swimming or riding a bicycle. Refrain from any vigorous exercise for 24 to 48 hours during this recovery period. This will allow your body to recover, heal and adapt to the demands of the game at the level you are playing. Because tiredness can delay recovery when you are young, regularly monitor how you feel, the quality of your sleep and the length of time it takes for your stiffness to subside and your normal energy levels to return. If by two days following the game you are fine, then carry on with your regular regime. If not, then seek advice from your coach and explain how you feel so that someone else can monitor the amount of energy you are expending and the type, amount and quality of nutrition you are taking in.

PERSONAL EQUIPMENT

Many situations in training and playing can cause slight injury. Therefore, you should take the precaution of wearing the safety equipment allowed in Laws of the Game (see figure 3). You might consider wearing light shin guards to protect your legs from scrapes.

Wear only legal and well-fitting
shoulder pads and head guards.

Make sure your gum shield
is fitted by a dentist.

Keep your tetanus
protection up to date.

Warm up thoroughly
before each game.

Wear only legal studs and
have them inspected regularly.

Wear shin guards for
added protection.

Use a simple ankle strap
for extra support.

Figure 3 Safety equipment allowed in Laws of the Game.

Every player on your team should be fitted with a gum shield. This helps to protect your teeth and jaw and often prevents concussion if there is a clash of heads. Gum shields that are not fitted by a dentist should be avoided, as they are easily dislodged in contact.

Simple protective horseshoe strapping on your ankles prevents injury. No other strapping should be considered. If you need heavy strapping on any part of the body, you should not play. Playing with an injury risks making that injury much worse. An extra week away from the game is a far better option.

The Laws allow you to wear shoulder protection, and there are many protective vests on the market. Your personal preference will help you decide which one to wear. Choose one that gives the protection you need but also allows you to move freely so that you can play. It is common practice for many players to train and play wearing a head guard. Once again, your choice can be based on personal preference, but make sure

that the guard is legal in rugby Law, that it doesn't impair your field of vision and that it allows you to move freely.

Make sure that you are up-to-date with a preventive course of tetanus injections to help prevent serious infections in even the slightest of wounds.

As you prepare for a match, you should adopt good habits. Always pack your kitbag the night before you are due to play. Make sure everything in your kit is clean, and check laces for fraying. Pack your tie-ups for your socks and your protective equipment. Check for any excessive wear on your studs and, if necessary, replace them with new ones. Make sure you understand all meeting arrangements for the pregame period so that you can arrive promptly. Lateness is a very bad habit and cuts down on the time you have to prepare mentally and physically for vigorous exercise.

Remember to clean your boots after the match if the ground was muddy, so they can dry out. This will help your feet to breathe during the next match.

RESOURCES

The Web addresses noted here are starting points for anyone wishing to take up the game as a player or coach, research rugby history or view recent changes to the Laws.

The major rugby-playing nations have their own home Web addresses. Using a good search engine, you should be able to find information about local rugby in your community, women's and girls' rugby, wheelchair rugby and rugby for those with disabilities no matter where you live.

International Rugby Board (IRB): www.irb.com

England: www.rfu.com

Ireland: www.irishrugby.ie

Scotland: www.scottishrugby.org

Wales: www.wru.co.uk

France: www.ffr.fr

Italy: www.federugby.it

New Zealand: www.nzrugby.com

Australia: www.rugby.com.au

South Africa: www.sarugby.net

Argentina: www.uar.com.ar

Canada: www.rugbycanada.ca

United States: www.usarugby.org

To learn about some of the major international tournaments, go to www.rbs6nations.com or www.trinationsweb.com. For general research about rugby, http://sportsv1.com/rubgy-union/links features numerous links to a variety of rugby Web sites.

Key to Diagrams

○	Attacker	→	Direction of run
●	Defender	▪	Pitch marker
- - - →	Direction of pass or kick	◑ ✦	Ruck or maul
◗	Scrum	▢	Player with tackle shield
◖◗	Player in scrum	◢	Areas to attack or defend
▬	Line-out	⬗	Direction of push in scrum
●	Rugby ball	Ⓒ	Coach
		▮	Tackle bag

Ball Handling

All rugby players need good ball-handling skills to cope with the various demands of the attacking game: running with the ball, passing and catching at actual game speed, also called pace. Great teams have players who take the fullest advantage of attacking situations. To do this, they must keep possession of the ball. To truly succeed as a rugby player, you must be skilful in executing the basic techniques required to successfully complete the drills in this chapter.

The position you may play in the future is of little importance in comparison to your overall range of skills. The drills and practices shown in this step will help you develop basic running and handling techniques that you can use in the changing situations in a game.

During play the ball may arrive at various angles, heights, speeds and forces. A ball that arrives at a difficult angle may affect your ability to keep possession. For example, a pass that arrives from behind at knee height may be difficult to catch and bring to your waist while you are running at pace and attempting to maintain balance. Becoming used to the unique shape of the ball early on will give you confidence and help you cope with the unexpected when it happens—such as a ball bouncing wildly off the turf or a pass thrown too high or away from you.

The modern approach to the game is to try to retain possession for as long as possible. Often, this must be done while in contact with the opposition. The running and handling drills in this first step will increase your chances of retaining possession in close-contact situations.

When practising these techniques, use a ball that is the right size for your hands so that it is easy to grip.

HANDLING THE BALL

It is to your advantage to carry the ball in two hands whenever possible. This allows you to either pass or keep the ball safe when a tackler grabs hold of you. It also allows you to make a more accurate pass in open play. When holding or moving the ball around your body, grab it firmly in your hands with your fingers spread across the seams (figure 1.1). The seams will help you maintain your grip. Use your fingers to control the ball, not your palms.

Figure 1.1 Use your fingers to control the ball.

1

You might carry the ball along your forearm or tuck it into your ribs near your elbow when running in the open field. This is a safe carrying style that allows you to run more quickly because you can pump your arms with the running motion. However, by tucking the ball, you may have difficulty readjusting it to pass. When you run with the ball tucked in, you must always be prepared to quickly readjust your grip to pass with two hands on the ball.

To get used to the eccentric shape and movement of an oval ball, try the following introductory practices before you go to the drills towards the end of this step.

Stand with your feet shoulder-width apart, with the ball held in two hands at waist level out in front, fingers spread across the seams of the ball. Move the ball clockwise around your body, changing hands from front to back, and then counterclockwise.

Always try to move your body in rhythm with the pace and movement of the ball and reach for the ball as far around your body as you can. Always keep the ball off the palms of your hands; use your fingers to control and grip the ball. Also, try to keep the ball away from your clothing so that you do not drop it.

Once you have mastered this simple practice, you can increase the difficulty by moving the ball faster around your body. Increase the number of repetitions to 20 each way, or use a larger ball. Occasionally work against a stopwatch to see how many repetitions you can do in a certain time.

Introduce movement to the practice by passing the ball around your body and walking with your eyes closed. Make sure that you have plenty of space around you with no obstacles. Slowly walk forward, gradually increasing your speed. Move the ball around your body as fast as you can over a 22-metre distance.

If you find this practice very difficult, use a small, round ball, or slow down the movement around your body.

Once you find this kind of handling easy, move on to something far more difficult. This is a great exercise that combines movement with ball-handling practice. Stand with your feet slightly farther apart than your shoulders and your legs bent slightly at the knees. Bend over at the waist, keeping your back as flat as possible. Hold the ball in both hands, with your fingers spread across the seams and away from your body in front. Move the ball around and behind one leg with one hand (figure 1.2a), passing it between your legs around to the other hand in front (figure 1.2b). Allow your body to sway with the movement of the ball. Repeat the movement around the back of the other leg and between your knees, finishing with the ball in front. The ball will have followed a figure 8.

As soon as you can perform this with ease, make it more difficult. Move the ball as quickly as possible at the edge of control. Try closing your eyes while moving the ball. Reverse the direction of the movement so that you move the ball behind your knee first. Remember to concentrate on moving the ball smoothly, spreading your fingers across the seams and allowing your body to sway sideways with the movement of the ball.

a

b

Figure 1.2 Figure 8 juggling drill: *(a)* the ball goes around one leg; *(b)* the ball comes between the legs to the other hand.

Once you have mastered the figure 8 juggle, try it as you walk. At first you may try to lift your leg a bit to allow the ball to pass under, but this will make it extremely difficult to walk, especially because you may need to take much longer strides to make space for the ball to pass under your legs. Try to walk normally at first and at a good pace while moving the ball around your knees. Then try to increase your speed to a jog.

This is a very difficult exercise to do well, but if you are able, try to move the ball as quickly as possible at the edge of control, or reverse the direction of the movement so that you move the ball behind your knee first.

As with the previous exercise, simple adjustments will help you improve very quickly. Concentrate on moving the ball smoothly. Spread your fingers across the seams. Allow your body to sway sideways with the movement of the ball. Walk or jog normally with slightly longer strides.

During play, the ball sometimes arrives at an odd height or speed, making readjusting it awkward and difficult. Here is a practice that simulates the ball arriving low and slightly behind you as you move forward.

Stand with your feet shoulder-width apart. Hold the ball in both hands away from your body, arms straight. Lift one leg, bending it at the knee (figure 1.3a). Pass the ball from one hand to the other around the outside of your thigh and under the lifted leg (figure 1.3b). Lower that leg, raise your other leg and repeat by passing the ball around the other leg. Aim for developing a smooth movement involving both legs.

If you managed to do this drill successfully, add a movement forward to make it more difficult. Walk forward, lifting your knee high as you pass the ball under each leg in turn. Reverse direction, moving the ball from inside and under your leg to the outside. Close your eyes and work by touch. Make sure that you spread your fingers wide across the seams of the ball.

All of the practices so far required that you keep the ball in your hands so that you become accustomed to the feel and behaviour of the ball as it moves. Before you move on to passing and receiving the ball, practise releasing and regathering the ball so that you begin to experience

a

b

Figure 1.3 Under your leg drill: *(a)* lift one leg; *(b)* pass the ball under the lifted leg.

how a ball flies and how it behaves once it is not being held.

This practice focuses on simple catching movements. More detailed information on passing and receiving comes later in this step. Stand with your feet apart and hold the ball in both hands out in front of your body. Throw the ball up above your head, watching it as it flies (figure 1.4a). Follow the ball with both hands so that your fingers point at it. As the ball falls, spread your fingers (figure 1.4b).

As it touches your fingers, pull it down in both hands and to your lower chest area, keeping your elbows close to your ribs (figure 1.4c).

a *b* *c*

Figure 1.4 Catch above your head drill: *(a)* throw the ball above your head; *(b)* spread your fingers as the ball falls; *(c)* pull the ball to your chest.

It is very simple to make this practice far more difficult. Try the following in competition against a friend. Remember to watch the ball into your hands and pull it to your chest, cradling it firmly in your hands and arms.

- Throw the ball three times and clap before each catch.
- Increase the number of times you throw, clap and catch until you can do it successfully for 1 minute.
- Try to clap twice before each catch.
- Throw a little higher, touch your hips, clap and then catch.
- Throw, touch your knees, touch your hips, clap and catch.
- Throw, touch the ground, touch your knees, touch your hips, clap and catch.

Sometimes in a match—especially if you've misjudged a kick or the wind is blowing—you may have to turn to catch the ball. Once you can throw the ball above your head and catch it, begin to practise throwing the ball slightly over one shoulder so you have to turn to face in a different direction to catch it.

Hold the ball in both hands in front of your body (figure 1.5a). Throw the ball above your head and slightly over one shoulder. Watch the flight of the ball closely and turn your body so that your chest is facing the falling ball, but keep your feet still (figure 1.5b). Catch the ball with your palms facing you and your hands slightly higher than your eyes. As the ball touches your fingers, pull it to your lower chest, tucking your elbows into your ribs (figure 1.5c).

After you can do this successfully, throw the ball higher and slightly farther from your body. To catch now, you will need to turn not only your

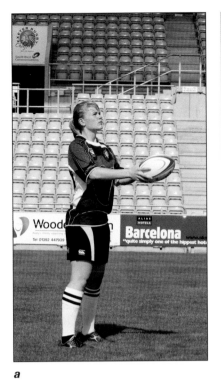

a   b   c

Figure 1.5 Twist and catch drill: *(a)* hold ball in front of your body; *(b)* throw the ball above your head and slightly over one shoulder, twisting so your chest faces the falling ball; *(c)* catch the ball and pull it to your chest.

chest, but also your feet so that you turn around to face the ball as it drops.

As you master the turn and catch, repeat the drill with a jump, turn and catch. Many match situations demand this skill. As you jump, lift your front knee up to waist level, reach for the ball (figure 1.6*a*), timing your jump so that you catch the ball in the air (figure 1.6*b*), and finish in a safe squat position. Tuck the ball firmly to your lower chest area (figure 1.6*c*).

a   b   c

Figure 1.6 Jump, turn and catch drill: *(a)* jump and reach for the ball; *(b)* catch the ball in the air; *(c)* tuck the ball to your chest.

Don't introduce the following variations to the practice until you can successfully and regularly repeat the throw, jump, turn and catch sequence. For the following sequences, turn in the air and land facing a different direction than the direction in which you started. As you improve, you should be able to jump closer to 360 degrees and still successfully make the catch.

- Throw the ball three times, clap as you jump and turn before each catch.
- Increase the number of times you throw, clap, jump, turn and catch until you can do it successfully for 1 minute.
- Try to clap twice before each catch.
- Throw a little higher, touch your hips, clap and then catch.
- Throw, touch your knees, touch your hips, clap and catch.
- Throw, touch the ground, touch your knees, touch your hips, clap and catch.

- Jump to catch after turning through a full circle.

These simple practices are like shadows of certain skills needed in the game. Because every player must be able to catch a ball coming from a height, you must master this skill. Remember the following simple rules:

- Watch the ball.
- Tuck your elbows into your ribs and lift your front knee to waist height when you jump to catch.
- Pull the ball to your chest, cradling it firmly in your hands and arms.

All of the simple practices detailed so far should familiarise you with the shape, feel, reaction and flight of a rugby ball. It is now time to get down to preparing to play a game.

GAINING THE ATTACKING EDGE

Now that you have begun to master some simple handling techniques, it is time to begin moving with the ball and practise some simple passing movements. Accurate, early passing prevents the defence from dominating the attack. If you constantly move the point of the attack, the defence will find it impossible to become set. Teams that play like this need to be very fit, because attackers and defenders have little opportunity for rest. The ball is passed continually away from would-be tacklers, so the passing team needs many players running in support of the ball carrier. The main purpose of this strategy is to make the attack so overpowering that at some stage there will be more attackers in one area than there are defenders. With accurate passing and receiving, the attacking team can strike around the edge or through the defence to score.

The main types of rugby passes are the lateral pass, which travels sideways or backwards; the switch pass, which changes the direction of the play; and the loop pass, which helps to put a player either through a gap in the defensive line or into space around the far edge of the defence (overlap). Other passes in rugby (e.g., the gut pass and screen pass) are simply slightly different ways

of making lateral passes. More details about these kind of passes can be found in step 5.

Accuracy is the most important characteristic of an effective pass. The height at which the ball arrives is crucial. If it arrives below chest height, the receiver will have to look down to catch it. This means that the player will look away from the defence and may lose sight of an attacking opportunity. Passing too high has the same effect and will also expose the receiver's ribs to a hard tackle. The ideal pass arrives at about chest height, with enough power (whether soft or hard) to allow the receiver to play to the best advantage of the team.

Sometimes you may be required to pass with power; and other times, softly. A soft pass may draw the receiver towards the ball. This may help keep the attack moving towards the goal line, the defence will be unable to drift across to the edge of your attack, and therefore space around the edges of the defence will be maintained for the next attempt at a score. A powerful pass may push the receiver away from the most effective running line, which is normally parallel to the touch line. Your receiver may be forced to run slightly sideways, which makes tackling by the defence easier and the attack less likely to penetrate or overlap the opposition because it lessens the space outside the edge of the defence.

Once you can control the power of your pass and understand when to use it, you will begin to send out passes that will allow other players to make the best use of the available attacking options.

Although there are few basic passes, there are various ways to pass the ball. All involve some movement of the arms, wrists and fingers. A short, punched lateral pass may require just a strong flick of the wrists and fingers. For long passes you may need to use the full swing of your arms and also the larger parts of your body, such as your shoulders, hips and legs.

There are no right or wrong ways to pass the ball. You may have already developed a style that allows you to send out accurate passes that you can easily vary in height, length and power. If not, then try various techniques during practice sessions. Any style that suits you is correct. Your main concern is to develop a technique that allows you to send accurate passes that vary in length, height, power and direction.

PASSING SITUATIONS

During play, attacking players will have many opportunities to create space for support players to run into. The task of the attackers nearest the space is to recognise it in advance or to create situations in which the attack outnumbers the defence: two attackers versus one defender or three attackers against two defenders, and so on. A key ingredient of success in these passing situations is to draw the defenders towards you—committing them to tackling you—to create space for another attacker to run through (see figures 1.7 and 1.8). The passing drills that appear later in this step will help you practise these skills. As you develop your passing game, you should seek to create and take advantage of these situations.

When practising passing and receiving skills, defensive players should initially use two-handed touch tackling (touching the ball carrier on the hips with both hands) instead of full-contact tackling. This technique allows players to refine passing skills under defensive pressure without exposing them to injury.

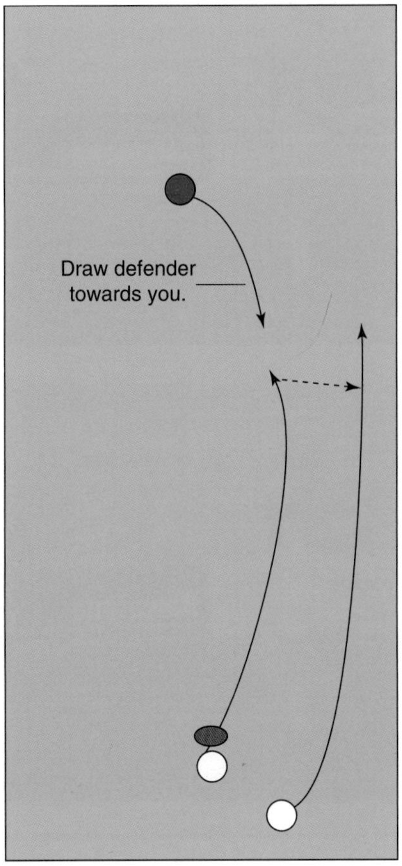

Figure 1.7 Drawing the defender towards you.

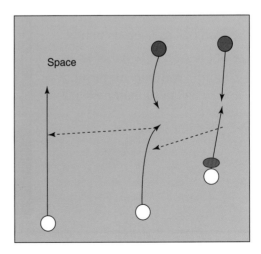

Figure 1.8 Creating space for the extra attacker.

7

LATERAL PASS

To move the ball up the field, you can run in any direction, but you may pass the ball only sideways or backwards. Therefore, the lateral, or sideways, pass (figure 1.9) is the basic pass.

Figure 1.9 | Lateral Pass

PREPARATION

1. Hold ball in both hands; only fingers in contact, across seams
2. Carry at chest height
3. After checking opponent, look at receiver when preparing to pass
4. Choose speed, direction, height, distance and power

a

EXECUTION

1. Swing arms towards receiver
2. Push ball with rear hand
3. Guide and steady ball with other hand
4. Flick wrists and fingers as ball leaves hands

b

FOLLOW-THROUGH

1. Watch ball as it leaves hands
2. Point fingers at target area
3. Change running angle and follow ball to support new ball carrier

c

Misstep
You continually miss the target when passing.

Correction
Follow through after the pass so that your fingers point to the target area. Concentrate on accuracy, not speed.

Sometimes a pass travels a short distance; at other times, much farther. Sometimes a soft pass floats towards the receiver, but on other occasions the pass may travel much farther, spinning with great power and speed as it arrives in the player's hands. No matter which kind of pass you send, you should remember a number of basic techniques for the lateral pass.

 Misstep
Your soft passes spin towards the receiver.

Correction
Your rear hand is pushing up and over the top of the ball as you release it. Keep both hands level, fingers pointing to the target.

Always try to pass the ball with both hands. Spread your fingers around the seams, keeping your palms away from the surface of the ball. Carry the ball at chest height when you are ready to pass, but also practise passing the ball from other heights—for example, near the knees or above the head—so that you are prepared for any eventuality in the game. When you prepare to pass, you must decide how far, at what height and how powerfully to send the ball to determine your passing action. For short, soft (pop) passes, hold the ball at chest height and flick your fingers and wrists slightly upwards towards the receiver (figures 1.9b and c). You can also use this type of pass if you pick up a rolling ball and wish to flick it on to another player. For slightly longer passes, which you might make when you are running as an attacking line, you need only extend the action by allowing your arms to move farther across your body towards the receiver.

For passes that miss out (skip over) players running in the line, you may have to swing your shoulders and turn at the waist to add more power. Sometimes you may want a pass to travel over a long distance and arrive as quickly as possible. To do this, the ball must spin point first, rather like a bullet. The easiest way to spin the ball is to use the hand behind the ball to push towards the receiver and then quickly move it up the side and over the top of the ball (figure 1.10). Your other hand guides and steadies the ball. In all cases your hands and fingers must complete the follow-through and finish pointing at the intended target.

Figure 1.10 Spinning the ball on a lateral pass.

SWITCH PASS

At times in a match the defence is tight and your attack is running out of space. To confuse the defence or create a little more space, you might consider using a switch pass (figure 1.11). This pass can quickly change the direction of an attack or hide the ball for a split second from the defence so that you create a little time or space before the defence responds.

To execute the switch pass, you must first run as a threat towards a defender. Once the defender begins to follow your running line and you are closing towards each other, alter your running line to go across that of the receiver (figure 1.11*a*). As you and the receiver cross close together, turn at the waist with the ball facing the receiver behind you, look at the receiver's hands and softly flick the ball up into the space in front of the receiver's hands (figure 1.11*b*).

A gently lobbed, soft pass will allow the receiver to accelerate on to the ball and at the same time keep the defence in sight. Once you have passed the ball, you must work hard to rejoin the attack as a support runner, even though you initially may be running in a different direction from the next ball carrier.

Figure 1.11 | Switch Pass

PREPARATION

Ball Carrier

1. Hold ball in both hands; only fingers in contact, across seams
2. Carry at chest height
3. Threaten defender
4. Quickly change running angle to go between defender and receiver

Receiver

1. Make a target
2. Watch defender and ball carrier
3. Accelerate as ball is passed

a

EXECUTION

Ball Carrier

1. Deliver soft, lobbed pass up in front of target
2. Turn while passing so that ball is hidden from defender

b

FOLLOW-THROUGH

Ball Carrier

1. Run to support new ball carrier

c

For the switch pass to be successful, the ball must always be visible to the members of your own team, especially to the player who is going to receive the pass. If you are running to the right, you will turn around with the ball behind your right hip (figure 1.12a); if you are running to the left, it will be behind your left hip (figure 1.12b).

a

b

Figure 1.12 Receiving the switch pass: *(a)* when running to the right; *(b)* when running to the left.

Misstep

You find it difficult to make a quick pass.

Correction

Catch the ball in your fingers, not the palms of your hands. Flick the ball towards the receiver, using wrists and fingers plus some of the power of your forearms.

Usually, a switch pass is used to redirect the attack from parallel to the touch lines; to put a player back at an angle to, and in a gap through, a defence that is running across the field (figure 1.13); or to change the direction of the attack (figure 1.14).

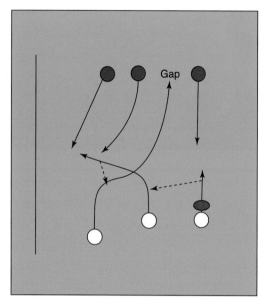

Figure 1.13 Playing back at an angle to the defence.

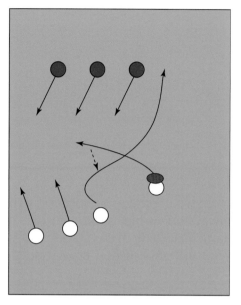

Figure 1.14 Changing the direction of the attack.

LOOP PASS

There are only three ways to beat the defence: go around it (overlap), go through it (penetrate) or go over it (kick). The loop pass (figure 1.15) is a ploy that allows you either to create an overlap by putting an extra pair of hands in the attack or to penetrate the defence by putting another player into a gap.

Figure 1.15 Loop Pass

PREPARATION

1. Receiver makes target
2. Ball carrier watches defender
3. Determine length of pass
4. Use arms, wrists and fingers to fire pass
5. Look at target area and pass into gap

a

EXECUTION

1. Receiver holds ball in both hands; only fingers in contact, across seams

2. Carry at chest height

3. Original passer runs around receiver to pull defender away from pass direction

b

FOLLOW-THROUGH

1. Original passer runs to support or receive return pass

c

The loop pass is another version of the standard lateral pass that offers the ball carrier some options. One option is for the ball carrier to pass to the player next in line and then immediately run behind the new ball carrier and reenter the line to receive a return pass, as shown in figure 1.15. Another option for the ball carrier is to deliberately miss the next player in line with the pass, so that the third player receives the ball. The middle player then runs behind and outside the new ball carrier to receive a pass.

The loop pass is executed in much the same way as the lateral pass, except that the new ball carrier does not pass the ball directly at the looping player, but into the space in front of the gap the looping player is attacking (figure 1.16). This

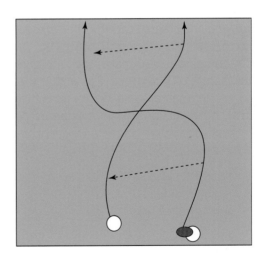

Figure 1.16 The ball carrier passes into the space in front of the gap being attacked by the looping player.

ensures that the receiver is brought onto the effective running line and is able to either penetrate the defence or pass out for the overlap.

By running at the defence first, as the ball carrier you will attract a defender towards you and create a gap farther out along the attacking line (figure 1.17). If you are the support runner, make sure that you are on your intended running line before you receive the pass. Accelerate as you receive the ball, and penetrate the defence through the gap that has been created.

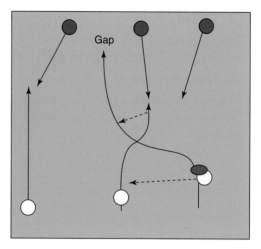

Figure 1.17 Creating a gap farther along the attacking line. The receiver accelerates and penetrates the defence.

Misstep

You always seem to be in front of the passer as he is about to deliver the ball.

Correction

Keep your depth on the ball carrier. A simple way is to always be able to read the ball carrier's shirt number. Accelerate only when you see that the ball is on its way through the passer's hands.

As with the switch pass, it is possible to use the looping player as a decoy runner (figure 1.18). Make a dummy pass and then pass to another player in a better position, or have the decoy runner exchange passes with the ball carrier or pull the last defender towards you and create space for the ball carrier to pass to the outside attacker (figure 1.19).

Of all the passes you make, the loop gives the greatest range of outcomes. It is a skill that you should try to master as soon as possible. It is effective, however, only if your support players also understand the variations and options. A loop pass is usually a planned move. However, the more you practise with the same players, especially those who play in the positions nearest to yours, the more you will be able to read their body language and instinctively react to them should they improvise and go for the loop.

Practising against a static defence can help you achieve the timing required to make a successful loop pass; however, the sooner you can advance to a more active defence, the better.

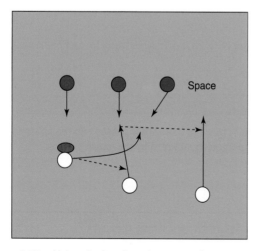

Figure 1.18 Using the looping player as a decoy.

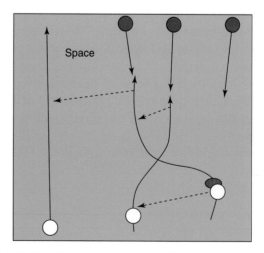

Figure 1.19 Creating space for an attacker out wide.

RECEIVING A PASS

In a match, attackers with and without the ball must make instant decisions. Ball carriers need to quickly choose the angle at which to run towards the defender, when to pass, the type of pass to make and how to quickly return to effective support once the pass is completed. Receivers' options are just as varied: They must determine their running angle in relation to the defence and ball carrier, provide a target with hands ready to receive the ball, run in within sight of the ball carrier, determine where the next attack will be and so on.

To receive the ball successfully, you should always make a target with your hands. The best way of providing a target is to hold out your hands towards the passer at about chest height with palms facing the ball (figure 1.20). The target is then quite easy for the ball carrier to see, and it can also act as a decoy to attract the defender should the ball carrier dummy the pass or send out a pass that deliberately misses you and is collected by the next player in line. The passer should look at your target just before passing and aim the ball so that it arrive just in front of your hands. Passers

Figure 1.20 Making a target.

should always try to pass from low to high and use sufficient power so that the ball arrives at the target just past the highest point on its trajectory.

Misstep
You continually fail to catch the ball.

Correction
Watch the ball all the way into your hands. Make a target with your fingers pointing upwards. Close your fingers and thumb around the ball as it arrives.

Misstep
Each time you receive the ball, you lose sight of the nearest opponent.

Correction
Either your target is too low or your partner is passing the ball below chest height. In both cases, you need to look down for the ball and so lose sight of the defender. Make a higher target for the passer to aim towards.

If the ball is aimed at you, it should arrive just in front of your outstretched fingers so that you can either reach and collect it or accelerate and collect it. In either case you should allow the ball to arrive into your fingers and not the palms of your hands. Your fingers should grip the ball naturally, allow you to readjust the ball in your hands if necessary before passing it on, and making it easier for you to pass the ball quickly.

DUMMY PASS

Each of the pass situations described in this step provide opportunities for you to use a dummy pass. It is best to use a dummy pass when you see that the defender is beginning to take up a running line towards your support player in anticipation of your pass. It is essential that you use the same actions for the dummy as you would when actually intending to pass the ball. This will convince both attacker and defender that you are about to release the ball. At the last moment keep your fingers wrapped around the ball, and bring it back into the carrying position in front of your chest. However, if you always use a dummy pass, you will soon become known for it, and it will cease to be a surprise to the defence. Your attacking options will be therefore fewer.

You can practise the dummy pass in your normal passing drills. Occasionally keep hold of the ball when you see the defender anticipate the pass.

PASSING AND RECEIVING EFFECTIVELY

For the greatest success at passing, you should always keep the ball in front of your body throughout the passing movement. Turn your chest to face the receiver when passing to a player running 2 or 3 metres away and slightly behind you. This will allow you to use the same passing technique as normal and should result in an accurate pass.

It's important to practise passes of various lengths when developing your passing skills. As you and your teammates work wider apart, you will find that more and more parts of your body become involved in making the pass. Very short passes will use just your forearms, but long passes will involve your arms, shoulders, back and legs. The longer you pass, the less able you will be to immediately run to support the new ball carrier. This is because the effort needed for making the long pass often pushes you away from its intended direction.

You will find that swinging the ball with straight arms is not very effective when you and your teammates begin to move much wider apart. Although you use the same pendulum motion for long passes, you now add a flick of the wrists and fingers to pass the ball on to the next player. It also helps if you bend your arms slightly to shorten the length of the swing; this allows you to use more shoulder and back muscles to add power to the action.

The support runner may not always be in the ideal position to receive the ball. Therefore, you must develop your ability to deliver the ball to either side or to any depth. Your support runner will arrive from various angles and distances. Sometimes you will pass well behind; at other times you may be able to make a flat pass, almost parallel to the goal line. No matter what the situation, you must make sure that your pass arrives safely to the support player.

If you are the support runner, you must select your intended running line before the ball arrives. Good players select one line but run on a slightly different one until the ball is in the air and then change very late, on to the best one. This fools the defender and often results in the ball carrier breaking through the defensive line.

When you work against a more active defence, you may find that you have to readjust the timing of your pass. Your coach will tell you when the defence can change from touch to tackle. It may be better for you to concentrate on passing rather than tackling for the time being.

CAUTION Always wear protective equipment in both practice and match situations. Although not every drill in this section anticipates contact with a player, a piece of equipment or the ground, by its very nature rugby invites contact, sometimes by accident. It's better to be safe than sorry.

Passing and Receiving Drill 1. *Three-in-a-Line Passing*

This drill gets you started with the basic passing motion.

In groups of three, begin by walking side by side and close together. Allow your arms to swing while passing the ball. The player on the end has the ball and reaches out with it to the next person, who is close enough to pick the ball out of the ball carrier's hands (figure 1.21*a*). In one movement the passer's arms swing the ball down (figure 1.21*b*), across and back up into the next pair of waiting hands (figure 1.21*c*). Move the ball to the next player as soon as you receive it. Once the ball has gone across the line of players, players pass in the opposite direction and return it to the starting point.

Now, widen the spaces between you. Start about 1 metre apart and gradually extend the distance until you are about 3 metres apart. If this distance is too wide, move a little closer. You should not be farther than 3 metres apart until you've mastered this drill.

To Increase Difficulty

- Try the same exercise with a variety of balls, such as tennis balls, basketballs, hockey balls, foam balls, and so on. (Try this also with an egg—it will really help you concentrate on sending the pass to the correct place and receiving it in the fingers.)

To Decrease Difficulty

- Stay close together.
- Walk steadily and take your time with the pass.
- Walk over a short distance; then come back in the opposite direction.

Success Check

- Watch the ball into your hands; then turn to look at the target.
- Spread your fingers wide across the seams, holding the ball upright.

Score Your Success

Walk the length of the field with no dropped passes = 5 points

Walk the length of the field with 1 dropped pass = 3 points

Your score ___

a

b

c

Figure 1.21 Three-in-a-line passing drill: *(a)* the player at the end of the line hands the ball to the next player in line; *(b)* the player swings the ball down; *(c)* the player swings the ball across and up into the hands of the next player.

Passing and Receiving Drill 2. *Passing Lines*

Now that you have practised the basic passing motion, this drill provides practice in getting into proper running lines.

Stand in a line one behind the other with the front person holding the ball. The ball carrier begins to run forward steadily, and the remaining players fan out to one side in an arc, ready to catch and pass (figure 1.22). Players behind the ball must work hard to run sideways and then forward onto their running lines before receiving the ball.

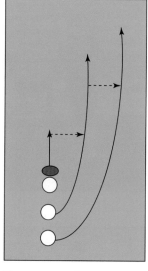

Figure 1.22 Passing lines drill.

To Increase Difficulty

- Work in 5-metre channels.
- Try the same exercise with a variety of balls, such as tennis balls, basketballs, hockey balls, foam balls, and so on. (Try this also with an egg—it will really help you concentrate on sending the pass to the correct place and on receiving it in the fingers.)

- Use a wider work channel. The front person calls 'Left' or 'Right' to decide which way the support runners have to run.

To Decrease Difficulty

- Stay close together.
- The ball carrier shouts out the direction before the players begin to run.
- Give the receiver time to run into position before you make the pass.

Success Check

- Watch the ball into your hands; then turn to look at the target.
- Spread your fingers wide across the seams, holding the ball upright.
- Use soft passes.
- Be on the intended running line before receiving the ball.

Score Your Success

Run the length of the field with no dropped passes = 10 points

Run the length of the field with only 1 dropped pass = 5 points

Your score ___

Passing and Receiving Drill 3. *Zigzag Passing*

Work in a confined area—no more than a 10-metre square—with two other players. As you continuously jog and change direction, pass the ball to a support player, who immediately passes on to the third player. Support players always join the action from behind but alongside the ball carrier. All potential receivers should show the ball carrier a target and call for the ball. The ball carrier selects which target to hit and chooses the type of pass required to deliver the ball accurately.

To Increase Difficulty

- Change direction while running.
- Make passes as soon as you can after changing direction.

- Add a defender who tries to knock the ball to the ground after each pass.

To Decrease Difficulty

- Walk rather than jog.
- Make slower, softer passes that are easy to catch.
- Remove the defender.
- Work along a channel without a change of direction.

Success Check

- Follow behind the ball carrier until the direction changes.
- Keep your eyes on the ball.
- Make a target.
- Call for the ball.
- Stop ball movement with the hand farther from the direction of the pass.
- Push the ball on with the other hand.

Passing and Receiving Drill 4.   2v1 Passing

Start with a defender about 10 metres away and a support player directly behind the ball carrier (figure 1.23). The distance from the defender helps the support player avoid jogging in front of the ball before the carrier is ready to pass the ball.

The ball carrier's running line should go towards the defender and slightly away from the direction of the pass. Once the defender

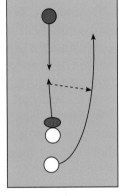

Figure 1.23   2v1 passing drill.

becomes fully committed to that defensive line, the ball carrier turns to look for support and gets ready to pass the ball as soon as the defender can no longer threaten the receiver.

Remember, finding the support runner is as important as the support runner catching up to you. If the support runner is not close, either slow down or run across and towards the running line of the defending player.

The pass receiver will recognise when the pass is about to be made because the ball carrier will look for the target. At that precise moment, the pass receiver makes the target and accelerates from behind the ball carrier to collect the pass. The defender will have no chance to tackle because the pass receiver takes the ball quickly behind the defence.

Allow a number of attempts to beat the defender. Remember to start from different sides of the area you are working in, so that you practise passing to the left and right. After every pass the receiver should try to score over the end line.

After you feel comfortable with this drill, take some time to practise the dummy pass. Surprise is important for the dummy pass to be successful, so when the defender holds back to anticipate a pass, you'll need to switch from an intended to a dummy pass. Do not worry if the defender is not fooled by your dummy pass. Having the confidence to try it is what's important.

To Increase Difficulty

- Run at about 75 percent of full speed.
- Start with the ball on the ground. Run in and pick it up as you attack the defence.
- Shorten the space between you and the defender.
- Have the support runner start outside the work area, in a different place each time.

To Decrease Difficulty

- The defender must follow the first ball carrier, not the pass or the receiver.
- The defender may walk only.

Success Check

- Take the defender away from the direction of the pass.
- Pass when the defender is committed to tackling.
- Keep both hands on the ball when passing.
- Find the support runner.
- Focus on the defender and the support runner.

Score Your Success

10 consecutive successful passes and scores on alternate sides with no forward passes = 10 points

6 to 9 consecutive successful passes and scores on alternate sides with no forward passes = 5 points

Fewer than 6 consecutive successful passes and scores on alternate sides with no forward passes = 1 point

3 successful dummy passes and scores = 5 points

Your score ___

Passing and Receiving Drill 5. *3v2 Grid*

Succeeding with a 3v2 passing situation is very difficult unless you are generally successful with the 2v1 situation. The most important elements in the loop are the lines of running of the players who create the space, or gaps, in the defence. To be successful with the 3v2 situation, you must fix the first and second defenders and hold off the pass long enough to put the next, or link, ball handler under pressure. The link player then has to catch the pass in one movement to avoid being tackled. In a successful 3v2 situation, this sequence of movement is executed so close to the defenders as to make it impossible for either of them to drift across from one attacker to the next.

You also must angle your running lines to drag both defenders away from the area you and your partners wish to attack. The person you pass to must be able to give and take a pass in one running stride. Otherwise, the defenders will be able to move across and tackle the outside running player before the goal line can be threatened.

Give yourself plenty of width to begin with—20 metres will be sufficient—and play over a distance of about 15 metres. The defenders should stand on the far goal line 2 metres apart and should move forward as the practice begins. The first defender must be responsible for the ball carrier. The other defender is free to defend against either of the other two attackers.

The ball carrier takes the first defender towards the nearer touch line to create space for the next two attackers. Once the defender is fully committed to that running line, the ball carrier turns to look at the support and make ready to pass (figure 1.24).

The support runners run 2 metres behind the ball carrier. This will give the next ball receiver time to pass the ball on if it comes to his target. If the first support runner's running line copies that of the ball carrier, space is created for the third player and the defender will be dragged away from where the pass is intended to go.

Defenders often approach at various speeds and from a variety of angles, so you must practise for such situations. Always practise at match pace so that you prepare for the game realistically. After you have mastered the original grid, widen the space in which you work.

Mastering simple practices such as these helps you to become more successful in the game. You should try to misshape the defence to create a situation in which an attacker can run at a gap in the defence. Sometimes this gap is between two of the players, and at other times it will be around the outside edge. In the full game, this situation most often occurs when the centres and full back have managed to confine the defence into a narrow

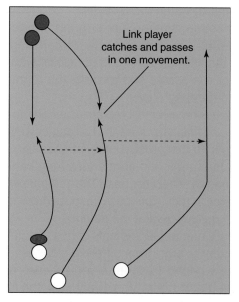

Link player catches and passes in one movement.

Figure 1.24 3v2 grid drill. The ball carrier draws the first defender towards the nearer touch line.

space and give the winger a clear run down the touch line. Many of the game's best tries have been scored in this way.

To Increase Difficulty

- Work at game intensity in the grid.
- Shorten the distance between the ball carrier and the defenders.
- Have the support runners start from various points along the side of the work area.
- Start by having a coach or the ball carrier roll the ball into the area. This is the trigger for everyone to move.
- Narrow the work area.

To Decrease Difficulty

- Defenders follow their designated attackers only.
- Defenders may walk only, but attackers may run.

Success Check

- Make a target for the pass.
- Stay behind the ball carrier until the ball is about to be passed.
- Accelerate to the ball.
- Choose a running line that creates space for others.
- Pass only when the defender is committed.

Score Your Success

5 consecutive successful scoring attempts = 5 points

3 or 4 consecutive successful scoring attempts = 3 points

2 consecutive successful scoring attempts = 1 point

Your score ___

Passing and Receiving Drill 6. *Switch Passing Down a Channel*

This drill provides pair practice of the switch pass and introduces variable defensive pressure.

Mark out a channel to run down. Space the markers evenly down the edge of both sides of the channel (figure 1.25). After making a switch pass at the centre of the channel, run outside the next pair of markers and across the centre again for another switch pass. Practise this drill until you make no mistakes with any passes as either receiver or passer. When receiving the ball, remember to take the ball at chest height so that you do not have to look down when catching it.

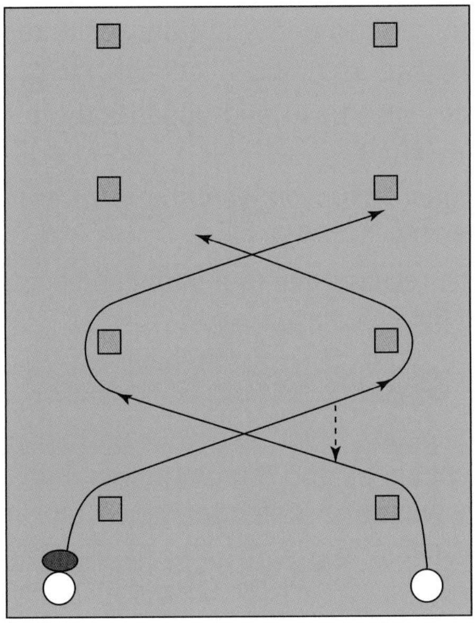

To Increase Difficulty

- Alter the angles of your running lines so that they do not match. Sometimes run parallel to the side of the channel.
- Change your running speed so that the receiver is running flat out as you deliver the pass. You will have to practise the correct timing sequence for the safe delivery of the pass.

To Decrease Difficulty

- Place a marker at the centre of the channel in each square, and make your passes directly over the top of the marker.
- Run quickly but never at full speed to control the movement of the ball.
- Pass early with a little more height.
- The passer and the receiver talk to each other to coordinate passing and catching.

Figure 1.25 Switch passing down a channel drill.

Success Check

- Keep the ball visible to the receiver.
- Lob the ball gently in front of the receiver's hands.
- Turn your head and upper body to look at the target.
- Signal when you want the receiver to cross behind.

- The receiver makes a target and accelerates to the ball.

Score Your Success

Score 5 points if you and your partner move up one channel length and back without making any passing or receiving mistakes.

Your score ___

Passing and Receiving Drill 7. Switch Passing Down a Channel With a Defender

Practise the timing of the pass against a defender. Although this is not a realistic position from the defence's point of view, start by allowing the defender to stand at the centre of the grid. Once you become used to playing close to the defender, you can allow the defender to move and also touch tackle the ball carrier.

Your aim is to make the defender touch tackle the wrong person—that is, not the ball carrier. You can do this only if you introduce the dummy switch into the game. As the practice develops, the ball carrier and the support player can begin to alter the angles at which they run, and they can stay within the channel rather than going outside the marker cones. Sometimes the run can be shallow; at other times, much more angled to the other player. The defender too can alter positions, so that all three players become used to putting the opposition at a disadvantage.

You may have as many defenders in the channel as you wish, but there must be at least 10 metres between them so that you can practise running at the correct angles for making a switch pass. Defenders should change their starting positions so that you can practise working at various angles.

To Increase Difficulty

- Alter the angles of your running lines so that they do not match. Sometimes run parallel to the side of the channel.
- Change your running speed so that the receiver is running flat out as the pass is delivered. You will have to practise the correct timing sequence for the safe delivery of the pass.
- Defenders try to touch the ball carrier. Introduce the dummy switch to confuse the defenders.
- Defenders may move from side to side.

To Decrease Difficulty

- Place a marker at the centre of the channel in each square, and make your passes directly over the top of the marker.
- Run quickly but never at full speed to control the movement of the ball.
- Pass early with a little more height.
- The passer and the receiver talk to each other to coordinate passing and catching.
- The defender may not knock the ball down, but must say if the ball was visible to the defence at the point of release.

Success Check

- Keep the ball visible to the receiver.
- Run at the defender.
- Lob the ball gently in front of the receiver's hands.
- Turn your head and upper body to look at the target.
- Signal when you want the receiver to cross behind.
- The receiver makes a target and accelerates to the ball.

Score Your Success

Score 5 points if you and your partner make it up the channel, and 5 more points if you make it back without a defender touch tackling the ball carrier.

Your score ___

Passing and Receiving Drill 8. *Five Lives*

Another variation of the channel drill is called five lives—five attempts at scoring against three defenders with 15 metres between the defenders. As the attack develops, try to work in a switch pass. Defenders may move sideways only.

To Increase Difficulty

- Allow defenders to move forward as soon as the one in front is beaten.
- Roll the ball into the grid, chase it, pick it up and begin play.
- Let the defender throw the ball in the air for you to retrieve, and then attack.
- Narrow the game channel.

To Decrease Difficulty

- Allow more space between defenders.

Success Check

- Keep the ball visible to the receiver.
- Run at the defender.
- Lob the ball gently in front of the receiver's hands.
- Turn your head and upper body to look at the target.
- Signal when you want the receiver to cross behind.
- The receiver makes a target and accelerates to the ball.

Score Your Success

5 successful scoring attempts = 10 points

3 or 4 successful scoring attempts = 5 points

1 or 2 successful scoring attempts = 1 point

Your score ___

Passing and Receiving Drill 9. *Loop Pass*

Practise loop passing in pairs and then threes without opposition. Work down a 15-metre-wide channel and continuously loop around the ball carrier (figure 1.26). The ball carrier must always angle any run slightly away from the direction of the next pass to create space for the next player to run into. The ball carrier should pass into the space with sufficient power for the ball to go no higher than the receiver's shoulder. He should pass only when he has seen the receiver move into the space to his side. The receiver should accelerate to the ball and through the gap in front of the ball carrier.

After completing 10 loop passes with no mistakes, add three defenders and practise attacking the gap between two of them (see figure 1.17, page 14). Be sure to run hard at the defence. In a real game this makes defenders focus their attention on the ball carrier and not on the looping player. The first ball carrier must attract the defence. Having fixed the first defender, the first ball carrier can then pass and loop. If the second ball carrier runs slightly back and across, receivers will find it easy to loop around. If not, they may find themselves running slightly back towards their own goal line in order to hit the gap. Therefore the ball carrier should accelerate hard to make it easier for a receiver to head downfield as he receives the pass in the gap.

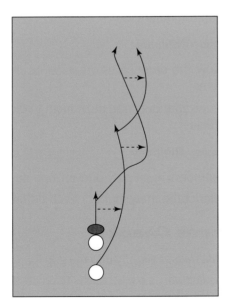

Figure 1.26 Loop pass drill.

To Increase Difficulty

- Catch and pass in one stride to the looping player. You can do this only if you are committed to a running line back towards the looping player.

- Assume the receiver will get there! Pass without looking.

- Bring the defenders a little closer to shorten the time to make the pass.

- Work at match pace.

- Complete a sequence of lateral passing once the loop pass has been made.

- Include a fourth defender as a full back and try to complete the score.

To Decrease Difficulty

- Hold the ball for a few strides before passing, but be sure that the receiver does not run ahead of you before you can make the pass.

- Talk your way through the passing sequence so that the receiver knows when you will pass.

- The defenders play one-on-one defence so that gaps occur.

Success Check

- The runner hits the gap at pace parallel to the touch lines.

- Pass at shoulder height into the gap.

- Create space for the pass.

- Do not pass until the receiver has started to run.

- Move onto the running line before receiving the pass, and accelerate hard.

Score Your Success

10 loop passes with no mistakes = 10 points

6 to 9 loop passes with no mistakes = 5 points

2 to 5 loop passes with no mistakes = 1 point

Your score ____

Passing and Receiving Drill 10. *Playing Against an Active Defence*

Now that you have experienced various types of passing against a limited defence, it is time to allow the defence to react more as it would in a match. In this drill the defence is allowed to drift across from one attacker to the next. You will find that fixing your opponent is very important. At times you may need to use a dummy pass to create a gap for another player or yourself. Also, see if you can recognise situations in which you might use either a switch or loop pass instead of a lateral pass.

Set up your defence at various angles, and also alter the shape of the attacking line. Sometimes begin flat with the players close together; at other times begin deep or with a combination (first two players deep from the first passer and others much flatter). See which gives you the most options for attack. Where you are when you start to run is not important, but rather, where you are when the ball is passed. If you are too flat, you may overrun the pass; if you are too deep, you may collect the passer's tackler as well as your own.

In this practice you should try to attack the spaces that are already there. Sometimes you may have to widen them by running at an angle. Then, by making a loop pass or a miss (skip) or a dummy loop, continue the attack by passing to other players who are in better positions to either penetrate or overlap the defence.

To Increase Difficulty

- Allow the defence to organise its defensive system.

- Allow defenders free movement to tackle any attacker.

To Decrease Difficulty

- Defenders must play one-on-one defence.

- Restrict the movement of each defender.

Success Check

- Float passes slightly into the gap for accuracy.

- Pass upwards so the ball is taken at shoulder height.

- Check the running lines to hold the defence.

Passing and Receiving Drill 11. *Passing Sequences*

The purpose of this drill is to link a range of action sequences together to practise attacking a multi-layered defence. Throughout the game of rugby, recurring situations sometimes require improvisation; others require a structured attack. Good players recognise such needs immediately and respond accordingly. This drill puts you in such fluid attacking situations and demands a range of decisions from you. You may need to use a lateral pass to penetrate or outflank the defence, or a switch or loop pass to create space, or you may need to improvise a pass to meet the need of the attack. If it works, it is correct!

Use a channel approximately 22 metres wide and 50 metres long. Place four or five defenders at random in the channel. As you become more proficient, you can add more single defenders to the opposition. Initially, you may restrict the defenders to moving only sideways, but eventually they should be allowed to defend their goal line as they wish.

To Increase Difficulty

- Gradually make each layer of the defence active.

- Allow any defender who has been passed to follow the attack from behind to try to stop the momentum of the ball carrier.

To Decrease Difficulty

- Defenders may defend only their zones.
- Defenders defend an individual attacker, leaving other players free to run.

Success Check

- Misshape the defence each time you go for a score.
- Attack the approaching defence—use your eyes!
- Pull defenders from where they want to be into positions of disadvantage.

SUCCESS SUMMARY OF BALL HANDLING

Although many skills are needed to be a good rugby player, ball handling is a very important piece in the jigsaw puzzle of required skills. To improve, you must spend a great deal of time with the rugby ball in your hands. Make up your own ball-handling exercises and drills. It's a fun and useful way to practise new skills. Quality practice helps make quality rugby players.

You may be a naturally gifted player who does not need the structure of a drill to develop your skills. You might prefer to learn by playing modified rugby games and return to practice drills only when you need to learn a handling technique in a controlled and structured environment. Have a coach or teammate check your technique against the photos and technique points described earlier in this step. Remember that you should not alter your passing style if it is successful in delivering a wide variety of passes with sufficient accuracy to allow the receiver a range of options.

On the other hand, you may be new to the game and need to use the practice drills to improve your skills. If you are just starting out, it is essential that you realise that you must always carry the ball so that you can pass it to someone in a better position than yourself. Direction is given by holding the ball in the fingers and pushing towards the catcher with your hands. The receiver can assist the passer by making a target with the hands at chest height, palms facing the ball carrier. This assists greatly when the ball needs to be passed in close-contact situations. As you gain experience, you will discover that rugby is a game of running, passing, catching and collision. To avoid collisions with your opponents, you will need to master passing skills.

Before moving on to step 2, Footwork, evaluate how you did on the ball-handling drills in this step. Tally your scores to determine how well you have mastered the skills of ball handling, passing and receiving. If you scored at least 80 points, you are ready to move on to step 2. If you did not score at least 80 points, practise the drills again until you raise your scores before moving on to step 2.

Passing and Receiving Drills

1.	Three-in-a-Line Passing	___ out of 5
2.	Passing Lines	___ out of 10
3.	Zigzag Passing	___ out of 10
4.	2v1 Passing	___ out of 15
5.	3v2 Grid	___ out of 5
6.	Switch Passing Down a Channel	___ out of 5
7.	Switch Passing Down a Channel With a Defender	___ out of 10
8.	Five Lives	___ out of 10
9.	Loop Pass	___ out of 10
10.	Playing Against an Active Defence	___ out of 10
11.	Passing Sequences	___ out of 10
Total		___ **out of 100**

Footwork

Many game situations may isolate the ball carrier. It is as much the responsibility of the ball carrier to find support as it is for the support to find the ball carrier, but the reality is that occasionally you cannot help becoming isolated when you're carrying the ball. This may occur when you have been put through a widening gap, and you may have only one player to beat in order to score. At times like this you will have to rely on different ways of beating the last defender.

Pure speed is probably the best and easiest way of beating a defender, but sometimes the defender is in a position that makes it difficult for you to use speed alone. Also, you won't always be as fast as your opponent. Therefore, you need to develop some dodging skills.

Besides pure speed, basic evasive skills consist of changing pace, swerving and sidestepping. If you can run at speed while moving on and off a straight line, any tackler will have difficulty lining you up for a decisive tackle. This type of running is difficult to develop if you do not have basic agility. If you play a number of sports, you will very likely develop agility quite naturally while practising and playing. If you do not play other sports, consider taking up a sport such as basketball, or work with a group of friends to develop a series of running practices that encourage changes of speed and direction. You can also play tag and dodge games with the group, which also will develop your evasive running skills.

A player who can beat a defender using speed or agility or a combination of both is an asset to any team. Such players have the ability to make the defence focus on them, which allows them to set up an attack, take on the last defender and score, or breach even the tightest of defences to create opportunities for others. To help you achieve the most from your running ability, and to select the best options for a given situation, this step introduces you to the basic evasive skills of changing pace, sidestepping and swerving and offers drills to help you develop these skills.

Each player in the team should practise evasive skills to make the unit more efficient. As with all your other practice, it is best to start with a passive defence to become used to the pressure that a defender exerts. Make sure that you dominate the defender at all times. The defender should react to you, not the other way around.

INCREASING RUNNING SPEED

Most athletic clubs have specialist coaches for sprinters. If you wish to increase your running speed, consult your nearest specialist coach for advice; however, you can begin by increasing the speed of your leg movements (cadence) and the length of your stride.

Increase stride length by improving the flexibility of your leg joints and by increasing the length and suppleness of your leg muscles, especially the hamstrings. Leg speed will improve only if you use a range of exercises specifically designed to work on your knee lift, stride, speed of contact and lift from the ground. As you mature, you will begin to develop running power through constant practice and specific strength work.

EVADING A DEFENDER USING A CHANGE OF PACE

Tacklers calculate where the tackle will occur by judging the speed and direction of the ball carrier and then set off to intercept the ball carrier's running line (figure 2.1). When faced by a tackler, you have a range of decisions to make that depend on the tackler's angle of approach and the space available in which to use your skills. If you have little space on the outside and the inside gap is covered, your sideways movement options are limited; you will likely need to pull the defender towards you by using a change of pace as a ploy and then accelerate away (figure 2.2).

To use this skill, you must first slow down slightly and run as if you were going to run behind the tackler. This will force the tackler to change direction onto a new defensive line. Once the tackler commits to this new angle of approach, accelerate away. Your change of pace also may include a swerve away from the direction of the would-be tackler. All players should try to perfect this evasive skill because it puts the tackler at a disadvantage and allows the ball carrier to stretch the defence.

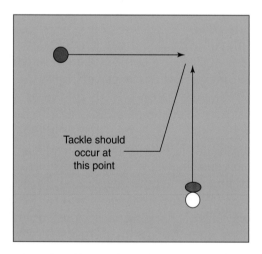

Figure 2.1 A tackler running to intercept the ball carrier's running line.

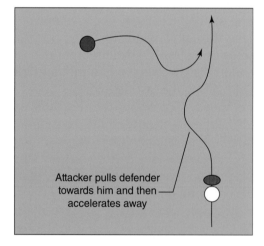

Figure 2.2 Changing your pace and accelerating away.

Misstep
You find it difficult to change speed when running.

Correction
You probably are running too quickly to begin with and so have little control. Slow down at the start and you will be able to change speed and direction more easily.

SIDESTEPPING

When running towards an opponent at an angle, sometimes you will wish to quickly change the direction of the attack. To do this, trick the defender by running in one direction and then quickly stepping off one foot to head off at a different angle. This move is called a *sidestep*. Many young players can do this quite naturally, especially if they play other team sports in which they have to dodge and weave.

To perform a sidestep well, you need to understand the basics. First, you must decide where you next wish to attack and then begin to angle away from that area. As the defender begins to close in on you, accelerate, then step wide with the outside leg while at the same time leaning your body weight directly over the top of that foot (figure 2.3*a*). This will suggest to the defender that you are trying to attack the outside space. As the defender also moves outwards, drive off the outside leg back inside (figure 2.3*b*), thus 'wrong-footing' the defence. Accelerate through the defence or look for a pass to a support runner (figure 2.3*c*).

Figure 2.3	Sidestep

PREPARATION

1. Choose running angle to take defender away from chosen attacking line
2. Hold ball in both hands

a

EXECUTION

1. Plant outside foot, shifting weight over that foot
2. Shift weight quickly away from planted foot and drive past defender to the inside
3. Watch defender constantly

b

FOLLOW-THROUGH

1. Accelerate into open space
2. Look for support or the goal line

c

Misstep

Your sidestep is ineffective against a defender.

Correction

You probably are approaching the defender directly head on. Run at an angle away from your intended attack area. As soon as the defender commits to your running line, change direction.

Sidesteps are easy to learn but difficult to execute, especially against a defender. Usually, the quick change of direction causes the most difficulty for attackers. A simple way to experience the feel of a sidestep is to step onto a slope and use the incline to push against (figure 2.4). As you become better at the skill, decrease the slope until you can perform the sidestep well on a flat surface.

Figure 2.4 Stepping onto a slope to learn the feel of a sidestep.

Misstep

You have difficulty changing direction with your sidestep.

Correction

Practise driving your foot hard into a slope to develop your change of direction. At the same time allow your body weight to move over the foot on the slope. Shifting your body weight persuades your opponent that you intend to continue running in that direction. Then drive off into the space behind the nearest defender.

SWERVING

Sometimes ball carriers use the swerve when they have committed to a running line and the defender is very close to making a tackle. If you are in this situation, draw the defender in close (figure 2.5a) and then alter your running line to take your legs away from the defender's outstretched arm and accelerate away (figure 2.5b and c).

Figure 2.5 **Swerve**

PREPARATION

1. Run towards defender's inside shoulder
2. Hold ball either to the ribs or in both hands
3. Control your pace

a

EXECUTION

1. As defender moves towards you, accelerate away hard
2. Use edges of feet to help you lean away and swerve
3. Watch defender constantly

b

FOLLOW-THROUGH

1. Run into space, towards goal line
2. Look for support

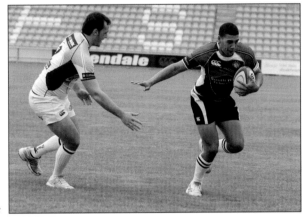

c

Misstep
You always seem to be caught by the defender when you have a decision to make.

Correction
Your priority is to run at the space away from where you next intend to attack. Leave plenty of space between you and any defender. Slow down slightly, if necessary. As soon as the defender slows or commits to a change of direction, make your decision and commit to it.

If you are swerving to the left, run on the inside edge of your left boot and the outside edge of your right one as you travel past the defender. When you swerve left, hold the ball with your left hand and arm and pull it in to the left side of your chest. Use the opposite side when swerving to the right. At the same time, try to lean towards the defender with your shoulders, and if it is allowed in your game, fend off the defender with your arm and hand.

Sometimes you may receive a pass when there's space between you and the defender. When this happens, threaten the space behind the defender and then lean and swerve away, accelerating as hard as you can. If you can also add a controlled change of pace into your swerve, you will be very difficult to tackle.

Misstep
Even though you have a good swerve, defenders catch you easily.

Correction
Either you are running too close to the defender before you swerve, or your running line is too shallow. Try to run first at the space behind the defender before you accelerate and change direction.

CAUTION Always wear protective equipment in both practice and match situations. Although not every drill in this section anticipates contact with a player, a piece of equipment or the ground, by its very nature rugby invites contact, sometimes by accident. It's better to be safe than sorry.

Footwork Drill 1. *Speed Up and Slow Down*

Before you try to beat a defender, you should become used to the feeling of accelerating hard from a running start. To accelerate, increase your stride length and leg speed. Practise accelerating from various speeds–for example, from jogging to three-quarters speed, and from three-quarters speed to full pace. As you accelerate hard, swerve to the left or the right. Try to reach your target speed as quickly as possible. A smooth, slow build-up of speed allows the defender to speed up as well. Surprise is everything.

Although a change of pace may occur on a long run in for a try, the actual change of pace covers only a few metres, so you should practise over relatively short distances of approximately 20 metres. When you try the change of pace, it is a good idea to set out a range of markers to follow so that your running line and acceleration distance are clearly visible when running.

To Increase Difficulty

- Make your swerve more pronounced by moving the markers outwards.
- Work at three-quarters to full pace.

To Decrease Difficulty

- Practise down a straight line.
- Work slowly until you've mastered a variety of speeds.

Success Check

- Accelerate smoothly and quickly.
- Change pace quickly.
- Keep your head up and scan the area for any would-be defenders.

Score Your Success

5 times through the markers without slipping or touching a marker = 5 points

3 or 4 times through the markers without slipping or touching a marker = 3 points

2 times through the markers without slipping or touching a marker = 1 point

Your score ___

Footwork Drill 2. *Defender Chase*

To practise your change of pace, always have the defender approach from one side and slightly behind so that you find it impossible to sidestep. It is up to you to draw the defender in close by slowing your run and then accelerating hard away and slightly outwards, provided there is room between you and the touch line.

For the first part of the drill, place markers from the 10-metre line to the goal line. The defender will approach from behind you as you enter the 22-metre area (figure 2.6). The defender must wait for you, as ball carrier, to start your run. After starting your run, move into the 22-metre area quickly so that you attract the attention of the defender. As soon as you can, slow slightly to pull the defender towards you; then accelerate hard and swerve away to score at the goal line.

In the second part of the drill, practise scoring as well as evasion. Use the lines marked on the field to gauge where the markers should be placed. Always mark the goal line at the end of the channel. Set the defender's markers slightly behind those for the attacker.

Your intention is to win the race for the score between the markers near to the corner (figure 2.7). If the defender's markers are too far to the side, you will score too easily; too far in, and you will never beat the defender. Choose a defender who is about your speed or slightly faster–this is the only way to improve. Place the markers by gauging the speeds of each player and altering the distances accordingly.

The race begins when the defender passes the ball to you. The defender will be close as you round

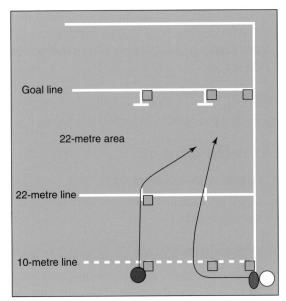

Figure 2.6 Defender chase drill, part 1.

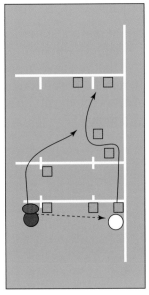

Figure 2.7 Defender chase drill, part 2.

the first marker, so you should keep looking to decide when to accelerate hard: too late and you will be caught, too early and you may slide as you round the marker.

To Increase Difficulty

- Move the goal line sideways in favour of the defender.
- Move the defender's and ball carrier's markers closer together.

To Decrease Difficulty

- Move the goal line sideways in favour of the ball carrier.
- Move the defender's and ball carrier's markers farther apart.

Success Check

- Control your speed.
- If you have space, beat the defender using speed alone.
- Pull the defender close; then accelerate and swerve away.
- Watch the defender constantly.

Score Your Success

9 or 10 evasions = 10 points

6 to 8 evasions = 5 points

3 to 5 evasions = 1 point

Your score ___

Footwork Drill 3. *Slalom Course*

Organise a slalom course using as many corner flags or markers as you can find. Set up each row of gates so that you have to change direction to go from one set to the next. The more gates you have, the more you can practise your agility running and the more quickly you may improve.

To feel the rhythm required to swerve through these obstacles, begin by walking and gradually increase your pace. It is almost impossible to work at maximum speed, so you must control your speed through the gates. Except when racing side by side with an opponent for the goal line, you must control your running speed to take best advantage of your opportunities when trying to beat a defender in a game.

You should now be ready to practise at match pace. This is not necessarily running as fast as you can. Run so that you are still in control of your body weight and can dodge and weave. The faster you can do this under control, the better.

To Increase Difficulty

- Put a team of players at the opposite end of the slalom course working in the opposite direction so that you have to pass one of their players (figure 2.8). Keep your eyes open and look for players coming at you so that you can avoid any contact.

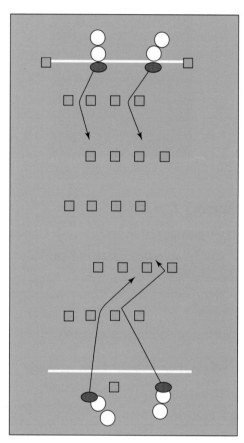

Figure 2.8 Slalom course drill with teams moving in opposite directions.

- Use a number of teams at each end of the slalom course so that you must avoid players working in the same and in the opposite direction.

To Decrease Difficulty

- Widen the spaces between the gates.

Success Check

- Run at a controlled speed.
- Look ahead and plan which gate to go through next.

Score Your Success

Earn points based on the following scale for the normal drill. If you increase difficulty and have another team working towards you, add 5 bonus points to your score if you avoid colliding with any opposing players.

Move quickly through all gates without touching any 5 times = 10 points

Move quickly through all gates without touching any 3 or 4 times = 5 points

Move quickly through all gates without touching any 2 times = 1 point

Your score ___

Footwork Drill 4. *Sidestepping a Single Defender*

Work against a defender in a 10-metre by 10-metre square. Both of you start at the same time but from different corners along the same edge of the square. As you approach the defender, head towards one corner; then drive your outside leg hard into the ground and drive back inside at the gap (figure 2.9). Lower your body weight as you do this in case you have to drive through an outstretched arm. Score on the goal line.

To Increase Difficulty

- The defender starts closer to the attacker.
- Narrow the channel.

To Decrease Difficulty

- The defender starts farther away from the attacker.

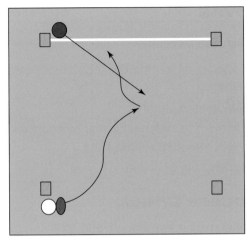

Figure 2.9 Sidestepping a single defender drill.

Success Check

- Run at pace with control.
- Drag the defender sideways quickly.
- Sidestep as the defender overtakes you slightly.
- Vary your attack. If the defender is expecting a sidestep, attack using speed.

Score Your Success

Score 9 or 10 times = 10 points

Score 7 or 8 times = 5 points

Score 5 or 6 times = 1 point

Your score ___

Footwork Drill 5. *Avoiding a Slap*

You need to be able to swerve to both sides. Practise against a line of other players, each of whom holds out an alternate arm with a clenched fist or open hand. Practise swerving first to one and then to the other side. In this practice you should try to lean towards the 'tackler' as far as you can, but keep your body away from the hand (figure 2.10). Shift the ball from one side of your body to the other so that it is always at the side farther from a tackler.

To Increase Difficulty

- Allow the tacklers to try to slap the runner's thigh with an open hand.
- Move the tacklers closer together.

To Decrease Difficulty

- Increase the distance between the tacklers.

Success Check

- Run at pace with control.
- Stay close to the fists without touching them.
- Use the outside and inside edges of your boots to increase traction.
- Keep the ball away from the tacklers.

Score Your Success

Start with 10 points. Subtract 1 point each time you touch a fist or a player in line slaps your thigh (increase difficulty variation).

Your score ___

Figure 2.10 Avoiding a slap drill.

Footwork Drill 6. *Combining Moves*

Set out a row of markers for yourself (the attacker) and a defender along a channel at uneven intervals.

Set out the defender's markers so that the defender approaches from various angles depending on which marker is rounded (figure 2.11). The defender decides which marker to run around. You must react to the defence that comes at you. If the defender comes from behind, use speed; if the defender comes directly from the side, consider swerving; if the defender comes from straight ahead, use your sidestep.

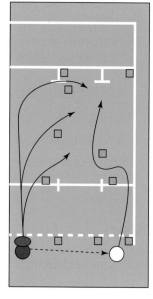

Figure 2.11 Combining moves drill.

To Increase Difficulty

- Introduce the full tackle when your coach thinks you are ready.
- Narrow the channel.

To Decrease Difficulty

- Specify which marker the defender will run around.
- Widen the channel.
- Move the defender's markers farther from your intended running line.
- Widen the goal line.

Success Check

- Keep your eyes open and look for players coming at you so that you can avoid any contact.
- Allow the defender to come close only in a narrow channel.
- Always dominate the defender.
- Drag the defender away from your intended attack area.

Score Your Success

5 scores = 10 points

3 or 4 scores = 5 points

2 scores = 1 point

Your score ___

SUCCESS SUMMARY OF FOOTWORK

You may already possess the agility vital to rugby, but if not, you can develop it by constant practice against a defence that gradually exerts more and more pressure on you. Agility is only one way of helping your team overcome a defence. Although most footwork skills are done when running quickly, they are most easily performed when running at a speed at which you can control your balance. Focus on timing, on staying balanced and on making strong moves to evade your defender. Have a coach or another player check your fundamentals against the photos in figures 2.3 and 2.5.

Before moving on to step 3, Tackling, evaluate how you did on the footwork drills in this step. Tally your scores to determine how well you have mastered the footwork skills of changing pace, sidestepping and swerving. If you scored at least 45 points, you are ready to move on to step 3. If you did not score at least 45 points, practise the drills again until you raise your scores before moving on to step 3.

Footwork Drills

1. Speed Up and Slow Down   ___ out of 5

2. Defender Chase   ___ out of 10

3. Slalom Course   ___ out of 10

4. Sidestepping a Single Defender   ___ out of 10

5. Avoiding a Slap   ___ out of 10

6. Combining Moves   ___ out of 10

Total   ___ **out of 55**

Tackling

Winning teams spend at least 50 percent of their time practising defensive techniques and systems to prevent the opposition from scoring. This is because often rugby is 50 percent defence, and good tackling helps to win games. If all members of your team improve their tackling technique, you will increase the amount of pressure you put on the opposition and force them to make mistakes, which will create more opportunities for you to regain control of the ball and therefore control of the game.

If your team never misses a tackle, the opposition will find it very difficult to score against you. When you make first-time tackles, you prevent your opponents from going forward and force them back towards their own goal line. Well-timed tackles could stop your opponent from passing the ball, making defence easier for the rest of your team. Pressure tackling could force the opposition to knock on, or make a forward pass, giving you the advantage of the put-in at the subsequent scrum and controlled possession from which to launch your next attack. You may also gain an advantage by immediately regaining possession of the ball from your opponent's mistake, in which case the referee will often allow you to play on and make progress by attacking what is usually a disorganised defence. You should regard defence as attack without possession.

In this step, you will learn how to tackle opponents from various directions—from the side, behind and directly in front—because the opposition will attack you from various angles. You often

may have to chase back to tackle a player as well. The tackling techniques and practices in this step are carefully structured to create confidence and improve tackling ability and therefore improve your efficiency in game situations. The drills in this step will lead you gradually up the staircase to tackling success.

Before you take part in any practice that involves contact, make sure that you wear your gum shield and any other protective equipment that you would normally wear in a game. As the intensity of the practices increase, you may be asked to wear further protection in the form of a tackle suit so that no one is injured while learning the basic tackling techniques.

Initially, the best way to practise tackling against a partner is from a kneeling position. Gradually progress to walking, jogging and finally full-paced tackling. It is a good idea to take off your boots or trainers for your first tackling session, which should be on soft ground or spongy gym mats. Make sure that you practise with someone about your own size and weight and that you are thoroughly warmed up before you start tackling practice. Use some noncompetitive strengthening exercises, such as piggyback walks and bear hug lifts and walks over a 5- or 10-metre distance, to prepare for contact practice.

When tackling, never attempt to trip up your opponent with your feet. Tripping is dangerous and illegal. You also are not allowed to tackle around the neck or above shoulder height because it is very likely to cause serious injury to the ball carrier.

As part of tackling practice, be sure to practise making contact with the ground safely when you fall. Although this will be dealt with in more detail in step 5, be aware of safe falling practices as you take your tackling up to speed. When being tackled, go with the flow of the impact because this will help you to land and roll naturally. Round your shoulder as you prepare to hit the ground, and land mainly on your back and side. Shrug your shoulders and tuck your chin into your chest as you land. Bend your knees, keeping them tucked up, and resist the urge to put a straight arm or hand out to break your fall because you may injure yourself. After you execute a tackle, always get back on your feet as quickly as possible to rejoin the game.

Rugby Union Laws state that a tackled player must pass or release the ball immediately, move away from the ball and get up off the ground before playing the ball again. If the ball carrier falls down with the ball without being held by the tackler, he can get up and continue running forward. When you tackle the ball carrier, grip your opponent tightly as you both land on the ground to ensure that the player has to release the ball. It's only a tackle if both players go down together and if the tackler holds the ball carrier.

Once you become a skilled tackler and seasoned rugby player, you will find that executing a good tackle can be as satisfying as scoring a good try.

SIDE TACKLE

Start your practice of the side tackle with both you and your partner in a kneeling position. As your partner (the ball carrier) approaches, prepare for the tackle by keeping your head up, your chin off your chest, and your back flat. With your shoulders braced for impact, seek to place your head behind the ball carrier's legs, going 'cheek to cheek' (figure 3.1a). The best contact is made in the dip where your shoulder meets your neck. Wrap your hands around the player's legs and drive up and through with your legs, keeping your eyes open and holding on tightly. Try to fall on top of the ball carrier (figure 3.1b). Keep hold until the tackled player is stationary on the ground.

Misstep
Your tackle is unsuccessful because you put your head in front of your opponent's legs.

Correction
Remember to go cheek to cheek, with your head and face behind your opponent's buttocks.

Figure 3.1   Side Tackle

PREPARATION
1. Watch ball carrier
2. Keep head up, chin off chest, back flat
3. Look forward
4. Place head behind ball carrier's legs, cheek to cheek

a

EXECUTION

1. Brace shoulder; contact thighs
2. Wrap arms around thighs; pull and hold tight
3. Don't intertwine fingers
4. Keep eyes open
5. Use legs to drive up and through ball carrier
6. Try to land on top of ball carrier

b

Misstep
You completely miss the ball carrier.

Correction
Keep your head up. Use your eyes to aim for the point of contact, usually around the thigh region.

FRONT TACKLE

There are two ways to execute the front tackle. One way is to use your opponent's forward momentum to your advantage to complete the tackle. Don't try to drive the attacker backwards until you are a lot more experienced and stronger. Start learning the front tackle from a kneeling position or squat position; then progress to a crouching or standing start.

As the ball carrier approaches, look up into the legs and ribs and move your head and neck to one side of the ball carrier's body (figure 3.2a). Shrug your shoulders on contact and drive your shoulder into the attacker's rib cage as you wrap your arms around the thighs. Using the ball carrier's momentum, sit and fall backwards as you turn (figure 3.2b). This will allow you to bring the attacker over your shoulder as you fall on top (figure 3.2c).

Figure 3.2 — Front Tackle Using Ball Carrier's Forward Momentum

PREPARATION

1. Watch ball carrier
2. Look up into thighs and ribs
3. Keep back flat
4. Move head and neck to one side of ball carrier's body
5. Go cheek to cheek

a

(continued)

Figure 3.2 *(continued)*

EXECUTION

1. Shrug shoulders on contact
2. Drive shoulder up into lower ribs
3. Wrap arms around ball carrier's thighs and hold tight
4. Follow ball carrier's momentum as you sit, fall backwards and turn

b

FOLLOW-THROUGH

1. Allow ball carrier to fall over your shoulder
2. Turn ball carrier sideways and land on top

c

Misstep

You make contact with your hands only and are brushed aside.

Correction

Get closer and drive your shoulder at a point about 1 metre beyond the ball carrier. Get into a low, driving position. Hold on tightly when you fall to the ground and release only when you are sure that you have made the tackle.

The second way to execute the front tackle is to generate your own forward and upward momentum into the ball carrier. This is achieved by making stronger contact upwards into the lower ribs—low to high—with one of your shoulders. Remember to move your head and neck to the side of the ball carrier's body (figure 3.3a) as the ball carrier approaches. At the same time the arm on your contact shoulder side wraps around the ball carrier's back and your other arm picks up the nearer leg (figure 3.3b). (Note: It is dangerous to lift a player high and tip him over onto his shoulders or head, and you should not complete the tackle in this way.) This effectively disrupts the player's balance, and you can then tip the player sideways and backwards so that you land on top (figure 3.3c). If you are able to stay on your feet, attack the ball, which the ball carrier should have released.

Figure 3.3   Front Tackle, Forward and Upward Momentum

PREPARATION

1. Eyes on ball carrier
2. Look up into ribs
3. Keep back flat, chest low
4. Move head and neck to one side of ball carrier's body
5. Go cheek to cheek

a

EXECUTION

1. Shrug shoulders on contact
2. Drive shoulder up into lower ribs
3. Wrap inside arm around ball carrier's back and hold tight
4. Drive shoulder into body and pick up ball carrier's outside leg to disrupt momentum and balance

b

FOLLOW-THROUGH

1. Keep driving forward
2. Turn ball carrier sideways
3. Land on top of ball carrier

c

Misstep
You do not have any power in the tackle.

Correction
Bend your knees, lower your hips as you explode, and drive hard from your legs through the tackle. Make shoulder contact first.

REAR TACKLE

Sometimes you need to turn and run up behind to catch and tackle an opponent to prevent the player from scoring or gaining ground. To do this at pace, you need to time your tackle carefully to be sure you make solid contact. Remember to practise in training shoes or bare feet when you first try this type of tackle.

To execute the rear tackle, place your head behind or to the side of the ball carrier's buttocks (figure 3.4a) as you grip tightly around the thighs and drive forward with your shoulder (figure 3.4b). Pull the ball carrier's legs towards you and try to fall on top (figure 3.4c).

Figure 3.4 | Rear Tackle

PREPARATION

1. Watch player; time your contact
2. Head up; back flat
3. Head and neck behind player's buttocks or to side

a

EXECUTION

1. Shoulder into buttocks
2. Arms around thighs, squeeze tight
3. Drive forward with shoulder

b

FOLLOW-THROUGH

1. Pull ball carrier's legs to side
2. Land on top

c

Misstep
You are caught on your heels out of position.

Correction
Move forward quickly. Shepherd the attacker into a space you can control, often towards the touch line, leaving the attacker only one direction to move in. Stay up on your toes and balanced.

Sometimes, especially near your own line, a smother tackle is useful. For a smother tackle, wrap your arms around your opponent's arms and the ball, preventing a pass to support players.

Becoming comfortable and successful with tackling a ball carrier from any angle takes practice. Start from a static tackling position and progress to walking, jogging and then full movement. For more effective tackling, rather than waiting for the attacking player to control your movements, move towards the attacker, keeping infield, and force the attacker towards the touch line before you pounce. Never attempt to trip up your opponent or tackle around the neck or above shoulder height: It is illegal and dangerous.

Once you master the basics of tackling, it is time to put your technique under pressure by increasing the speed of the ball carrier and the impact made by your shoulder. At this stage, it is a good idea for the ball carrier to wear a tackle suit during practice to help prevent injury. You should always have your gum shield in and wear any other protective equipment that you would use in a match. In some drills, it is a good idea to have the attacker carry a tackle shield as well to protect the ribs and provide a firm, safe area for the tackler to target and hit.

CAUTION Always wear protective equipment in both practice and match situations. Although not every drill in this section anticipates contact with a player, a piece of equipment or the ground, by its very nature rugby invites contact, sometimes by accident. It's better to be safe than sorry.

Tackling Drill 1. *Kneeling Side Tackle*

Work in a small (8-metre by 8-metre) grid. Kneel down next to your partner, who is also kneeling and holding a ball. Get into the starting position to make a static side tackle on your partner. Remember to practise 'cheek to cheek' and to grab your opponent around the thighs. Make three successful static tackles leading with your right shoulder, followed by three successful static tackles leading with your left shoulder.

To Increase Difficulty

- Begin with both players kneeling. Tackle your partner as he moves forward to prevent him from scoring on the opposite side of the grid.

To Decrease Difficulty

- Use the shoulder you feel more comfortable tackling with.

Success Check

- Keep your eyes open and look at the target.
- Keep your head behind your opponent's legs and seat and go cheek to cheek.
- Make contact with your shoulder on the player's thigh.
- Hold on tight.
- Drive with your legs.

Tackling Drill 2.   Standing Side-Tackle Progression

Work in the same 8-metre by 8-metre grid as used in tackling drill 1. Stand and crouch. As the attacker walks forward, tackle him from the side. Remember to keep your head up, drive your shoulder into your opponent's thigh and hold on tight. Leading with your right shoulder, make three successful tackles. Then make three successful tackles leading with your left shoulder. Progress from a walk to a jog and finally to a run.

To Increase Difficulty

- Starting on the sideline, your partner carries a ball and tries to get past you to score. After each try by your opponent, you must touch the opposite sideline before your next tackle attempt. How many tries can your partner score in 30 seconds?

To Decrease Difficulty

- Start on your knees or go back to having your opponent walk.
- Use the shoulder you feel more comfortable tackling with.

Success Check

- Keep your eyes open and look at the target.
- Keep your head behind your opponent's legs and seat and go cheek to cheek.
- Make contact with your shoulder on your opponent's thigh.
- Hold on tight.
- Drive with your legs.

Tackling Drill 3. *Front Tackle Practice*

Work in an 8-metre by 8-metre grid. Face your partner and crouch down to prepare to make a front tackle. Your opponent walks alternately to your left, then right shoulder. Remember to sometimes use your opponent's forward momentum to your advantage when tackling: sit, fall backwards and turn to execute the tackle. You should also begin to use the front tackle that alters the ball carrier's centre of gravity by lifting and driving through the contact point. Execute three successful tackles leading with your right shoulder, and then three successful tackles leading with your left shoulder. Switch places with your partner.

To Increase Difficulty

- Have your opponent try to jog, then run past you.
- Roll a ball to your partner, who picks it up and attempts to jog past you and score on the goal line. Your partner can choose on which side to try to pass to you to keep you guessing. If your partner scores, both of you should turn around immediately and attempt to score on the other goal line. Trade with your partner after three tackles; then move up to running.
- See how many tackles you can make in 10 seconds.

To Decrease Difficulty

- Ask your partner to walk towards the shoulder you feel more comfortable tackling with.

Success Check

- Move your head to the side of your opponent's body.
- Hold on tight.
- Use the opponent's momentum and weight to your advantage.
- Turn the opponent, and land on top.

Score Your Success

3 successful tackles leading with the right shoulder = 5 points

3 successful tackles leading with the left shoulder = 5 points

Your score ___

Tackling Drill 4. *Rear Tackle Practice*

Work in an 8-metre by 8-metre grid. After your partner kneels, kneel down slightly behind your partner, both facing in the same direction. Get into a comfortable starting position to make a rear tackle (see figure 3.4, page 44). Complete three successful tackles while leading with your right shoulder and three while leading with your left shoulder.

Try this variation: Say 'Go' and have your partner try to move forward as quickly as possible while still kneeling to avoid your diving tackle. Don't forget to hold on tightly.

To Increase Difficulty

- You and your partner start in push-up positions on all fours next to each other. On your 'Go', your partner tries to crawl away before you can make the tackle.
- Standing in a crouched position, have your partner walk from behind you carrying a ball. As your partner walks past, dive to tackle. Repeat at a jog; then at a run.

To Decrease Difficulty

- Use a static kneeling starting position.
- Tackle with the shoulder you are more comfortable with.

Success Check

- Keep your eyes open and look at the target (upper thighs).
- Keep your head and neck to your opponent's side and go cheek to cheek.
- Push your shoulder into your opponent's buttocks, put your arms around the thighs and grip tightly.
- Land on top.

Tackling Drill 5. 6v1

Create a grid that is 8 metres by 8 metres. Six ball carriers stand in a line behind each other at the end of the grid and one by one try to score at the opposite end. You, the tackler, start on the sideline and go from one side to the other after each attempted tackle. It is your job to prevent a score. Practise all of the tackles.

Success Check

- Keep your eyes open and look at the target.
- Keep your head behind your opponent's legs and go cheek to cheek.

- Hold on tight.
- Drive with your legs.
- Land on top.

Tackling Drill 6. 3v3

In preparation for your role in a defensive system, it is time to start working in a small group of tacklers. Practise moving up as a line to shut down the space of a group of attackers and also to tackle any ball carrier. Work in an 8-metre by 8-metre grid, with three defenders against three attackers. Each attacker has a ball. On the coach's signal, attackers gently jog forward in a line. Defenders also set off and make contact at the same time with their opposite number. At this stage it is sufficient to hit with the shoulder, grab the body and lift the leg. Gradually increase the speed. When everyone is capable and confident, defenders may complete the tackle by landing on top of the ball carriers.

To Increase Difficulty

- Make the area 20 metres by 8 metres. In a line of three, ball carriers walk or jog and try to break through the defensive line. Ball carriers can go only the way the coach points. Otherwise, there is a danger of colliding with the other ball carriers

Success Check

- Keep your eyes open and look at the target.
- Keep your head behind your opponent's legs and go cheek to cheek.
- Hold on tight.
- Drive with your legs.

SUCCESS SUMMARY OF TACKLING

If every player in your team works hard to develop tackling techniques, you will be a difficult team to beat. Before you start any contact practice, warm up thoroughly with some noncompetitive strengthening exercises with a partner about the same size as you. These could include a variety of partner lifts and walks over a 5- or 10-metre distance—for example, piggyback walks and bear hug lifts and walks. Ask a friend or coach to watch your tackling practice and give you feedback on your technique and progress.

If you are determined, you will be successful and have a lot of fun making try-saving tackles. Remember to practise cheek to cheek: no one can run without legs.

Before moving on to step 4, Kicking, evaluate how you did on the tackling drills in this step by tallying your scores. If you scored at least 65 points, you are ready to move on to step 4. If you did not score at least 65 points, practise the drills again until you raise your scores before moving on to step 4.

Tackling Drills

1.	Kneeling Side Tackle	___ out of 10
2.	Standing Side-Tackle Progression	___ out of 30
3.	Front Tackle Practice	___ out of 10
4.	Rear Tackle Practice	___ out of 10
5.	6v1	___ out of 10
6.	3v3	___ out of 10
Total		___ *out of 80*

Kicking

Accurate kicking wins games, and poor, aimless kicking often loses them. If you learn to kick the ball accurately and with precision, you will make an important contribution to your team. Usually, the scrum half, fly half and full back do the most kicking. However, almost every player on your team should be able to kick with some degree of accuracy and skill.

All your teammates also should be able to catch a ball safely and under control, to regain and maintain possession of the ball. If your opponents are accurate kickers, you will probably be under extreme pressure when trying to catch the ball. Teammates greatly respect—and spectators greatly admire—players who can keep their concentration and secure the ball for their team with a safe catch when they are surrounded by chaos. If you knock the ball forward, you will give away a scrum to the opposition and lose possession of the ball for your team.

Although we encourage you to run and pass the ball as much as possible, at a crucial moment in the game your best option may be to kick the ball. It may be in your best interest to keep the ball in play and avoid touch (placing the ball out of bounds). Make sure you don't aimlessly kick away your possession.

Kicking the ball downfield and within 5 metres of the touch line will ensure that your opponents have only a narrow angle from which to kick back to touch, which will hopefully make a long clearance impossible. This will give you an opportunity to regain possession by having control of the throw-in at the subsequent line-out. This proves that you need to kick with purpose, rather than as a last resort because you cannot think of anything else to do.

Accurate kicking can help relieve pressure on your team when you are in a deep defensive position, and well-placed attacking kicks that are chased well can be powerful additions to your team's threat. Inaccurate kicking can spoil much of the hard work you may have done in gaining possession and will probably put your team under pressure by giving away the ball.

In this step, you will learn how to execute the most important kicks in Rugby Union and also how to catch a kicked ball.

THE ROLE OF KICKING

When you kick the ball, you must know why you are doing it and what advantage you hope to achieve over your opponents. Your teammates, especially the chasers who are directly involved, must know when to expect a kick, and the entire team should know where the ball should land.

During a game you are likely to kick the ball both in attack and in defence. Grubber, chip and high kicks should help your teammates regain possession behind a defence, having moved the ball across the gain line so that it is in front of all attacking players. You may kick the ball into a space to gain ground and take play deep into opposition territory to expose your opposition's defensive weakness and to ease defensive pressure on your backs. For example, a high punt in the air (bomb) is an attacking kick that makes it difficult for the opposition to control the ball because they have to retreat to cover the catcher. If the catcher is the last defensive player, deep in her own territory with the opposition bearing down, she may decide simply to kick the ball off the field to stop the game and allow time for the team to regroup and start again. It is essential that all players understand the effects of kicking in both attack and defence and also their roles once the ball is kicked. Teams that have an effective kicking strategy are often very difficult to play against because they can keep their opponents pinned down in their own half.

If you want to play international rugby, you must practise kicking using both feet. In match situations you would normally kick with the foot furthest from the opposition. For this reason, being able to kick effectively with only one foot is a problem.

In preparation for games, identify who your opponent's main kickers are, whether they kick with both feet equally well, and if not, which is their dominant foot. Once you have done this, you can prepare a kicking strategy to position your opponents so that they have to use their weaker kicking foot to kick the ball.

Practice to improve the accuracy, height and distance of various kicks is also a good opportunity for teammates to practise receiving the ball, on the ground or from the air, and also to practise chasing kicks to regain possession. Except when you are kicking from deep in your own territory, try to keep the ball in play so your team can either regain possession or put the opposition under pressure with a good kick chase.

TYPES OF KICKS

There are two basic ways of kicking the ball: from your hands (punt, drop punt, chip kick, box kick, grubber kick and crossfield kick) and from the ground (place kick and drop kick). Each type of kick plays a distinct and important role for the team with possession.

Kicks From Your Hands

There are a number of types of punt. A high up-and-under bomb allows chasing players to regain possession behind the defence. For this punt, you need to give the ball enough height to allow time for your chasers to race upfield and catch the ball or put pressure on the catcher. A long touch kick

(kicking the ball off the field) is used to gain field position or territory. If you wish to have the throw-in at the subsequent line-out, a long, rolling kick near the touch line will force the opposition to put the ball into touch. Though similar to a grubber kick, this kick is usually much longer. If you know that the opposition's full back cannot kick a long way, you might consider a long, rolling kick to the centre of the pitch, near the posts. A defender picking up the ball here will find it very difficult to hit a long touch, especially with a good chase arriving at the same time, and may even be unable to kick the ball long enough to go over the touch line. This would give your team an attacking opportunity deep in your opponents' defensive zone.

Misstep
You have difficulty kicking the ball into touch.

Correction
Select a target area 5 to 10 metres beyond the touch line. Overcompensate to make certain that the ball reaches touch.

A chip kick is kicked just over the top of an advancing defence, when you see a space behind the defence. Try to catch the chip kick before the ball hits the ground.

The scrum half executes a box kick from the base of the scrum, often on the right-hand side of the field so the right winger and centres can chase the ball and put pressure on the defence. You need to get the ball to hang in the air to buy time for your chasers. (Note: A box kick is similar to a bomb kick, but the technique is notably different.)

Use a grubber kick to move the ball along the ground in such a way as to make it difficult for opponents to control. When you find yourself isolated outside of your 22-metre safety area, use this kick to gain territory or to force a line-out. If the defence is coming up quickly, direct an angled grubber kick through a gap between the opposition players. Often, one of your backs can regain possession. It's also a useful restart kick in wet weather and can lead to the opposition's knocking on.

The crossfield kick is a diagonal kick behind the defence for wingers to chase. A fly half will use this kick if the defence is coming up fast, making it difficult for the centres to play, and there is a space out wide behind the defence. Such kicks often make it difficult for the defence to turn and get back in time to prevent forward movement up the playing field. The type of punt normally used is a drop punt, which flies straight and accurately when done well.

Kicks From the Ground

A place kick is used for penalty and conversion attempts at goal. To start and restart the game, the drop kick is used. You can also use a drop kick to score 3 points in a game.

The drop kick is a vital skill for the fly half to master. Aim to drop kick the ball over the crossbar and between the upright posts. It is an excellent skill that should be learned by as many players as possible. For example, a New Zealand number 8 forward scored a spectacular 45-metre drop goal against England in the semifinal of the 1995 World Cup.

PUNT

To punt accurately and well, you need to have good balance and timing. First, you must select your target, decide where you want the ball to land, and point the ball in the direction in which you want to kick. To start the motion, hold the ball at about waist height and at arm's length from your body (figure 4.1a). Hold the ball at a 45-degree angle to the axis of your foot to get maximum contact with your kicking foot. To kick with your right foot, hold the ball underneath with your right hand near you and your left hand farther away at the top and side of the ball. For a left-footed kick, exchange hands, right hand below left. Your hands create a channel through which you kick.

Misstep
You throw the ball upwards before you kick it and lose control of the ball, resulting in loss of direction and distance.

Correction
Hold the ball away from you at about waist height and bring your foot to the ball. Imagine that you are placing the ball on a shelf. Remember to follow through.

In one controlled movement, place the ball at waist height as if you were stacking something on a shelf; then drop it (figure 4.1b). Point your toes down. Contact the centre of the ball just above your boot laces with your extended ankle and the hard upper bridge of your foot to impart full power (figure 4.1c). Your nonkicking leg must provide a firm foundation for an accurate kick. As your foot contacts the ball, your leg should accelerate to maximise the force imparted to the ball.

When on the run, slow and steady yourself just before kicking. You will find that control, timing and a natural fluid action often produce better results than attempting to whack the ball out of the grounds. The best type of kick here would be a drop punt. A drop punt will allow you to hit the ball and maintain your stride pattern as you punch the ball up through its point and bring your foot back to the ground quickly. For accuracy, point the ball in the direction in which you are going to kick it, point your toes and kick (punch) the point in the line with the panel seams and bring your foot back to the ground quickly so that you can keep going forward without breaking your stride pattern.

Misstep
You lean backwards and lose your balance, which results in a poor punt.

Correction
Steady yourself if you are on the run, and create a firm base with your nonkicking foot. Keep your head down and your body over the ball.

For proper follow-through, keep your head down and your body over the ball. Try to finish with a high follow-through, with your foot above head height (figure 4.1d). Keep your leg straight and your toes pointed. For a right-footed kick, your left hand should be almost touching your right foot, and your left shoulder should be forward.

Figure 4.1   Punt

PREPARATION

1. Select target
2. Keep eyes on ball
3. Point ball in direction of kick
4. Hold ball at 45-degree angle
5. Hold ball at waist height and arm's length
6. Hold ball in right hand, left hand at top and side of ball (right-footed kick)

a

RELEASE

1. Point toes down
2. Release ball

b

CONTACT

1. Contact centre of ball just above boot laces
2. Use nonkicking leg to provide firm foundation
3. Accelerate leg at impact
4. Use good control, good timing and fluid action

c

FOLLOW-THROUGH

1. Head down; body over ball
2. High follow-through; foot above head
3. Leg straight; toes pointed

d

Misstep
You keep slicing the ball in the wrong direction.

Correction
Hit the belly of the ball, and point your toes down to keep a firm kicking foot.

BOMB KICK

This kick is similar to the punt for touch or down-field, but incorporates a special technique that helps the ball hang in the air, allowing time for your chasers to regain possession and making it difficult for the opposition to catch. Often, it is aimed at the opposition's goalposts, and the ball rotates end over end. To execute the bomb kick, hold the ball vertically (upright) with one hand on each side and release it, aiming to kick the bottom point of the ball (figure 4.2).

Figure 4.2   Executing the bomb kick.

GRUBBER KICK

Lean forward with your head and eyes over the ball while holding the ball upright across its side seams with one hand on each side (figure 4.3a). Release the ball and make contact with it just before it lands upright on the ground. Point your toes towards the ground (figure 4.3b), and make contact with your laces while keeping your bent knee slightly ahead of the ball. Make contact with the upper half of the ball. Follow through with a low, straight leg so the ball moves along the ground (figure 4.3c).

Misstep
The ball lands awkwardly because you made poor contact with your foot.

Correction
Hold the ball across the side seams, with one hand on each side to steady it, and allow it to drop vertically. Try kicking the ball with your instep or the side of your foot for more control.

Figure 4.3   Grubber Kick

PREPARATION
1. Select target
2. Keep eyes on ball
3. Keep head over ball
4. Lean forward
5. Steady yourself if running
6. Hold ball on each side across side seams
7. Hold ball upright

a

(continued)

Figure 4.3 *(continued)*

EXECUTION

1. Release ball to fall upright
2. Make contact just before ball lands
3. Point toes down; make contact with laces
4. Keep bent knee slightly ahead of ball
5. Make contact with upper half of ball

b

FOLLOW-THROUGH

1. Punch ball along ground
2. Keep leg low and straight

c

Misstep
You have difficulty coordinating the movement.

Correction
Remember to slow down and keep your eyes on the ball, not on your opponents, after you have selected the target area.

DROP KICK

Hold the ball on each side with your fingers pointing down or forward (figure 4.4a). Hold the ball out in front of you at waist height, with your elbows bent slightly inwards. Keep your eye on the ball, and release it to drop vertically, upright and angled slightly towards you. As the ball lands on the ground, use your instep to connect with the ball on the half-volley, and sweep through to kick the ball into the air (figure 4.4b). For the follow-through, your kicking foot swings through high, above head height, and your nonkicking leg supports your weight (figure 4.4c). Remember to keep your eyes on the ball and the point where it initially lands throughout your drop-kicking action.

Misstep

You have difficulty controlling the drop of the ball.

Correction

Hold the ball on each side, with your fingers pointing down or forward, and simply release the ball in front of you.

Figure 4.4 — Drop Kick

a *b* *c*

PREPARATION

1. Select target
2. Keep eyes on ball
3. Hold ball in front at waist height, elbows bent slightly in
4. Hold ball along sides, fingers forward or down

EXECUTION

1. Keep head down over ball
2. Drop ball upright, angled slightly towards you
3. As ball lands, instep connects with ball

FOLLOW-THROUGH

1. Nonkicking leg bears weight
2. Kicking foot swings above head height
3. Eyes on ball and point on ground where it landed

Misstep

You have difficulty timing the drop and the kick.

Correction

Relax and keep your head down and eyes on the ball all the time, especially when it hits the ground.

Misstep

You are unable to get any height on the ball.

Correction

Your head is coming up too early. Keep it down and use a long follow-through with your leg.

PLACE KICK

A place kick is used for a penalty kick at goal and a conversion attempt after a try has been scored. The kicking tee, a bit like a golf tee, lifts the ball off the turf, which helps you make better contact with the sweet spot. An accurate, reliable place kicker is a very important member of the team because successful penalty kicks and conversions keep the scoreboard ticking over. Each international team has a specialist place kicker, who usually practises kicking at least five days a week to develop a kicking routine and almost infallible technique.

Place kickers place the ball on the tee at various angles and use a variety of approach runs. We will concentrate on the 'round the corner' method. If you do not have a kicking tee, use a marker cone or sand or just place the ball upright on the ground. (You may need to use your heel to make a dent in which to balance the ball.) Experiment with angles until you find one that allows the ball to fly straight and accurately and at the same time allows you to kick the ball with good elevation.

 Misstep

You keep kicking the ball along the ground.

Correction

You are making contact too high up on the ball, and your nonkicking foot is probably too near the ball. Remember to aim for the sweet spot about a third of the way up the ball.

To execute the place kick, place your left foot alongside the ball and your right foot behind it (right-footed kicker). Take three to seven strides back from the ball, and two to the left side, remembering that the more strides you take, the more you risk becoming unbalanced as you approach the ball. Align your shoulders with the intended path of the ball. Select your target area, midway between the posts and high above the crossbar. Align the ball with the posts, using the seams like gun sights, with one seam facing the posts and one facing you. Focus on a particular spot between and beyond the middle of the posts. Visualise the path of flight to the target. Relax, take a couple of deep breaths and focus on success. See the ball soaring between the posts.

 Misstep

You cannot get the ball to travel in a straight line.

Correction

Select your target area. Lean the ball at a slight angle away from your foot. You need to concentrate on where you place your nonkicking foot. Ask a friend to point out where you plant your foot. It should land to the side of the ball at a distance that allows your kicking leg to swing freely. Kick through the middle line of the ball, not to the left or right side.

With your focus on that particular spot between and beyond the middle of the posts (figure 4.5a), and while keeping your eyes on the sweet spot of the ball, approach the ball with a balanced, controlled stride. Plant your nonkicking foot alongside the ball with a long last stride (figure 4.5b). Keep your head down and your weight on your left leg, and make contact with your instep or the top of your big toe while holding your left arm out for balance (figure 4.5c). To finish the place kick, keep your head down and follow through the line of the ball (figure 4.5d). Keep your kicking foot along the line of the trajectory.

Figure 4.5 Place Kick

PREPARATION

1. Tee ball up at angle that suits your kicking style
2. Select target between posts; visualise path to target
3. Align ball with posts
4. Place left foot beside ball, right foot behind it
5. Take three to seven paces back and two to the left (right-footed kick)
6. Align shoulders with proposed trajectory of ball
7. Focus on particular spot between and beyond middle of posts
8. Look at sweet spot and visualise successful kick between posts to land on your focus point
9. Look up at posts and at focus point
10. Breathe deeply, relax, focus on success and look back at sweet spot

a

b

c

d

APPROACH

1. Approach ball at slow, steady speed
2. Plant nonkicking foot beside ball with long last stride
3. Keep head down
4. Hold left arm out for balance

CONTACT

1. Keep kicking leg extended
2. Make contact with instep or top of big toe on sweet spot
3. Keep weight on nonkicking leg

FOLLOW-THROUGH

1. Keep head down after kick
2. Punch kicking leg through ball towards posts
3. Kicking foot follows along ball flight and finishes in line with trajectory

Misstep
You are having trouble kicking the ball far enough.

Correction
Your last stride may be too long, preventing your kicking foot from swinging through with power. You could be kicking under the ball and making contact too low on the ball.

CATCHING A KICK

Catching a kick in a controlled manner is as important a skill as kicking the ball. If the kick is slightly too far for the chasers to contest, you may be able to keep your feet on the ground and catch with a very stable base.

To execute the catch properly, keep your eyes on the ball and call 'My ball!' to communicate your intentions clearly to your teammates. Then move quickly to the spot where the ball will land, making sure your body is side on to the attackers. Create a wide base by making sure your legs are at least shoulder-width apart to ensure good balance (figure 4.6a).

Raise your arms, spread your fingers and turn relaxed palms upwards. Catch the ball in your spread fingers and pull it down to your chest and arms (figure 4.6b). As you pull the ball in, sink your hips into a stable, crouched position, sideways to your opponents with your shoulder braced to accept contact (figure 4.6c). Maintain control of the ball.

Figure 4.6 Catching the Kick

PREPARATION

1. Call 'My ball'
2. Keep eyes on ball
3. Move quickly to where ball will land
4. Keep body side on to attackers
5. Have feet at least shoulder-width apart
6. Raise arms, spread fingers, turn relaxed palms upwards

a

b

c

EXECUTION

1. Catch ball in spread fingers
2. Pull ball down to chest and arms

FOLLOW-THROUGH

1. Sink hips to stable crouch
2. Use sideways stance with shoulders braced
3. Maintain control of ball

If the ball has been kicked so that the chasing players will arrive with the ball, you will need to jump to have the best chance of claiming the ball. To time your run, watch the ball as it descends, and move close to and behind where it will land. At the right time, take a couple of strides to go under the ball, form a triangle with your thumbs and index fingers and stretch your arms upwards so that you can see the ball through the triangle (figure 4.7a).

Jump up and into the trajectory of the ball. At the same time lift your front knee to protect yourself (figure 4.7b) and catch the ball at full stretch. According to the Laws, no other player may tackle you when you are in the air, but if someone jumps against you, your knee will act as a buffer to keep him away from the ball. As you land, try to turn away from the chasing team and towards your own. Sink into a strong braced position with a wide base (figure 4.7c).

Figure 4.7   Jumping to Catch a Kick

PREPARATION

1. Call 'My ball'
2. Keep eyes on ball
3. Move quickly to within a couple of strides and behind where ball will land
4. Make a triangle with thumbs and index fingers as you prepare to jump

a

(continued)

Figure 4.7 *(continued)*

b

c

EXECUTION

1. Raise arms
2. See ball through triangle
3. For protection, lift front knee as you jump
4. Catch ball in spread fingers

FOLLOW-THROUGH

1. Land and sink hips to stable crouch
2. Have stable sideways base
3. Keep control of ball

CAUTION Always wear protective equipment in both practice and match situations. Although not every drill in this section anticipates contact with a player, a piece of equipment or the ground, by its very nature rugby invites contact, sometimes by accident. It's better to be safe than sorry.

Kicking Drill 1. *Punt Kicking for Accuracy*

Work within a four-sectioned grid, with each section measuring 8 metres square (figure 4.8). Stand in grid 1; your partner stands in grid 3 or 4. Punt the ball accurately to each other so neither of you has to move to catch the ball. Constantly change positions within the two grid areas after each kick to test your punting accuracy.

To Increase Difficulty

- Ask a friend to pass you the ball before you kick.
- Pick up a rolling ball; then punt.

- Kick; then chase your ball to put the catcher under pressure.
- Use your weaker foot.

To Decrease Difficulty

- Shorten the distance you have to kick over.
- Stand with your kicking foot back and walk gently into the kick over three paces. As you start the third pace, drop the ball onto your foot as you swing it through and make contact along the long axis with all of your laces. Remember to follow through.

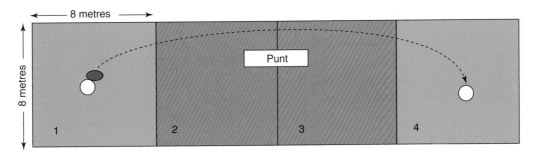

Figure 4.8 Punt kicking for accuracy drill.

Success Check

- Select a target.
- Keep your eyes on the ball and your head down.
- Point your toes down.
- Keep both hands under the ball.
- Make contact with the top of the foot on the belly or up through the point along the axis of the ball.

Score Your Success

9 or 10 accurate punts = 10 points

7 or 8 accurate punts = 5 points

5 or 6 accurate punts = 1 point

Your score ___

Kicking Drill 2.   *Up and Under*

You can use kicking drill 1, punt kicking for accuracy, to help you master the up-and-under (bomb) kick, but to further increase the difficulty and effectiveness of your practice, try the following drill. The bomb kick must stay in the air long enough for the chasers to arrive as it comes down. For the chasers to cover 25 metres to get under the kick, the ball needs to be in the air 3.5 seconds (figure 4.9). Covering 35 metres requires about 5 seconds. Set markers at 25 metres and 35 metres. Practise accuracy and measure timing and height by counting the seconds that the ball is in flight.

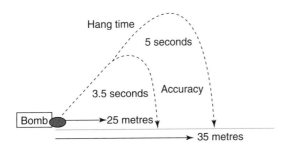

Figure 4.9 Up and under drill.

To Increase Difficulty

- Ask a friend to pass you the ball before you kick.
- Pick up a rolling ball; then punt.
- Practise the bomb with your weaker foot.
- Move the targets to the left or right of the kicker and reduce their size.

To Decrease Difficulty

- Kick just for accuracy and slowly build up the height.
- Make the targets bigger.

Success Check

- Select a target.
- Keep your eyes on the ball and your head down.
- Point your toes down.
- Keep both hands under the ball.
- Make contact with the top of your foot.

4 or 5 accurate bomb kicks that stay in the air for at least 4 seconds = 10 points

2 or 3 accurate bomb kicks that stay in the air for at least 4 seconds = 5 points

1 accurate bomb kick that stays in the air for at least 4 seconds = 1 point

Your score ____

Kicking Drill 3.   Grubber Kick for Accuracy

Use an area 24 metres long and 8 metres wide divided into three sections. Place cones on the four corners of the work area (figure 4.10). Stay in grid 1 and attempt to grubber kick past your partner in grid 3 to score between the two marker cones in grid 3. You and your partner are not allowed in grid 2. Your partner can guard any area in grid 3 to prevent a score. Your partner then attempts to grubber kick the ball past you from where the ball was stopped.

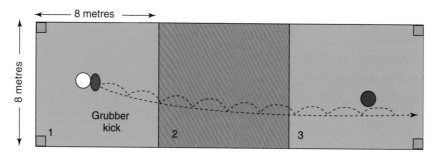

Figure 4.10   Grubber kick for accuracy drill.

To Increase Difficulty

• Make the middle grid narrower.

To Decrease Difficulty

• Grubber kick the ball along the ground by using the side of your foot or instep.

Success Check

• Select a target.
• Hold the ball upright with your hands on either side of the ball.

• Keep your head down.
• Drop the ball onto your foot.
• Punch the ball along the ground.

5 goals or more in 1 minute = 10 points

3 or 4 goals in 1 minute = 5 points

1 or 2 goals in 1 minute = 1 point

Your score ____

Kicking Drill 4.   Drop Kick for Three Points

Place cones 10, 15, and 22 metres directly in front of the posts. Receive a pass from your partner and attempt a drop kick over the bar and between the posts (figure 4.11). Make three drop kicks from each distance. Remember to keep your eye on the ball and to drop the ball directly onto its point slightly in front of your kicking foot as you make contact on the half-volley. Kick straight through the ball, and follow through in line with the flight of the ball.

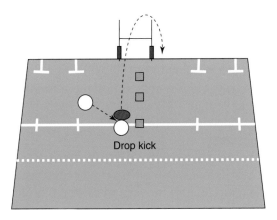

Figure 4.11 Drop kick for three points drill.

To Increase Difficulty

- Kick with your weaker foot.
- After passing the ball, your partner runs towards you, creating pressure like that of an opposition flanker.
- Move 10 metres to the side at the same distance from the posts to change the angle required of your drop kick.
- Gradually move farther away and at wider angles as you become more successful from short distances.

To Decrease Difficulty

- Take all your drop kicks from 10 metres away.
- Remove the passer, and start in a more controlled, static position with the ball already in your hands when you drop kick.

Success Check

- Look at the target area.
- Keep your eyes on the ball.
- Drop the ball onto its point, slightly in front of your kicking foot.
- Make contact on the half-volley.
- Kick straight through the ball and follow through.

Score Your Success

3 successful kicks from each distance = 10 points

2 successful kicks from each distance = 5 points

1 successful kick from each distance = 1 point

Your score ___

Kicking Drill 5. *Daily Dozen Place Kick*

Attempt 12 kicks at goal from various distances and angles. Start with three kicks from a marker placed 15 meters directly in front of the posts. Remember to practise good place-kicking form: Align the ball, focus on a point between and beyond the posts, keep your eyes on the sweet spot, approach the ball under control, and swing through and beyond the ball along the line of flight.

To Increase Difficulty

- Increase the distance from and angle to the posts.

To Decrease Difficulty

- Take all 12 place kicks from the 15-metre mark in front of the posts.

Success Check

- Align the ball.
- Focus on a point between and beyond the posts.
- Keep your eyes on the sweet spot.
- Approach the ball under control.
- Plant your nonkicking foot alongside the ball.
- Keep your head down.
- Swing through and beyond the ball.

Score Your Success

10 to 12 successful kicks = 10 points

7 to 9 successful kicks = 5 points

4 to 6 successful kicks = 1 point

Your score ___

SUCCESS SUMMARY OF KICKING

You will have a lot of fun learning to kick accurately. Set yourself high standards and lots of challenges. Initially, concentrate on perfecting technique, then accuracy and finally power. Remember that good kicking wins games and poor kicking can lose them, so be patient with yourself.

Kicking over the approaching defence is one way of getting the ball over the gain line and in front of your players. Communicate with your team so everyone knows when, why and where you are going to kick to help your chasers regain possession and pressure your opponents. Learn what type of kick is required for any given situation in a match.

In the early stages of learning to kick and catch, you may find that what you learn inhibits your natural ability. However, as you master the various techniques, your natural skill will come through. Have a teammate or coach check your fundamentals against figure 4.1 through 4.7. Remember to practise kicking with both feet for distance, height and accuracy.

If you are expected to kick the ball in either attack or defence, you have a major responsibility to the team. Before moving on to step 5, Contact, evaluate how you did on the kicking drills in this step by tallying your scores. If you scored at least 40 points, you are ready to move on to step 5. If you did not score at least 40 points, practise the drills again until you raise your scores before moving on to step 5.

Kicking Drills

1. Punt Kicking for Accuracy   ___ out of 10

2. Up and Under   ___ out of 10

3. Grubber Kick for Accuracy   ___ out of 10

4. Drop Kick for Three Points   ___ out of 10

5. Daily Dozen Place Kick   ___ out of 10

Total   ___ *out of 50*

Contact

It might not seem like it to you when you are watching or playing a game of rugby, but most of the time players are attempting to avoid contact. Your aim should be to use contact as a last resort, and you should view a ruck or maul situation as a continuity failure—that is, a failure to keep the ball moving forward. In reality there is very little chance of avoiding contact for the duration of the match, and so eventually you will find yourself in contact with opponents, your own teammates and the ground. You need to prepare for and know how to make contact so that you stay in control of your body and the ball to ensure that your team keeps possession.

You have to decide whether to pass or present the ball before, during or after contact. Your decision is based on the closeness and shape of the defence in front of you and the positioning of your support players.

Step 3 focused on tackling and stopping opponents from progressing down the playing field. Here we will look at ways of keeping possession of the ball and using the ball in contact situations. Successful techniques such as the offload, gut pass, ruck and maul will help you remain in control of the game. You will need to practise these techniques with your teammates to familiarise yourselves with each other's body language so you can learn to react to produce a coordinated sequence of support movements. This will enable your team to control possession.

During the game you may find yourself attempting to drive through the opposition or supporting the drive of another member of your team who has made contact. Sometimes this contact is as powerful as the contact you make with the opposition, because you want to ensure that you retain possession of the ball and keep it moving forward against the defence. If you remain straight legged and upright, you will make no impact on the opposition. Imagine you are pushing a car that has run out of petrol. Your body position is low, with shoulders higher than hips, head up, knees bent and legs driving hard. It's important to stay on your feet to prevent toppling over and landing flat on your face. The principles are similar for making contact in rugby.

To maintain the continuity of the attack, the ball carrier must find support, and support players must try hard to stay close to the ball carrier. One of the best ways to find support is to practise the offload and make it a strength of the team. The offload keeps up the tempo of the attack and takes away the time the defence needs to reset.

However, you will not always be able to offload the ball to your support. Sometimes you will have to go into contact. Control the speed at which you go to ground by staying strong at the moment of contact and taking up a good body position to dominate the tackler. As you make contact with the ground, make the best use of the ball by either placing or rolling it to the best advantage of your arriving players. The first support player to arrive at a ball on the ground can pick up the ball and run forward, pick up the ball and pass, or secure the ball for his team to stop the opposition from getting it.

Every player on the team must understand contact techniques to take maximum advantage of the many contact situations that occur in each game. Develop confidence by systematically practising contact techniques in a safe environment, so that these become a natural part of your game.

When practising contact techniques, always have defenders either carrying tackle shields or wearing tackle suits as protection for both of you. As you grow bigger and stronger, tackle suits become an essential piece of equipment for practice sessions.

At the beginning, or learning, stage, the defender should not interfere with the ball.

The defender must take a wide stance with one shoulder pointing towards the ball carrier, so that there is some resistance at contact. Be thoroughly warmed up before you start contact practice with a partner, and remember to always wear your normal body protection and gum shield.

At some point in a game you will make contact with the ground, so you need to learn to fall safely. We will look at falling in this step as well. The state of the pitch will change depending on the weather: Sometimes it will be wet, soggy and muddy; and at other times, dry, hard and with little grass cover. There's nothing like a hard pitch to keep you on your feet!

BUMP

The ball carrier has a range of options for making contact with an opponent. The first to consider is the bump.

As you near the defender, begin to lead with one shoulder. Lower your body towards the ground and push the ball back and away from the contact area, still holding it in both hands. Just before you make contact, take a long, low last stride and bump up and into your opponent's shoulder (figure 5.1). If you make very strong contact, your opponent will step back a little, creating time and space for you to offload the ball to a support player.

If you create enough space with the bump, use your front leg as a pivot, roll your back towards your opponent, swing your rear heel through 180 degrees and drive powerfully off that foot past the defender. Then link up with your nearest team member.

Figure 5.1 Executing the bump.

OFFLOAD

Use the offload just when you make contact with an opponent or immediately after you hit the ground during a tackle attempt. The offload maintains the tempo of the attack and keeps pressure on the defence. Teams that successfully offload regularly often find that they play at high speed and are able to turn defence quickly into attack, which is bad news for the opposition.

Offloads can occur in most contact situations and can be deliberate ploys to beat your direct opponent. Keep the ball in both hands when offloading because you may be in vigorous

contact when you have to offload, making it very easy to spill the ball if it is not secured. However, some of the best offloads occur when defenders believe they have stopped any further passing and either a ruck or a maul is about to form. If a pass is made at that time, then two or three defenders may be committed and taken out of the defensive pattern. Often, offload passes are made with one hand or at odd angles and varying heights, arriving at various speeds. Make sure you practise these many variations so there are no surprise situations when you begin to play.

The more practice you take part in, the more quickly you will see offload opportunities. In many of the tackle drills in step 3, you could add an offload practice by having a support player follow you into the tackle. As you fall, your role is either to make a pass to your support or to place the ball on the ground so that any support player can immediately pick it up and continue to play.

A big and strong player might be able to hold off a would-be tackler with one hand and arm, stay strong and low and make an offload with one hand to a support player (figure 5.2). Once again, this needs a lot of practice on the training field against very active opposition.

Figure 5.2 Offloading with one hand.

GUT PASS

If you have been weaving slightly from side to side to prevent the defender from remaining in one place, you can use a gut pass. Make a long, low last stride into shoulder-to-shoulder contact, drive up and into the defender and roll your back into any other defensive player. Pivot on your front foot and turn through a quarter of a circle until you can see your support and your support can see the ball (figure 5.3a). From this position, you are ready to use the gut pass to move the ball to your support player.

Use both hands to move the ball away from your chest. Firmly push the ball up and into the lower chest region of your support player (figure 5.3b). The support player must lean in to the ball by lowering her shoulders, but keep them above hip height. She reaches out with one hand over and one hand under the ball. She pulls the ball to her chest, stays low and drives beyond the defender (figure 5.3c).

Figure 5.3   Gut Pass

PREPARATION

1. Lead defender away from where you intend to deliver ball
2. Lower shoulder and bend knees slightly
3. With long, low last stride, bump up and into opponent's lower chest or shoulder
4. Make contact with shoulder so ball remains visible to support player
5. Do not try to knock over defender; just make contact
6. Push ball backwards as you go

a

(continued)

Figure 5.3 *(continued)*

EXECUTION

1. Push or pass ball into support player's hands
2. Support player reaches one hand over, one hand under ball

b

FOLLOW-THROUGH

1. Support player stays low and drives past defender
2. Remain strong in contact area by maintaining wide base
3. Support new ball carrier immediately

c

RUCK

There are so many variables in a game of rugby—and situations change so rapidly—that you need to make instant decisions to best help your team. You need to be clear about the possibilities and difficulties associated with creating rucks and mauls.

A ruck is formed when the ball is on the ground and one or more players from both team are on their feet and in physical contact, closing around the ball. A ruck is a technique used by a group of teammates to retain or regain possession, usually when one team member has been tackled.

In some situations rucking is a good option because you are trying to disorganise the defence and retain or obtain the ball in a tackle situation. A ruck often produces a quick ball, meaning that the ball is in the hands of the scrum half before the defence has a chance to reset, in an attacking situation. Also, a ruck is more dynamic than

a maul and keeps you going forward, is technically simpler for support players and helps backs time their runs because they often can see the ball coming out.

To ruck well, players usually need to arrive at the contact or tackle situation before the opposition and then drive forward. To disorganise a defence and keep the ball moving forward quickly, try to set up a dynamic and fast ruck to produce a quick ball. The ball carrier should make contact first with his leading shoulder and attempt to bump the tackler away (figure 5.4a). If the ball carrier is held, he turns towards his support. The ball carrier goes to the ground slowly to buy time for his support (figure 5.4b). As he hits the ground, the ball carrier places the ball at arm's length towards his support players (figure 5.4c).

Misstep

As the ball carrier, you are turned as you go to the ground.

Correction

Drive your tackler back; then go to the ground under control.

Support players drive over the top of the tackled player and the ball and bind onto (wrap their arms around and grip tightly) the opposition or other support players (figure 5.4*c*). A support player drives forward with a low body position, keeping his eyes open and his head looking forward, with his chin off his chest and his spine in line with the touch lines. The support player keeps his back flat, his body heading towards the goal line and his shoulders always above his hips. He stays on his feet and keeps his opponents on their feet (figure 5.4*d*).

 Misstep

As a support player you fall over during the ruck.

Correction

Take a long, low last stride and keep your shoulders above your hips. Bind, with a firm grip, onto a teammate or the opposition.

After the tackle, the ball carrier gets back to his feet immediately to support the next piece of play (figure 5.4*e*). The support and driving players need to assess the situation and move to offer their support at the next stoppage or to join in the passing movement once the ball has moved away from the ruck.

Figure 5.4   Ruck

MAKE CONTACT

Ball Carrier

1. Make contact with leading shoulder
2. Try to bump tackler away

a

GO TO GROUND

Ball Carrier

1. If held, turn towards support
2. Go to ground slowly

b

(continued)

Figure 5.4 *(continued)*

FORM RUCK

Ball Carrier

1. Place ball at arm's length behind you, closer to support

Support Players

1. Drive over top of tackled player
2. Bind onto the opposition or other support players

c

DRIVE OPPONENT BACK

Support Players

1. Maintain low body position
2. Drive low and upwards to lift opposition
3. Keep eyes open, head looking forward, spine in line with touch lines
4. Keep back flat and shoulders always above hips
5. Shrug shoulders and loosen neck on contact
6. Stay on feet and keep opponent on his feet

d

FOLLOW-THROUGH

Ball Carrier and Support Players

1. After ruck moves on, ball carrier quickly gets to feet
2. Support players move to next stoppage or join in passing movement

e

Misstep
As the ball carrier you lose control of the ball as you attempt to place it on the ground.

Correction
Concentrate on landing on your side, not on the ball. Practise placing the ball with both hands.

Sometimes you will not be able to stop the defender from tackling you to the ground, and your support will be too far away for you to pass the ball. To execute the ruck in this situation, place the ball on the ground under control so your nearest support player can pick it up or drive over it and into the opposition before your team loses possession.

When preparing to make contact with the ground, it is important to go with the flow of the impact of the tackle because this will help you to land and roll naturally. Attempt to round your shoulder (figure 5.5a) and land mainly on your back and side. Bend your knees. Do not put out a straight arm or hand to break your fall. Tuck your chin into your chest as you land (figure 5.5b). The nearest support player can either stride across and above you, staying low to protect the ball (figure 5.5c), or drive over and beyond you, making contact with any opponent who is threatening to take the ball.

You can attempt to create rucks that have a particular balanced shape or structure, depending on the actions of the ball carrier and first support player. However, these are difficult to achieve in a dynamic game. It will depend on the quality and power of your opponents, who may be able to smash into your ruck and mis-shape it.

a

b

c

Figure 5.5 Going with the impact of the tackle: *(a)* round your shoulder; *(b)* tuck your chin into your chest as you hit the ground; *(c)* the support player strides over you, staying low to protect the ball.

 Misstep
As a support player you come to a stop as you make contact.

Correction
Keep pumping your legs quickly and take short, aggressive steps.

 Misstep
As a support player you arrive at an angle and drive across the pitch towards the touch line.

Correction
Make sure you arrive at the ruck through the gate at the back and behind the ball, with your spine in line with the touch lines. Drive straight down the length of the pitch to force the opposition backwards.

A 2-3-2 ruck (figure 5.6) is created when, because of close support players, the ball carrier decides to place the ball on the ground just before or as contact is made. The first two support players get low, bind on early and drive in on either side of the ball carrier. The next three players bind on and form a wider driving base. A 2-3-2 ruck also occurs when the ball is already on the ground, usually after a tackle, with an opponent trying to get the ball. If the first two support players arrive together, they should get low, bind onto each other and the opposition and drive the opposition out of the way to free the ball, with the help of other support players as they arrive at the tackle situation.

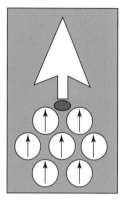

Figure 5.6 A 2-3-2 ruck when the ball is already on the ground.

A 3-2-3 ruck (figure 5.7) is created when the ball carrier is in contact with opponents and not on the ground, and the opposition seems likely to threaten the ball. The first support player decides to change the maul into a ruck by ripping the ball from the ball carrier, going to the ground and releasing the ball for the support players to drive over and the scrum half to

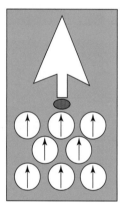

Figure 5.7 A 3-2-3 ruck.

pass away. In either case, you may not have to commit that number of players to win the ball, especially if the ball carrier has done everything correctly and made the ball visible and available to the nearest support players. The fewer you can put in the ruck, the better, because it means that you have more people available to run and help attack the defence. However the basic principles still apply—keep the shape balanced, moving forward and beyond the ball.

Sometimes an opponent may have got to the ball first and may already be picking it up from the ground close to the tackled player. In this situation you have two options:

1. Wipe out the player by driving in hard and taking the threat away in any direction.

2. Drive in directly over the ball, under the chest of your opponent, and force your arms through his and above the ball (figure 5.8). This will break his grip on the ball and you can then clear the area for your support to win the ball.

Figure 5.8 Freeing the ball from an opponent's grip.

Misstep

Your team has difficulty securing the ball at the breakdown because an opponent gets his hands on the ball.

Correction

The first player to arrive needs to decide whether to drive over or contest the ball. If an opponent has his hands on the ball, drive your arms between his and lift them away to clear the ball for your support. If not, drive in low and lift your opponent away.

If your opponent has fallen on or near the ball and play has been allowed to continue, drive in as low as you can and hook your hands and arms under this player and lift and drive to clear the ball. In all of these situations it is essential to have a 'go forward' mentality.

Misstep

Although you are strong in the ruck and you work hard, your team do not seem to go forward.

Correction

Check your driving positions and make sure your spines are in line with the touch lines.

MAUL

It is very difficult to ruck if you are not going forward. You may need to maul during a game if you are retreating and need to recover control of the ball or if your attack has been partially halted by the opposition. You also can use a maul as a deliberate ploy to disorganise the defence by quickly moving the ball to the back player and then driving downfield to suck in close defenders. The front players in driving mauls often trip over outstretched legs. All players must be aware of this and stay balanced enough so that, if any part of the maul falls, players who are still on their feet and driving forward can retain control of the ball. Mauls can produce problems if they are static, and a slow ball may be produced in attacking situations if too many players get their hands on the ball.

The ball carrier is the most important person in the maul because the first contact affects everyone else's reactions. By keeping the ball in his hands and off the ground, the ball carrier presents a target for support players. To execute the maul, the ball carrier drops his chin to his chest and shrugs his shoulders for protection as he makes contact with the point of his leading shoulder. The ball carrier drives from a low position up into the opponent's midriff (figure 5.9*a*). He spins slightly and towards the side of the opponent, holding the ball firmly to his chest with both hands. The ball carrier bends his knees to establish a wide, solid base and stay on his feet (see figure 5.9*b*). He keeps driving with his legs but keeps the ball visible to the first support player. If possible, the ball carrier passes to the support player.

Misstep

As the ball carrier you become isolated from your support.

Correction

Bump the tackler away and recoil to create time and space for your support players.

Misstep

As the ball carrier you lose control of the ball as you make contact.

Correction

If a pass is not possible as you make contact, hold the ball firmly to your chest with both hands, but away from the defenders, until your support arrives.

When you drive into the opposition, do not get isolated or turned towards your opponents. Rely on the nearest teammate to support you quickly so your team has four protective hands on the ball (figure 5.9*c*). Support runners must keep their eyes open and look at the ball. The nearest one should drive in under the ball and upwards, keeping shoulders square to the goal lines, and use the shoulder opposite to the ball carrier's to create a barrier. The support player has four basic choices:

1. Strip or take the ball and run with it.

2. Strip or take the ball and pass to another supporting player.

3. Secure and isolate the ball with the ball carrier and buy time for the next support player.

4. Keep the ball away from the opposition.

The rest of the supporting players need to drive the maul forward, protect the ball, and keep all players, including the opposition, on their feet (figure 5.9*d*). Move the ball to the back of the maul if the opposition prevents a roll around the edge of the maul (figure 5.9*e*). Try to release the ball to your scrum half while you are still driving forward (figure 5.9*f*).

75

Misstep

As the support player you lose sight of the ball as you go into contact.

Correction

Focus on the ball as the target.

Misstep

As the support player, after you drive in to the maul, the opposition still is able to put their hands on the ball.

Correction

When you drive in to secure the ball, lead with the shoulder opposite the ball carrier's.

Figure 5.9 Maul

PREPARATION

Ball Carrier

1. Keep eyes open and head up
2. Take a long, low last stride before contact
3. Keep low and aim to drive up into opponent's midriff
4. Keep body weight over leading foot

a

ESTABLISH POSITION

Ball Carrier

1. Drop chin to chest for protection
2. Establish wide, stable base

Support Player

1. Keep eyes open and on ball
2. Square shoulders to goal lines
3. Offer quick support

b

PROTECT BALL

Ball Carrier

1. Step to opponent's side to unbalance tackler
2. Make contact with point of leading shoulder
3. Drive from low and up into opponent's midriff
4. Hold ball firmly with both hands
5. Shrug shoulders on contact; turn slightly sideways
6. Look forward; keep driving with legs
7. Keep ball visible to support player

Support Player

1. Drive under ball and upwards
2. Use shoulder opposite to ball carrier to create barrier
3. Share ball with ball carrier: four hands on ball
4. Place one arm over top and one underneath ball

DRIVE AS A GROUP

1. Drive together, legs moving
2. Stay on your feet and protect ball

MOVE BALL

1. Communicate with each other
2. Take or uncouple ball and pass, run or roll out or move ball quickly to rear player
3. Stay on feet and pivot towards leading shoulder
4. Move ball back if opposition prevents roll around edge
5. If maul is about to collapse, move ball to players in maul who can stay on their feet and keep driving

c

d

e

(continued)

77

Figure 5.9 *(continued)*

RELEASE BALL

1. Release ball to scrum half while driving forward

f

Misstep
The defenders turn you, the ball carrier, away from your support.

Correction
Your last stride into contact should be long and low so you can sink your hips, bend your knees and create a wide, solid base with your feet and legs.

Misstep
As the ball carrier you fall over when you release the ball.

Correction
After releasing the ball, use your arms to hold up the support player to keep you both on your feet.

CAUTION Always wear protective equipment in both practice and match situations. Although not every drill in this section anticipates contact with a player, a piece of equipment or the ground, by its very nature rugby invites contact, sometimes by accident. It's better to be safe than sorry.

Contact Drill 1. *Falling Under Control*

In a grid 8 metres by 8 metres, follow your partner, who calls 'Down'. Both of you practise falling gradually; then getting up quickly. Now repeat the practice holding a ball, which you place under control at arm's length to the side of your body when you fall. The ball should remain still for your partner to pick up easily.

To Increase Difficulty

- After you place the ball on the ground, your partner straddles the ball or you, lifts the ball, runs forward five paces and then falls down. Get up quickly to get back into the game after your partner has lifted the ball. Alternate roles.

To Decrease Difficulty

- Start on your knees; then fall to the ground, placing the ball carefully for your partner to pick up.

Success Check

- Do not use your arms to break your fall or fall with your limbs extended.
- Tighten and round your landing shoulder.
- The ball should be the last thing to hit the ground.

5 falls with the ball well placed = 5 points

3 or 4 falls with the ball well placed = 3 points

1 or 2 falls with the ball well placed = 1 point

Your score ___

Contact Drill 2. Drive and Protect

Use an 8-metre by 8-metre grid. Your partner provides initially passive, controlled defence, so you get used to making contact with a defender. Pick up a ball, walk quickly to the side of your partner and make strong contact from low to high, shoulder to chest. Your partner, acting as a defender, holds you up, checks your technique and gives you feedback and marks on a 10-point scale for each attempt.

Progress to playing a 1v1 walking game across the 8-metre grid. Start with the ball on your goal line. Go forward and attempt to drive your partner back and score over the goal line. Alternate your lead shoulder each time you make contact. Your partner can tackle you to the ground. When you are tackled to the ground, both you and your partner have to get up quickly and regain your feet before you can play the ball again. Your partner can also rip the ball out of your hands.

To Increase Difficulty

- Play a 1v1 jogging or full-speed game across an 8-metre by 8-metre grid or a 16-metre by 8-metre grid.

To Decrease Difficulty

- Your partner stands still, holding the ball. Practise grabbing and turning your partner. Use your legs, shoulders, arms and back to make the turn. Your partner tries to drive you back over the goal line.

- Face your partner and take turns driving each other across the grid and then back. You can attempt this with or without a ball.

Success Check

- Keep your shoulders above your hips.
- Keep your eyes open.
- Make a long, low last stride.
- Hold the ball firmly.
- Turn slightly sideways to protect the ball.
- Drive your legs parallel to the touch line.

Score 3 times while leading with the left shoulder = 5 points

Score 2 times while leading with the left shoulder = 3 points

Score 1 time while leading with the left shoulder = 1 point

Score 3 times while leading with the right shoulder = 5 points

Score 2 times while leading with the right shoulder = 3 points

Score 1 time while leading with the right shoulder = 1 point

Your score ___

Contact Drill 3. *Continuity Practice*

Work in a grid 10 metres long by 5 metres wide. Three players attack one passive defender. You cannot pass the ball before contact. As the ball carrier, attack the edge of the defender, drive forward and then gradually sink to the ground, placing the ball at arm's length away from you. Alternate your lead shoulder each time you make contact. The first support player drives over you and the ball in a low body position, making contact with the defender and taking one step beyond you, leaving the ball behind for the second support player to pick up and score over the goal line. Start the practice at a jogging pace until you get used to it, to ensure safety.

Alternatively, try to stay on your feet and keep the ball visible and available to your nearest support runner. If you can do this, then try these options:

- Keep the ball close to your chest and stay on your feet until the first support player drives into you and rips away the ball.
- Gut pass or offload.
- Fend and feed.

To Increase Difficulty

- Choose to set up a maul, ruck or pass before, during or after contact. Support players start with their backs to you and turn and run only when you start to run towards the defender. The support players have to read your body language and react quickly. Start at a jogging pace. When you feel confident, try the drill at various running speeds.

To Decrease Difficulty

- Lie down in front of a defender and place the ball on the ground. The first support player jogs out and gently drives over you and the ball.
- Carry the ball into contact and stay strong and on your feet with the ball visible to the support. When the first support player arrives, get four hands on the ball and drive forward together. The first support player slowly goes to the ground, leaving you standing as a barrier against the opposition. This creates more time for a third support player to arrive and continue the attack.

Success Check: Ball Carrier

- Select a target.
- Take a long, low last stride.
- Drive forward; then turn to the support.
- Gradually sink to the ground or stay on your feet in a strong, low position.
- Place the ball at arm's length, or push it into the hands of your arriving support.

Success Check: Support Player

- Keep your eyes open and look forward.
- Go low early and keep your shoulders above your hips.
- Drive over the top of the ball carrier and ball or reach into the body of the ball carrier and rip the ball away or expect an offload.
- Bind on and drive the opposition backwards if you do not get the ball.
- Stay on your feet.

Score Your Success

5 tries leading with the left shoulder = 5 points

3 or 4 tries leading with the left shoulder = 3 points

1 or 2 tries leading with the left shoulder = 1 point

5 tries leading with the right shoulder = 5 points

3 or 4 tries leading with the right shoulder = 3 points

1 or 2 tries leading with the right shoulder = 1 point

Your score ___

Contact Drill 4. *Driving 2v1 and 3v1*

Work in a 10-metre by 5-metre grid. The ball carrier picks up the ball, which is half-way between the support player and the defender, and jogs to make contact with the defender's edge. The support player arrives, ensures that four hands are on the ball and drives forward through the area with the initial ball carrier to score. If there is any danger that the first ball carrier is about to go to the ground in a tackle, then the support player should rip the ball away and continue with the drive.

The 3v1 drill uses the same techniques as the 2v1 drill, but a second support player helps by binding into the gap between the players or over the back of the first ball carrier. The ball immediately is pushed backwards and into this player's hands. At the same time the two initial players gradually swing their hips inwards to make sure their spines are in line with the touch lines and bind tightly together to provide a barrier for the ball carrier, who also remains tightly bound. All three attackers attempt to drive the ball through the grid area to score over the goal line. Remember to stay on your feet. If there is any danger of the ball carrier being taken to the ground, then the ball should be moved through the hands to the back player, who can keep driving forward. Rotate positions.

To Increase Difficulty

- Play a 3v2 or 2v2 walking, driving and tackling game across a 16-metre by 8-metre grid. If tackled, the ball carrier has to release the ball for others to pick up, unless he gets back on his feet quickly to play the ball again. Experiment with pivoting, turning and rolling around the defenders; then driving straight. Keep in close contact with your support players and work as a team, sometimes holding each other up, sometimes trying to keep the ball alive by fending and feeding, offloading or driving and feeding.

To Decrease Difficulty

- Play a 1v1 keep ball game. Both of you have to stay on your feet and in the grid. You have to wrestle the ball away from your partner by pulling down on the ball when he pulls up, and vice versa, or by getting your hands between your partner's elbows and the ball and pulling down.

Success Check: Ball Carrier

- Make contact with your leading shoulder.
- Bump up and into the defender.
- Hold the ball away from the contact area and in both hands as your support arrives.
- Turn slightly sideways and shrug your shoulders.

Success Check: First Support Player

- Drive in and under the ball leading with your arm over the top of the ball.
- Use the shoulder opposite the ball carrier's.
- Share the ball with the ball carrier, and then push it back into the second support player's hands.
- Drive your hips together, keep your spine in line with the touch lines and drive forward.

Success Check: Second Support Player

- Bind over, not onto, the first ball carrier, or fill the gap, take the ball and drive.
- Drive your legs, keeping your shoulders above your hips.
- Keep your spine in line with the touch lines.

Score Your Success

5 tries = 10 points

3 or 4 tries = 5 points

1 or 2 tries = 1 point

Your score ____

Contact Drill 5. *Clearing the Ball*

Work in groups of six. Five players contest the ball but only go in if the ball remains tied in. The last player acts as the scrum half.

Lay four tackle bags on the ground at right angles to the players. At each bag an opponent mirrors a ruck situation. At the first bag an opponent threatens possession by standing with one foot on either side of the bag above the ball (figure 5.10a). At the second bag, the opponent has her hands on the ball (figure 5.10b). At the third bag, the opponent lies on the bag close to the ball (figure 5.10c). At the fourth bag, the opponent lies over the bag and ball (figure 5.10d).

a

b

c

d

Figure 5.10 Clearing the ball drill: *(a)* the opponent stands with one foot on either side of the bag; *(b)* the opponent has her hands on the ball; *(c)* the opponent lies on the bag close to the ball; *(d)* the opponent lies over the bag and the ball.

At each bag, the first player to arrive has to be decisive—drive over, contest possession, lift and drive or smash into contact in a controlled, aggressive movement.

To Increase Difficulty

- Arrange the bags in a square and work from the centre to the outside, coming back to the middle each time.
- The coach numbers the bags and calls out a different number each time you come back to the middle so that you have to react to a new situation each time.

To Decrease Difficulty

- Work through the bags in order, so that you know what situation will come next.
- Defenders do not put as much pressure on the area around the ball.

Success Check: First to Arrive

- Make a decision early.
- Go forward to clear the ball.
- Grab hold of and drive any defender away from the ball.

Success Check: Other Arriving Players

- Maintain a good body position—low to high and spine in line with the touch lines.
- Bind together tightly and work as a small unit.
- Drive beyond the ball.
- Grab hold of and drive away any defender.

Work through the circuit twice = 5 points

Your score ___

SUCCESS SUMMARY OF CONTACT

When contesting for possession of the ball, you will inevitably make contact. As you practise, contact will become a natural part of your game and you will make a significant contribution to your team effort. Remember, turning over possession gives your opponent the opportunity to attack. The main aim of rugby is to avoid contact and keep the ball moving forward to score tries. Rucks and mauls are temporary stoppages, but necessary techniques to master, to ensure that you retain possession when halted in your progress down the field.

Always practise contact work with someone the same size as you, and help each other to learn by being patient. Gradually progress from standing to walking to jogging and finally to running. By being sensible and learning the correct contact techniques, you will make contact in practice and game situations safe, effective and enjoyable. Don't forget to assess your progress in contact skills. Have fun, and remember that if you 'keep your spine in line, your drive will be fine', and if you 'stay on your feet, the opposition will retreat'.

The drills in this step have a combined total of 40 points. Add up your points to see if you are ready to move on to the next step. If you have scored fewer than 30 points, you may not yet be ready for the next step. Revisit those drills that you scored poorly on and improve your scores before you move on to step 6, Mini-Units in Attack.

Contact Drills

1. Falling Under Control		___ out of 5
2. Drive and Protect		___ out of 10
3. Continuity Practice		___ out of 10
4. Driving 2v1 and 3v1		___ out of 10
5. Clearing the Ball		___ out of 5
Total		___ *out of 40*

Mini-Units
in Attack

Players in a number of positions constantly interact with each other during a game. These players often make up trios—for example, the forwards in the front row and those in the back row. There are trios of backs: the fly half and two centres in midfield, and the full back and two wingers behind them. If you are a member of one of these mini-units, you should practise together to become a team within the team. If your mini-unit is efficient, you will add strength to the other sections of the team.

Sometimes the players in a mini-unit work together to create space for other players. In turn, those players also may work together to release other players into the attack. An example of a move that requires coordination between two mini-units is a back-row move that releases the three midfield players, who work hard to create space for the three backs. The midfield and back mini-units will line up in an M shape to make most effective use of any space or gap (figure 6.1).

If you have the ball in attack, other players become involved, so that a number of other mini-units form as a match develops. A ball carrier in open play or the scrum half from the base of a ruck or maul normally have two or three support players with whom to set up the next attack. These mini-units are not prearranged; they occur quite spontaneously during the game.

When the ball comes slowly from the ruck or maul or the ball carrier faces a covering defence, the attack sometimes struggles to be effective. At such times you need to apply the basic principles of playing in small units. These principles rely heavily on the vision of the ball carrier and the discipline of the support players, who should be in position to give the ball carrier a number of options to continue the play.

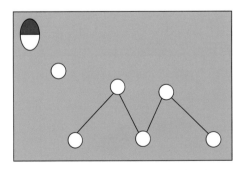

Figure 6.1   Midfield and back mini-units forming an M.

DEVELOPING MINI-UNIT SKILLS USING CHANNELS

Practising all your positional skills and individual skills together as a trio will help your mini-unit understand how to work together, so that under pressure during a game you will react instinctively to each other. Aim to run as a group during skill practice sessions so that you can specifically practise attacking ploys centred on your positions.

In the early stages of learning, practise in channels 5 metres wide and 22 metres long, without any defenders (figure 6.2). To begin with, respond to instructions from your coach so that the ball carrier or support runners can practise finding the gap in the defence. For example, your coach may tell you that the gap is in channel 3 and that your job is to move the ball quickly to that channel with a straightforward pass or a miss pass or other skill. When you can do this, introduce some passive defenders but leave one channel without a defender. Once your small group can spot and attack the empty channel, allow the defenders to try to stop the attack in any way they can but still leave one channel empty.

You can use a number of simple ploys to beat the defence in these situations. If you are the ball carrier at the outside, run forward and inwards towards the next channel, but do not enter it. The players in the other channels must keep their running lines parallel to the touch lines. When you reach the edge of the channel, you have three options:

1. Pop pass into the first channel to the first receiver.

2. Miss pass (skip over) across the next channel to the second receiver (figure 6.3).

3. Miss pass across two channels to the third receiver.

The player who catches the pass has another set of options, including a pass back, a miss pass farther out or penetration through a hole in the defence. The underlying principle of all of these attacks is that the players without the ball must run at spaces between the defenders ahead of them.

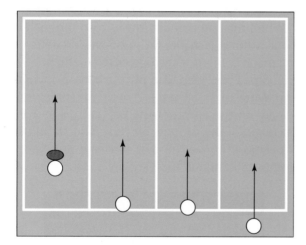

Figure 6.2 Practise in channels against no defenders at first.

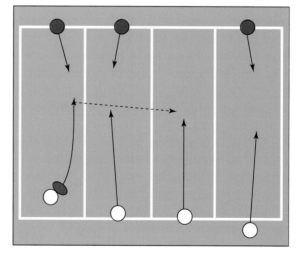

Figure 6.3 Miss passing across the channel to the second receiver.

Misstep

The sequences you practise do not work in the match.

Correction

Practise only against live opposition once you have learned the basic running and passing patterns of your moves. This is the only way to practise running lines and timing for entry into the attacking line. If the moves still do not work, work on the distance from your opponents at which your moves take place. You may be either too close or too far, and the timing of your passes may be either too soon or too late.

Now begin to change positions in the channels to practise decoy running and switching the direction of the attack. If you run with the ball from your original channel into another channel, the player occupying that channel takes up the space you left. This ensures that your attack continues to run parallel to the touch lines. At the point of the crossover, you have five options:

1. Execute a switch pass (figure 6.4).
2. Receive a pass back as a looping player.
3. Pop pass to the outside channel (figure 6.5).
4. Miss pass to the second receiver on the outside.
5. Make a dummy pass and run through a gap in the defence.

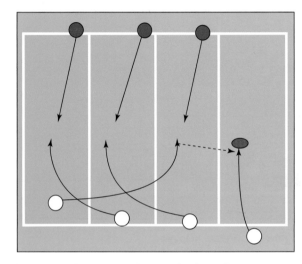

Figure 6.5 Pop pass to the outside channel.

However, if you run outwards and away from the other attackers, they should run to the same side of their channels so that the subsequent passes do not become too long (figure 6.6). Once you begin to run down the outside edge of your channel, you can pass to another player using any passing technique.

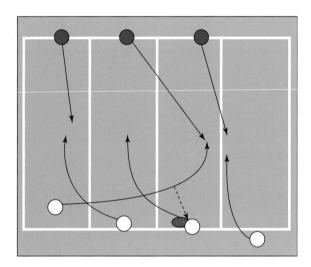

Figure 6.4 Switch pass.

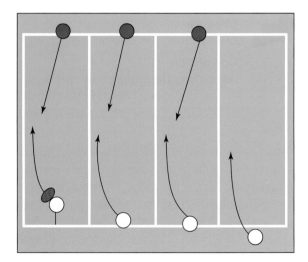

Figure 6.6 Supporting and following the ball carrier.

Now begin to practise a range of other options. You can run towards the support runners, make a pass before leaving your channel and continue to run behind the first-pass receiver to take the return loop pass into a gap (figure 6.7). If the gap closes, you can make another pass: pop pass outside, flick back inside, miss pass outside and so on.

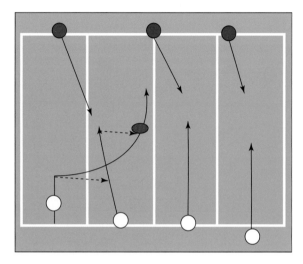

Figure 6.7 Return loop pass.

Adding opposition to the practice and taking away the marked-out channels will test whether your unit understands what you are trying to achieve. As the ball carrier, focus on these goals:

- Running at the defence and delivering the ball safely into a gap in the defence (figures 6.3, page 86, and 6.4, page 87).

- Running at an angle to the defence to misshape it; then passing to the support runner who is now running at the gap in the misshapen defence (figure 6.4, page 87).

- Running at an angle to the defence and passing to a support runner who has space around the outside of the defence (figure 6.5, page 87).

This simple attacking system can be used to attack any organised defence on either side of the ruck or maul, against the midfield defence from scrums or up the narrow side of the field from the base of a scrum when the full back and winger are supporting a penetrative run by the scrum half.

These practices can be used for any group of players but primarily the midfield backs or the back three. Also practise working in mixed groups of forwards and backs together. Try working in threes against two defenders in a channel about 10 metres wide. As with the previous practices, you should be able to create situations in which you can use a switch, loop or offload to a support runner. At this stage you may also begin to learn how to hold the ball in one hand, fend with the other and still make an accurate pass. Once you achieve repeated success, it will be time to add an extra defender and play 3v3.

 Misstep
After your run as the ball carrier, your options are reduced.

Correction
Watch how the support runners react to your running line. Do they run away from you or close down your space? Remind them that they should follow you, remain parallel to the touch lines or fill in the space you have left if you cross into their channel.

Another four players who work closely together as a mini-unit in attack are the back row and scrum half. Although most of their attacking moves may be orchestrated to take place at specific times and in particular places on the field, in practice they need to work together to develop an understanding of their moves and their ways of working. They should practise in an attacking channel against tackle bags or defenders who wear contact suits so that they become used to close-contact work, offloads and the running lines of the support runners. If they can shorten their reaction times to each other, they will be able to create space and misshape a defence for other players to take advantage of.

Back-row moves do not need to be complicated or intricate. They are designed so the back row can cross the gain line quickly, get in behind their first line of defence, attack the secondary defensive line and misshape the resulting defensive pattern. This can be achieved by simply moving the fastest back-row player to the number 8 slot at the scrum when the team is to use a back-row move. The role of the player is to pick up the ball, arc away to the right and forward from the scrum and drive past the back-row defence. Once the ball carrier is beyond the first tackler, it is up to the support runners to provide options—the scrum half and winger may be on the outside with one flanker on the inside. This will depend on the pace of the players and what your team is trying to achieve.

It is easy to work out a number of simple options for responding to the attacking patterns to the right-hand side of the scrum. One of the easiest ways is to put yourself in the defender's shoes and work out what would be the most difficult back-row moves to defend in certain positions on the field. Those are the back-row moves to develop. Whenever you play a back-row move to the right, it is to your advantage if your scrum can nudge its right shoulder forward of its left to take the back-row

defenders slightly away from the attack area (figure 6.8).

Caution Always wear protective equipment in both practice and match situations. Although not every drill in this section anticipates contact with a player, a piece of equipment or the ground, by its very nature rugby invites contact, sometimes by accident. It's better to be safe than sorry.

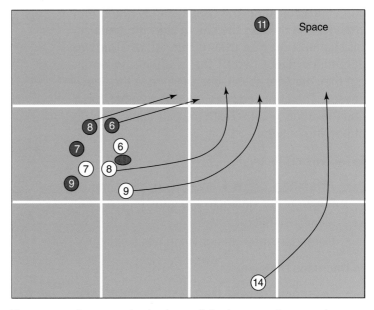

Figure 6.8 Scrum moving back-row defenders away from attack area to the right.

Mini-Units in Attack Drill 1. *Basic Attack Skills*

Use a set of markers to mark out four channels no wider than 5 metres and no longer than 15 metres. One player stands in each channel at one end, ready to begin. The ball carrier starts from one of the side channels and begins the practice by running forward. The support players react to the ball carrier's actions using the options discussed earlier in this step.

When a defender comes into the practice, the ball carrier must fix the defender to the ball-carrying channel by taking up a running line that threatens a score.

To Increase Difficulty

- Remove channels and add opposition, but always have one more attacker than there are defenders.

- Add an extra defender so that the numbers of defenders and attackers are the same.

- Move the attackers and defenders closer together.

To Decrease Difficulty

- Always have two or three more attackers than defenders.

- Allow defenders to jog only towards the attackers.

Success Check

- As a support player, react to the ball carrier but remain parallel to the touch lines unless the ball carrier crosses channels or runs away from you.

- Always run at a space in the defence, not a player.

9 or 10 correct patterns = 10 points

7 or 8 correct patterns = 5 points

5 or 6 correct patterns = 1 point

Your score ___

Mini-Units in Attack Drill 2.   *Playing Against Defenders*

Play 3v2 in three channels that are 5 metres wide and 20 metres long. The coach stands in the first channel and delivers the ball to start the practice. All channels may be used in the attack. The two defenders select two of the channels to enter, but they may not switch channels once they have chosen. The attackers, one in each channel, must find the empty channel with the ball, using a range of passing options.

To Increase Difficulty

- Attacking players start with their backs towards the defence and turn only on the coach's signal.
- Defenders may change channels at will.

To Decrease Difficulty

- Defending players start with their backs to the channels and turn only as the attackers receive the ball.

Success Check: Ball Carrier

- Run hard at the defence.
- Watch the shape of the defence as you approach it.
- Use the pass option that best suits the circumstances and gives the ball to the player in the empty channel.

Score Your Success

9 or 10 successful attacks down the empty channel = 10 points

7 or 8 successful attacks down the empty channel = 5 points

5 or 6 successful attacks down the empty channel = 1 point

Your score ___

Mini-Units in Attack Drill 3.   *4v3 in Channels*

The defenders have a third player and the attackers a fourth , both of whom can roam and join in any channel from behind the front three. The attackers must use the full width of the channels to create space for a player attacking from behind them to find the gap in the defence.

To Increase Difficulty

- Defenders may change channels to defend.
- Attackers play down the channels to begin with; then onto an open field with another defender to beat in order to score.

To Decrease Difficulty

- Add another attacker who also attacks from behind.

Success Check

- All players react to the ball carrier's actions.
- Attackers play close to the defence so they cannot shift their defensive formation once the first pass has been made.
- Attackers fix the defence in their defensive positions by the speed of their running.

Score Your Success

9 or 10 scores out of 10 attempts = 10 points

7 or 8 scores out of 10 attempts = 5 points

5 or 6 scores out of 10 attempts = 1 point

Your score ___

Mini-Units in Attack Drill 4. *Back-Row Moves Attacking Right*

Set up a 20-metre by 15-metre grid. Work in groups of 10 or 12 players. Nominate those to play as 6, 7, 8, 9 and 14 in attack and the equivalent players in defence. Defensive number 9 must decide whether to follow the ball around or stay behind his own scrum. If you decide to play full tackling rather than grip, defenders should wear tackle suits.

The aim is for the attacking back-row mini-unit plus two backs to link up and score a try. Begin with the ball at number 8's feet. As soon as the player touches the ball, the practice begins. After three attempts at scoring, change over so that those in defence become the attackers.

Remember that numbers 14 and 11 should take up a position 5 metres back from the hindmost feet of the back row until either number 9 or number 8 plays the ball with her hands (see figure 6.9).

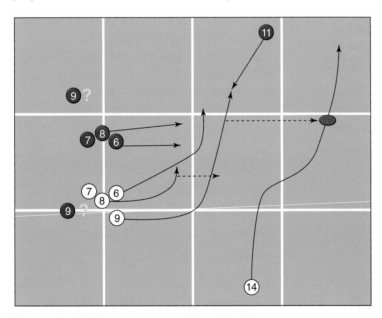

Figure 6.9 Back-row moves attacking right drill.

Many attacking options from this position are possible:

- Number 8 runs and arcs forward and goes for the line.
- Number 9 runs and arcs forward and goes for the line.
- Number 8 runs and feeds a running number 9.
- Number 8 runs to feed number 9 outside or number 6 back inside.

- Number 8 passes to number 9, who passes to number 14.
- Number 9 passes to number 8, who passes to number 14.
- Number 9 passes back inside to number 8, who goes to number 6 outside, who then goes to number 14.

The permutations are endless, but choose one, first, to match the abilities of your players and then, second, to have the greatest advantage against the team you are playing.

To Increase Difficulty

- Play a full tackling but conditioned game. If tackled, keep playing until you score, make an error or are turned over.
  - Allow the defending number 9 to put pressure on number 8's pick-up and pass or run.
  - Add another defender who stands behind the scrum but inside the defending number 11.

To Decrease Difficulty

- Play touch tackling or use tag belts to simulate tackles.
- Start the defending back-row players on their knees to create an attacking space.

Success Check

- Each player reads the situation, does not overrun and adds pace to the attack.
- Each attacker interests a defender with good running lines and footwork, creating space for the player about to receive the pass.
- Every pass is accurate and allows the receiver to put momentum on the attack.

Score Your Success

3 scores out of 3 attempts = 10 points

2 scores out of 3 attempts = 5 points

1 score out of 3 attempts = 1 point

Your score ___

Mini-Units in Attack Drill 5. *Back-Row Moves Attacking Left*

In this drill, the aim is to attack to the left of the scrum and score. Use the same set-up as in mini-units in attack drill 4, but use the left winger (number 11) in the attack and the right winger (number 14) in defence. If you decide to play full tackling rather than grip, the defenders should wear tackle suits.

Begin with the ball at number 8's feet. As soon as the player touches the ball, the practice begins. After three attempts at scoring, change over so that those in defence become the attackers.

Remember that numbers 11 and 14 should take up a position 5 metres back from the hindmost feet of the back row until either number 9 or number 8 plays the ball. The difficult part about attacking the left-hand side of the scrum is the positioning of the opponent's scrum half. If the defending number 9 is putting pressure on the attacking number 8, then it is difficult to attack to that side. If, however, number 9 stays back and allows space, then a number of attacking options are available from this position:

- Number 8 passes to a running number 9.
- Number 8 picks, goes left, hits or spins into defending 6 or 9 and pop passes to number 7, who passes on to number 9.
- Number 8 runs and goes for the line.
- Number 9 runs and goes for the line.
- Number 8 passes to a running number 9, who switches with or passes to number 11.

To Increase Difficulty

- Play a full tackling but conditioned game. If tackled, keep playing until you score, make an error or are turned over.
- Allow the defending number 9 to put pressure on number 8's pick-up and pass or run.
- Add another defender standing inside the attacking number 14.

To Decrease Difficulty

- Play touch tackling or use tag belts to simulate tackles.
- Start the defending back-row players on their knees to create an attacking space.

Success Check

- Each player reads the situation, does not over-run and adds pace to the attack.
- Each attacker interests a defender with good running lines and footwork, creating space for the player about to receive the pass.
- Every pass is accurate and allows the receiver to put momentum on the attack.

Score Your Success

3 scores out of 3 attempts = 10 points

2 scores out of 3 attempts = 5 points

1 score out of 3 attempts = 1 point

Your score ___

Mini-Units in Attack Drill 6. *Back-Three Counterattack to Score*

Mark out three channels that are 15 metres by 22 metres. One attacker stands at the end of each channel. Two defenders stand in the middle channel at the opposite end from the attackers. The practice begins when the coach throws a high ball to the attackers. Each defender selects one channel to defend and runs into it. The ball receiver cannot score but looks to see which channel is undefended and attacks into that channel. The ball carrier may run into any channel, but there may not be two attackers in the same channel. The support runners need to read the situation and, when necessary, swap channels while running in support of the ball carrier (figure 6.10).

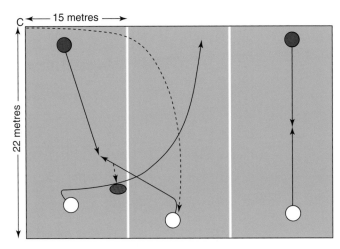

Figure 6.10 Back-three counterattack drill.

To Increase Difficulty

- Allow one defender to switch channels to follow the ball.
- Allow full tackling.
- Allow both defenders to switch channels once even if that means that both move into one channel to stop an attack.

To Decrease Difficulty

- Play touch tackling or use tag belts to simulate tackles.
- Allow attackers to switch channels at will, but there may be only one attacker in a channel at any time.

Success Check

- The ball carrier quickly spots the spare channel and takes up a running line that will attract one of the support runners down the unmarked channel for a pass.
- The support players communicate with the ball receiver as the ball is in the air so that quick decisions can be made.
- Every pass is accurate and allows the second receiver to put momentum on the attack.

Score Your Success

5 scores out of 5 attempts = 10 points

3 or 4 scores out of 5 attempts = 5 points

1 or 2 scores out of 5 attempts = 1 point

Your score ___

SUCCESS SUMMARY OF MINI-UNITS IN ATTACK

Teams with effective mini-units are normally very successful. Players understand their roles within the team's attacking strategy and know that if their attack has width, depth, pace and accuracy, the defence will be dominated, challenged and eventually overcome.

A strong back row or front row often means that your team might monopolise the possession in some area of play. Adding a back three that consists of players who run powerfully in support of a creative midfield or who counterattack with understanding and pace provides a team many of the ingredients for success.

Although the drills in this step are aimed at specific mini-units, players working through the drills in this step should have improved their general attacking performance and understanding. Add up your scores out of 60. If you scored 40 points or more, you are ready to move forward to the next step. If you scored fewer than 40 points, evaluate the skills that you need to improve and work on those before moving on.

Mini-Units in Attack Drills

1. Basic Attack Skills   ___ out of 10

2. Playing Against Defenders   ___ out of 10

3. 4v3 in Channels   ___ out of 10

4. Back-Row Moves Attacking Right   ___ out of 10

5. Back-Row Moves Attacking Left   ___ out of 10

6. Back-Three Counterattack to Score   ___ out of 10

Total   ___ *out of 60*

Mini-Units in Defence

Over the last few years greater emphasis has been placed on teams having a well-organised pressure defence, fully understood by individuals, mini-units and the whole team. In many ways defence is the ultimate team activity, with all players having specific roles and responsibilities at restart, line-out, scrum, kick chase and tackle area. It is a truism that you can be a great tackler but not a good defender if you cannot read situations.

You know you are in a good defensive system when the players on either side of you are in constant communication with you and clarify your role. In many ways your success individually and as a team is in the hands of mini-units of three people, which constantly change with the flow of the game. Together you have to build a brick wall that the opposition cannot penetrate.

After the attack has kept the ball for a few phases, you may find yourself as part of a team line spread across the pitch with as many of your players on their feet as possible and covering approximately a 2-metre space to either side of them. The first-up tackler needs to be clear about his role, as does the next defensive player on the team. Your actions and responses help the rest of the team to establish a defensive framework.

ORGANISATIONAL STRUCTURE AROUND THE CONTACT AREA

The tackler's key responsibilities are to defend within a unit, not as an individual; make the tackle; and get back on his feet, over the ball, and attempt to win the ball back for his team. If he cannot win the ball, he should slow down the ball to give the rest of the defence time to organise itself.

The priorities of the nearest defensive player to the tackler are to win the ball on the ground or prevent the offload and compete for the ball. If you cannot win the ball for your team, you need to slow it down by getting your hands on it, feet on it or foot or leg over it. You also could decide to counter-ruck your opponents, lift them over the top of the ball and drive them backwards so that the ball is on your side for your team to use.

When you know that you cannot get the ball, do not continue to fight for a lost cause and risk giving away a penalty. It is vital that you take up

95

a strong defensive position commonly known as guard, at the side of the contact or tackle area (figure 7.1).

Regardless of your usual position and the number on your shirt, you have to be prepared to take on the responsibility of being guard, bodyguard or third player at any point in the game. The scrum half will assist you in your role.

When you adopt the guard role, you must not move away or drift from your defensive area before the ball has gone to another area. You control the edge of the ruck or maul and must hold your position, waiting to put a positive tackle on any ball carrier who comes into your channel. As you establish yourself in the guard position, let all your teammates know with a verbal cue such as 'I am guard' and also a visual cue by putting up your hand. This will prevent teammates from competing for position and ensure that you maintain the width in your defence.

As a guard, you must physically dominate your area and prevent opponents from distracting you in their attempts to create space down your channel for their players to run into. Avoid being pulled into the ruck or maul, being tempted away from your position or being obstructed by the opposition. You may need to push the opposition away to maintain your guard position.

The next player to arrive after both guards have established their positions takes up the position of bodyguard. As the bodyguard, verbally or physically let the guard know you are ready to defend. You have the particular responsibility of watching out for the attacking number 9, who

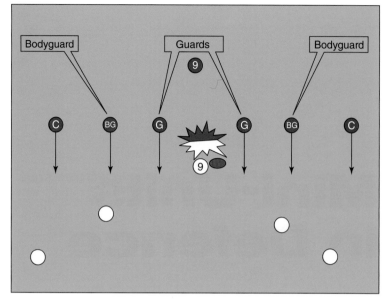

Figure 7.1 Guards' defensive positions.

may try to run across and drag the guard out of position. Shout 'I've got 9' to put pressure on number 9. If number 9 runs towards your third defensive player (C), be ready to defend against any player who cuts back into your channel. Cover the inside shoulder of the C defender and the guard in the event that the opposition manages to flood that channel with players to deliberately engage your guard and try to breach the defence there.

The player in the C position has a very important role. The C defender sets the speed of the team's defensive line and usually is responsible for defending against the opposition's first receiver. Also, the C defender calls the trigger word to move the defensive line forward. Most teams simply call 'In', and everyone immediately repeats the call and moves forward together and at the same speed.

Misstep

Attackers always seem to make ground when they attack the area in the line that the forwards are defending.

Correction

Your line should move forward only at the speed of the slowest player. Otherwise, a gap will open for attackers to exploit.

96

Misstep

Individual attackers seem to be able to step inside some of your defenders and penetrate the defence.

Correction

As defenders, stay in a line and move up and out together and make sure that no player goes out in front of the others.

The defending number 9 has the responsibility to be the eyes of the defensive structure. He must direct the guards and the C player immediately in front and remain free to cover any pick-and-go plays, chips over the top or sweeps behind the defensive line in case the opposition makes any line breaks.

The players in the bodyguard and C defender positions set the defence in motion. If the scrum half runs across the field and switches to a straight runner, the bodyguard and C defender set the speed of the line forward. The bodyguard tackles the scrum half, and the guard on the attack side tackles the runner coming into that channel (figure 7.2).

If the scrum half runs the same line, passes out to a wider runner but still uses a straight runner on the switch as a decoy, the same defenders set the speed of the line; but the C defender tackles the runner. The bodyguard tackles the scrum half, and the guard stays in place close to the contact area, keeping a close eye on the decoy runner (figure 7.3). In all cases it is essential that the three players to the other side of the contact area move forward and fill in the space to prevent a switch back to that side.

When the ball is passed out flat to the attacking number 10, the C defender sets the speed of the line. In this case, the attacking number 10 has to be tackled by the C defender. The guard and bodyguard stay close to the contact area and go forward and out only when the ball has gone away from number 10. Their running line is then at the inside shoulders of the attacking backs.

From this set-up, number 10 can bring a number of other players into the attack. For example, he could switch with the next player in line (figure 7.4) or make

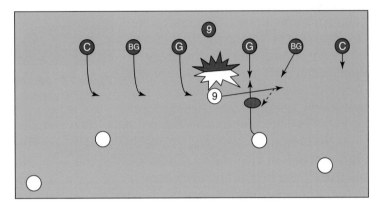

Figure 7.2 The bodyguard tackles the scrum half; the guard tackles the runner.

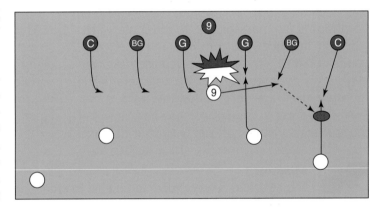

Figure 7.3 The C defender tackles the runner, the bodyguard tackles the scrum half and the guard stays close to the area of contact.

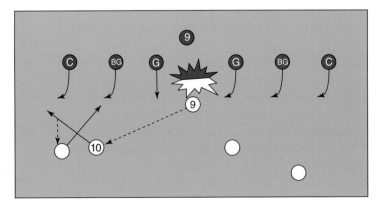

Figure 7.4 Number 10 switches with the next player in line. The bodyguard becomes the tackler.

a wider run to the line and pass back inside to a straight runner (figure 7.5). In all cases, if the first three in the defence are disciplined, they naturally will pick up the attacker running into their space.

The aim for the defence is to attack the opposition. It is very important that your team and the mini-units within it control the area around the contact point because this is where many matches are won or lost. Successful defence depends on each player making correct decisions and communicating clearly and loudly enough to be heard. First,

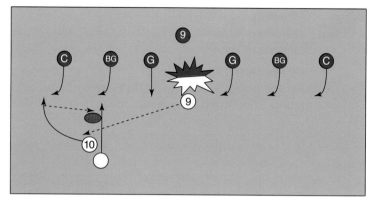

Figure 7.5 Number 10 runs to the line and then passes back inside to a straight runner.

you see, identify and understand the defensive problem in front of you; then you decide on the correct action to take and use the skills that you have practised to execute the action.

Good communication as well as good technique is extremely important. A good defensive team communicates constantly with each other on each side of the contact area as they equate numbers, nominate their roles, identify and nominate the players they are going to tackle and motivate their teammates when they are fatigued.

DEFENSIVE LINE AND DRIFTING

Committing too many players to the contact area when in defence is a common mistake many teams make. The moment the defence has more players on the ground than the attackers is the moment they are very vulnerable to a score. Therefore, don't commit players to a lost cause. Let the attackers win the ball and trust your defence.

The defensive line must be disciplined and stretch across the pitch with no large gaps, especially close to the contact area. All defenders should stand opposite the inside shoulders of their direct opponents. To be effective, establish equal numbers as soon as possible.

Misstep
The attackers always seem to be able to create an overlap.

Correction
Spread your defenders out a little more and make sure you have equal numbers.

As soon as the ball is passed away from the contact area, all defenders should move forward towards the opposition as a line and then out and across as the ball is passed. As soon as the attacker you are defending shifts the ball, shout to the next defender to move across and run on to the next pass receiver in the line (figure 7.6). In this way, you will always have a strong defence in front of the ball and be able to flood the outside channel with defenders so that the attackers will have no opportunity to pass back inside to other runners. After moving forward and then out to follow the ball, your role becomes to make the next tackle, assist the next defender or fill the inside gap to prevent a pass.

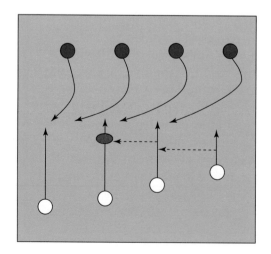

Figure 7.6 Moving out and across as the ball is passed.

DEFENCE OF LOOPS AND SWITCHES

Just as you should practise attacking in mini-units, you also should practise defending in the same way. Loops and switches don't happen only in the three-quarter line. They can happen all along any attacking line. For example, a scrum half might run a switch with a hard running forward to hit into the defensive line, or an outside centre might loop with the winger to create an overlap. No matter which position you play, you need to understand the fundamental principles of defending these plays.

Misstep

The attackers seem to penetrate your defence easily by bringing the ball back on either a switch or inside pass.

Correction

Make sure the defence goes forward first and sideways only after the ball is passed. Failure to protect the inside shoulder of the next defender creates weaknesses in the defensive line.

Essentially, even though you might be playing an up-and-out defence, you are in fact marking the 5-metre channel that you are standing in. Your role is to tackle any player coming into that channel.

If the small group in front of you plays a loop, the first defender moves up and then out as the ball is passed, leaving the second defender to move up and out to the looping player. If the ball carrier sends out a miss pass to the last player, then the third defender makes the tackle (figure 7.7a). Likewise, if the first player runs across the second and switch passes, the first defender tackles the player coming back into the first channel. If the first ball carrier keeps hold of the ball and does a dummy switch, then the second defender in the channel makes the tackle (figure 7.7b).

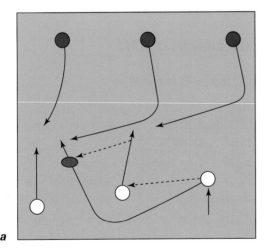
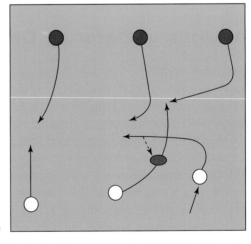

Figure 7.7 Defending against a loop: *(a)* the second defender tackles the looping player or the third defender makes the tackle after a miss pass to the last player; *(b)* the first defender tackles the player entering the first channel after a switch pass.

CAUTION Always wear protective equipment in both practice and match situations. Although not every drill in this section anticipates contact with a player, a piece of equipment or the ground, by its very nature rugby invites contact, sometimes by accident. It's better to be safe than sorry.

Mini-Units in Defence Drill 1. *Tackling*

Mark out three channels that are 5 metres by 15 metres so each defender becomes used to being responsible for a channel. Work in groups of six divided into three groups of two. One player in each pair has a ball; the other player is the defender. Make sure that you wear all of your normal personal protective equipment including your gum shield. The coach stands behind the defenders and faces the attackers. The practice begins when the coach points either left or right. That is the ball carrier's signal to run into the channel in the direction the coach signalled. The defenders run up and then out to make the tackle. In the first set of attempts, the attackers should run at a steady pace. After five attempts at scoring, attackers change places with defenders.

To Increase Difficulty

- Build up the speed of the attackers but keep the speed of the defenders low.
- Play at match speed.

To Decrease Difficulty

- Take the speed out of the practice and walk.
- Allow ball carriers to wear tackle suits so they will hit harder into contact.

Success Check

- Use an 'In' call to trigger the defensive line. Point and call out the ball carrier's name. Keep the line straight.
- As the defender, make sure your head is behind the leading thigh of the ball carrier (see step 3, figure 3.1, page 40).
- As the defender, drive through the hit. Land on top of your opponent and then get back to your feet as quickly as possible.

Score Your Success

Make 4 or 5 tackles = 10 points

Make 2 or 3 tackles = 5 points

Make 1 tackle = 1 point

Your score ____

Mini-Units in Defence Drill 2. *Numbering Off*

Mark out five channels that are 5 metres by 15 metres. Work in groups of 10. Pair off, with one player in each pair acting as an attacker and holding a tackle shield. All players must wear their normal protective equipment including a gum shield. One player in the attacking line gives the signal to move either forward, backwards, left or right. All of the shield holders move at the same time. The defenders stay alert and copy what the attacking line is doing until the call is given to move forward. Then the defenders quickly move up and make their tackles. Be sure to stay in your individual channel for safety's sake.

To Increase Difficulty

- Build up the speed of the attackers but keep the speed of the defenders low.
- Play at match speed.

To Decrease Difficulty

- Take all speed out of the practice and walk through it.

Success Check

- Use an 'In' call to trigger the defensive line. Point and call out the ball carrier's name. Keep the line straight.
- In a head-on tackle, make sure that your head is to one side of the tackle shield holder's thigh.
- As the defender, drive in and up under the rib cage. Land on top and get back onto your feet as soon as possible.

Score Your Success

Accurately mirror the attacking line 4 or 5 times = 10 points

Accurately mirror the attacking line 2 or 3 times = 5 points

Accurately mirror the attacking line 1 time = 1 point

Your score ____

Mini-Units in Defence Drill 3. *Numbering Off With a Sweeper*

Use the same set-up as mini-units in defence drill 2, but drop a defender in behind the other four in the line (figure 7.8) to act as the sweeper. When the shield holders move left, the defenders leave the attacker on the right in space. Similarly, when the attackers move right, the one on the left is free. The sweeper's role is to mark any free attacker. When the forward call is given, the sweeper comes around the end to tackle the free attacker. The other defenders attempt to tackle their attackers as well. Take turns being the sweeper.

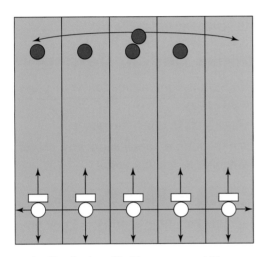

Figure 7.8 Numbering off with a sweeper drill.

To Increase Difficulty

- Speed up the changes of direction so that the sweeper has to make quick decisions.
- Each team can earn points for making or breaking tackles.

To Decrease Difficulty

- Walk through the practice.
- Reduce the number of movements given to the attackers.

Success Check

- Make quick, effective tackles that prevent forward movement in the free channel.
- Practise good communication as the sweeper, detailing who is to be tackled as the line changes course.

Score Your Success

Sweeper makes 4 or 5 tackles = 10 points

Sweeper makes 2 or 3 tackles = 5 points

Sweeper makes 1 tackle = 1 point

Your score ____

Mini-Units in Defence Drill 4. *Setting the Guard Area*

Ten players spread across the pitch between the 15-metre lines about 2 metres apart. They face the coach who is about 10 metres away with a ball. As a defence, you have to keep your line and mirror what the coach does. If the coach moves left or right, backwards or forward, so does your defensive line. As soon as the coach takes a step forward, your line takes two steps forward at speed, pointing and communicating. As you move up the pitch, you will begin to cross the marking lines. At each one, set your line (use 'Set' as a call). As the coach moves, all of you quickly move up and call 'In'. You must work hard to communicate with each other, especially those opposite where the ball is. Lower your body position to get ready to make tackles.

To Increase Difficulty

- When the coach moves and calls a number and rolls the ball to a defender, that many defenders have to join the contact area around the ball. The rest of the defenders move in quickly and set the guards, bodyguards and C defenders in place.
- On a signal, the coach takes the ball as the opposing scrum half and breaks to one side of the contact into the no-go area. Guards and bodyguards grab tackle.

To Decrease Difficulty

- Slow down the action by giving the defence plenty of time to react to signals.

Success Check

- Call loudly and move forward as a line.
- Use good communication with players on either side.

Score Your Success

Defensive line communicates well = 5 points

Defensive line moves as one in response to coach's movement = 5 points

Defenders show good body positions and are ready to move up and out = 5 points

Your score ___

Mini-Units in Defence Drill 5. Defending as a Line

Five attackers face five defenders in an area 22 metres by 30 metres. The long end lines are the try lines. At first, play player-for-player defence in which the defenders shadow the attackers as in the numbering off drills (2 and 3).

As defenders, practise your verbal communication and visual skills and try to put pressure on the attackers. Point at the attacker you are shadowing and call out 'Mine'. After your direct attacker has passed the ball along the line, drift across and defend on the inside shoulder of the next attacker to cover any switch or pass back inside.

If your defensive system works, you might create a turnover. If so, become the attackers and try to score over your opponents' try line.

To Increase Difficulty

- Use an extra attacker who plays as full back.
- Move two players to the touch line as defenders. They come into play as the first ball is passed. The attackers must try to bring a player back using either a switch or pass inside.

To Decrease Difficulty

- Have an equal number of attackers as defenders, but put one defender out as a full back to cover any break.

Success Check: Defenders

- Use good communication with players on either side.
- Quickly close down the space.
- Make double tackles on any player who attempts to make a break.

Score Your Success

Keep attackers from scoring = 5 points

Create turnovers in 2 to 5 attempts = 5 points

Your score ___

SUCCESS SUMMARY OF MINI-UNITS IN DEFENCE

Defence is an important individual, unit and team skill. Spend as much as 50 percent of your practice time perfecting it. To increase enjoyment in your practice, start with small-sided organisational games that use grip and hold tackling. Be enthusiastic about your defence and encourage the players around you to concentrate and work hard to stop the attack and try to regain possession of the ball. A good defensive team has to be very fit for running and contact. Improving conditioning will increase your work rate, speed up your reactions, help you enjoy defending more and make you a more effective defender.

Be aware of and avoid common defensive errors such as creating a defensive line that is too narrow; having a player who is in front of or behind the defensive line as it moves forward; or moving away too early or too quickly from the defender on your inside shoulder. Good teams control the game through their defence. Enjoy using your attacking defence.

This is a very important step. If you have not scored more than 40 points, identify your weak areas and return to those drills until you improve. If you scored more than 40 points, you are ready to move on to the next step.

Mini-Units in Defence Drills

1.	Tackling	___ out of 10
2.	Numbering Off	___ out of 10
3.	Numbering Off With a Sweeper	___ out of 10
4.	Setting the Guard Area	___ out of 15
5.	Defending as a Line	___ out of 10
Total		___ **out of 55**

The Front Five

The 15 players in each team are split into eight forwards and seven backs. These large units can be separated into smaller ones consisting of the front five, middle five and back five players. Each player within the unit has a range of specialist roles to play, especially the front five at scrum and line-out. These are ways of bringing the ball back into play and are commonly referred to as set pieces.

The purpose of the scrum is to bring the ball back into play after the attack fails as a result of an infringement and the opponents are unable to take advantage. The line-out brings the ball back into play after the ball or a player carrying the ball has left the field of play. In these situations, responsibility falls on the front five to gain possession for the team. This step addresses the roles of the front five: the ball providers.

The positions of the front-five unit are the loose head prop, the hooker, the tight head prop and the two locks (table 8.1). These players are the primary ball winners in the set pieces but nowadays are expected to play an important part in the many ball-winning and -using situations that occur during a match. Because of the possibility of injury to players during contact at the set piece, a number of safety factors must be considered, particularly at the scrum.

SAFETY FACTORS AND BODY POSITIONING FOR THE SCRUM

The front unit must understand many safety factors, and the referee must enforce the rules for both teams. The Laws demand that you make contact with the opposition in a very controlled way, and the referee will give you specific instructions that you must follow as they are given.

During a match the scrum may become uncontested, such as when there are not enough front-row players to constitute a full set as a result of injury. Some levels of rugby in some countries have already created or are considering creating a law that allows for only uncontested scrums to reduce the injury potential of the game. In an uncontested scrum, the team putting in the ball wins it because the opposition is not allowed to strike for it and no player from either team is allowed to push. These kinds of matches have no need for specialist props or hookers, but all other positions stay the same.

The whole scrum must be bound up and ready to engage before the referee calls you together. The scrums square with each other an arm's length away. Everyone must comply with the commands *crouch, touch, pause,* and *engage. Crouch* means exactly that—the front-row players bend at the waist and lower at the knee. On *touch,* the

Table 8.1　Front-Five Positions

| Position | Qualities and responsibilities | | | |
	Individual	Scrum	Line-out	Loose
Props: loose and tight head	Comfortable with contact; has overall core strength, but particularly in the shoulders, neck, chest, back and legs	Provides solid platform from which hooker wins ball Loose head prop: Resists the force from opponents Tight head prop: Holds strong, square position On opposition ball: Loose head prop counteracts any shove from tight head prop by driving or holding in square position; tight head prop attacks opposition loose head prop by driving straight, square and hard to help drive scrum backwards	Supports jumper in jump-and-catch sequence; quickly closes off any gaps; protects ball; sometimes acts as sweeper, gathering any loose balls; occasionally acts as forward, peeling around back or front of line-out On opposition's throw: supports any jumper who attacks ball; drives through any gaps and tries to retrieve the ball; joins in drives to slow down opponents' possession	Contributes to team attack and defensive sequences; is good head-on tackler; understands role in defence around rucks and mauls; stays on feet in contact; maintains good body position in rucks and mauls; drives dynamically into contact; moves quickly to support ball carrier, particularly at kick-off
Hooker	Comfortable with contact; flexible and strong in shoulders, lower back and hips; has overall core strength, but is particularly strong across shoulders and neck	Wins own ball; pressures opposition's	Throws accurately to jumpers; cleans up any spilled ball On opposition's throw: cleans up spilled ball; defends around edges of line-out and chases ball	Contributes to team attack and defensive sequences; is capable of attacking and defending out wide; stays on feet in contact; maintains good body position in rucks and mauls; drives dynamically into contact; runs in support of ball carrier
Locks	Has overall core strength, but particularly in legs, buttocks, lower back and shoulders; good ball handler, especially when jumping to catch at arm's length	Provides solid support for front row; exerts forward power when required; resists opposition's shove; binds tightly throughout scrum	Wins own ball; competes vigorously against opposition	Catches kick-off; contributes to team attack and defensive sequences; maintains good body position in rucks and mauls; drives dynamically into contact; runs in support of ball carrier

outside arm of each prop must reach up and touch the shoulder of the opposite prop. At *pause,* there is a slight pause before the referee gives the final instruction. At *engage,* both packs can go forward into contact with a steady force and bind onto each other as stated in the Laws. The force of this first contact should go slightly upwards to prevent a collapse.

All players in the scrum must adopt a safe scrummaging position (figure 8.1): head up, chin off the chest and back flat, legs bent slightly at the knees, and shoulders always above hips.

Figure 8.1   Scrummaging position.

PROP FORWARDS

There are two prop forwards in each unit. In the scrum, the main role of the prop forwards is to provide a solid platform and support for the hooker to win and control the ball quickly. The loose head prop forward plays on the left-hand side of the front row; and the tight head prop, on the right (figure 8.2).

A great deal of force is always directed through the props, so they must be strong and enjoy contact. It can be advantageous to have a short neck and broad shoulders because the force of the scrum goes through the props' spines into the opposition. Being particularly strong in the arms, back and chest also helps, as will very strong legs because most of your scrummaging stability comes from your thighs, buttocks and lower back. You will absorb much of the opposition's drive with your legs and should take short, backward steps only if absolutely necessary. Remember to keep your weight just in front of your stance, your hips square and your outside foot slightly forward. Your inside hip should be as close to the centre of the scrummage as possible, with your inside foot almost touching that of the other prop on your team. The thigh of the inner leg is almost vertical so that your knee is never ahead of your hip. Keep a wide stance by making sure your feet are as flat on the ground as possible.

Nowadays, props play a very important role after their positional responsibilities at the scrummage and the line-out have finished. They must be able to contribute to the attacking and defensive structure of the team.

As the prop forward, these are your main priorities:

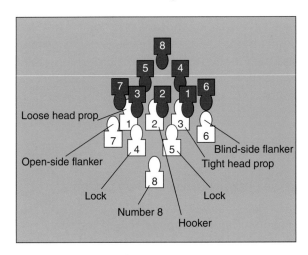

Figure 8.2   Players in the scrum.

At the Scrum

- Provide a solid platform for your hooker to win a good ball.

- As a loose head, resist the force from the opposition and support the hooker in every way.

- As a tight head, hold a strong, square position (figure 8.3).

Figure 8.3 Strong, square position.

At the Line-Out

- Support the jumper in the jump-and-catch sequence.

- Quickly close in on the jumper to shut off any gaps.

- Protect any ball that may have been secured.

- If required, take the ball from the jumper in order to give it back to the scrum half, or peel around the back or front of the line-out.

- On the opposition throw, try to go through any gaps that may occur after the opposition wins the ball, so that you put pressure on the opposition's possession.

- If the opportunity arises, try to take the ball from the opposition jumper.

In the Loose

- Stay on your feet in contact, keep the ball and resist the opposition.

- At rucks and mauls, drive in dynamically with good body position.

- At kick-offs, move quickly to any player who is about to catch the ball and help secure it.

- Occasionally, you may have to enter a contact situation and wrestle the ball free.

- Contribute to the team's tackle count.

- Understand what you are trying to achieve from all areas of play.

Position for the Scrum

In the scrum a good, safe body position is vital. It is against the Laws of the game to allow your shoulders to go below your hips. The golden rules of scrummaging are head up, chin off chest, flat back, shoulders above hips, legs slightly bent, wide stance, feet as flat as possible (figure 8.1, page 107). Practise this position against a suitably adjusted scrummaging machine, and progress to working against other players.

Misstep
When you are in the scrum, especially against live opposition, you are very unstable.

Correction
Make sure that your coach checks your body position (figure 8.1, page 107). If your position is safe and effective, check to make sure that your stance is wide enough (figure 8.3) and that your feet are slightly back from underneath your hips.

To position correctly, bind tightly with a wide stance and your outside foot slightly forward. Crouch and sight where you will put your head. Engage your opponent firmly and drive slightly upwards, with your hips and shoulders square.

Settle quickly; then keep movement to a minimum. Remember to keep your shoulders always above your hips. Remain static, with your shoulders horizontal. As soon as the ball is won, rejoin the support as quickly as possible.

Misstep
You never seem to be able to cope with the strength of the opposition's drive and constantly have to give ground slightly.

Correction
Make sure that you have as many studs in the ground as possible. Take as much of the drive force into your legs and hips as you can without becoming unstable. Use them like a spring that is compressed slightly. Move your feet backwards only if you feel as though you are about to become unstable.

Jumper Support at Kick-Off and Line-Out

In the line-out, one of the props normally stands at the front and the other stands third in line, although one of you might alternatively find yourself standing at the back. A jumper normally stands between the props. Your role as a prop is to lift and help protect the jumper during the contest for possession of the ball.

Safety is most important. While supporting the jumper, concentrate on not only lifting but also stabilising the jump and bringing the player down from the jump under control. You are allowed to pregrip the jumper, so take a good hold of him either on the upper thigh or on his shorts. Do not hold him in any position that creates an imbalance with the player behind him because this will cause him to topple over in midair. Normally, the player behind takes a slightly higher hold than the player in front to create this balance (figure 8.4). In the early stages of lifting, it is essential to hold from behind at hip level and in front from slightly lower. As you become more experienced, your hands gradually will go slightly lower on the jumper's body, and in return he will learn how to ride on your lift.

Figure 8.4 Props supporting the jumper.

Many supporting actions at a kick-off are very similar to those used at the line-out. The major difference is that at kick-off players are able to move a greater distance and in any direction. Once the jumper is in the air, you can safely support and control the landing (figure 8.5). Beware of taking hold of the player too early, because this might lead to instability. If you hold the player at or slightly above waist level, you should find that all landings are safe and under control.

Figure 8.5 Supporting and controlling the landing.

Misstep
Each time the ball is thrown into your line-out, your jumper moves before you can react.

Correction
Know the signals for the throw. Watch the jumper with your head up. Take up a stance that allows you to read the hooker's throwing style. Move as soon as you recognise the throw, and put your hands to the jumper early.

Supporting at a line-out and supporting at a kick-off are very similar. As soon as the jumper moves to catch the ball, react to the situation and play on. After the lift, your options are simple:

- Drive forward, bind onto and protect the jumper.

- Drive on to the jumper, strip the ball away and pass the ball to the scrum half or another player.

- Drive forward, strip the ball away and drive on.

- Drive forward, strip the ball and immediately give it to someone in a better position to continue the attack.

Which option is best depends on the game situation after the jumper has landed safely.

CAUTION Always wear protective equipment in both practice and match situations. Although not every drill in this section anticipates contact with a player, a piece of equipment or the ground, by its very nature rugby invites contact, sometimes by accident. It's better to be safe than sorry.

Prop Forward Drill 1. *Prop Forward's Body Position in the Scrum*

Most teams have an area designated for scrummaging, and some use a machine to help train correct techniques.

To simulate the correct scrummaging position, always go to the left of the player opposite you. If you are a loose head, scrummage against one player. If you are a tight head, scrummage against two or against a machine.

Remember to bind tightly with a wide stance. Engage your opponent firmly, drive slightly upwards, with your hips and shoulders square. Settle quickly; then keep movement to a minimum. Your shoulders should always be above your hips. As soon as the ball is won, rejoin the support as quickly as possible.

To Increase Difficulty

- Scrummage against the machine or opponents, keeping a good position, and then sprint 10 metres to the left around a marker and back to scrummage again.

- Repeat the preceding variation, but alternate sprinting to the left and to the right. Repeat 10 times in each direction for 20 sprints.

- Sprint from the scrum and rip a ball from another player's grasp.

- Between scrums, perform a simple sequence of movement (e.g., sprint, knock over a tackle bag, wrestle and rip a ball from another player and return to the scrum). Repeat 10 times.

To Decrease Difficulty

- Concentrate solely on the engage sequence. Step back 3 or 4 metres; then engage again.

Success Check

- Engage correctly: crouch, touch, pause, engage.

- Keep your head up, your chin off your chest and your shoulders always above your hips.

- Drive your shoulders slightly upwards and your hips slightly down.

- If your shoulders move forward or backwards, take short steps to reposition.

Score Your Success

10 consecutive firm nudges up and into the opponent, keeping a safe position = 10 points

8 or 9 consecutive firm nudges up and into the opponent, keeping a safe position = 5 points

6 or 7 consecutive firm nudges up and into the opponent, keeping a safe position = 1 point

Your score ___

Prop Forward Drill 2. *Prop Support of Receiver at Kick-Off*

Use an area about 10 metres wide by 25 metres long. The ball should be thrown over the distance you would expect it to be kicked (figure 8.6). In this practice you should have one receiver, normally a lock, two supporters (props) and another player to act as scrum half. When practising your support techniques as a prop, you will need to stand close to the lock you will be playing with in the next game. As soon as the ball is thrown, watch it as it flies and at the same time move in close to the catcher to offer some protection from your opponents by binding onto the receiver while he is in the air. Make sure that your bind is not below the catcher's centre of gravity. One player supports

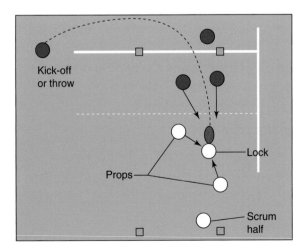

Figure 8.6 Prop support of receiver at kick-off drill.

111

from the front with his back to the opposition to protect the catcher. At first, practise without any opponents; then extend the practice to include two and then three chasers, who should try to prevent you from winning clean possession.

To Increase Difficulty

- Have two opposition jumpers follow the ball and jump against the receiver.
- Add two more chasers to try to drive the receiver and support players back towards their goal line. (Note: You must allow the catcher to be back on the ground before you can make contact.)

To Decrease Difficulty

- Decrease the number of defenders.
- Give tackle pads to the defenders. The defenders strike the catcher with the tackle

pads while he is in the air. This will allow the catcher to become used to contact while concentrating on the catch.

Success Check

- Use strong, safe lifting positions with a wide base and good grip at about waist height.
- Provide stable support while the jumper is in the air.
- Provide controlled support to bring the jumper down safely before releasing the support grip.

Score Your Success

5 out of 5 successful attempts at catching cleanly and supporting correctly and safely = 10 points

Your score ___

HOOKER

The hooker is one of the main ball winners on the team. In the scrum the hooker wins the ball by striking it down the channel between the loose head prop's feet and back into the scrum to finish up at the feet of the number 8. In the line-out the hooker is responsible for the throw-in from touch. Players in this position can be almost any shape or size, but in general it helps to have a short back and long arms to help bind around the props.

These are the main priorities of the hooker:

At the Scrum

- Make sure that you always win your ball by striking it cleanly down the target channel.
- Put pressure on the opposition's put-in by scrummaging hard and occasionally by contesting their ball.

At the Line-Out

- Throw accurately to the jumpers.
- Help protect any ball that has been won or tidy up any loose ball.

- Pose a constant threat on the short side of any rucks and mauls that may occur after the line-out.
- Defend the short side of any rucks and mauls that may occur after the line-out has ended.

In the Loose

- When necessary, play as a defender at rucks and mauls.
- Contribute to your team's tackle count.
- Mark the open side of the field at kick-offs.
- Be dynamic at rucks and mauls.
- Understand and involve yourself in attack and defensive roles in all areas of the field and in all situations.

Scrum Binding

When binding for the scrum, the hooker has a number of options. Rugby Laws dictate that hookers may bind over or under the arms of their props, around their bodies below or at armpit level (figure 8.7). There is no doubt that the most effective way is to bind both arms over those of the props. The loose head should bind first and must bind around your body onto your waist or middle chest. As the hooker, you may have a preference, which the front row should adopt. The tight head also has a choice of binding onto you: around your body, over the arm of the loose head and anywhere from your left hip to your mid-chest.

Figure 8.7   Binding both arms over those of the props.

At the scrum, engage your opponents in exactly the same way as the props. Pull firmly with your left arm and allow your weight to rest on your right-hand prop and your left foot (figure 8.8). Although you are allowed to turn your feet slightly towards the mouth of the tunnel, in the scrum you must not move your feet so far to your left

that you cause instability in the front row. Retain a hooking position at all times. Remember that your shoulders must always be above your hips.

You are always in a vulnerable position in the scrum because you are hanging between two other players with your body ever so slightly turned to face the mouth of the tunnel. Be sure to practise good body positioning at all times.

Hooking

To execute the hook, first settle early in the scrum, feet pointing slightly towards the mouth of the tunnel, hips lower than the props' hips. Look for the scrum half's hands. Your striking foot (normally the right) must be in contact with the ground. Signal for the ball. As the ball leaves the scrum half's hands, strike it back through the target channel. Complete the leg sweep and retake a firm stance. Contribute to any push in the scrum. Leave the scrum with the rest of the front row and rejoin in the support of the ball as soon as possible.

When you play hooker, you will develop your own style of hooking. This will depend on the quality of your props and also your flexibility, size and leg length. You will strike for the ball with your right foot only (figure 8.9). Your aim is to strike the ball and sweep back from in front of and beyond the loose head prop's right leg as soon as possible after the ball leaves the scrum half's hands. Your target channel is between the feet of the loose head prop.

Figure 8.8   Pulling firmly with the left arm.

Figure 8.9   Sweeping with the inside sole of the right foot.

The three basic techniques for hooking are as follows:

1. Sweep with the inside of the foot.

2. Stab and drag with the sole of the boot or the inside edge.

3. Stab and hit, normally with the heel.

To practise your hooking technique, find some way of resting on your right arm at the correct height for the scrummage. This may require a low wall, an exercise bar or the side of the scrummaging machine. Take the weight on your right forearm, sink your hips towards the ground and place your feet outside your left shoulder along the ground to simulate the hooking position. This will allow you to practise effectively. Remember, you must always be able to maintain a balanced position to help keep the scrum stable.

Misstep
When hooking, your legs do not seem long enough to reach the ball near the mouth of the tunnel.

Correction
This may be the fault of the scrum half. Ask for a much firmer delivery of the ball into the tunnel and you may find it easier to strike. Pull your loose head closer and move yourself nearer to the mouth of the tunnel.

As you grow older, increasing the speed of your strike will become less and less important, because the props in senior rugby are strong enough to protect the possession and will not succumb to the pressure exerted by your opponents. Your strike, however, always needs to be fast and firm. Remember, at every one of your own scrums you have the advantage because the ball is put into the scrummage from your left and you are half a body nearer to the mouth of the tunnel than your opponent (figure 8.10). You also have the advantage of using your right leg and its joints in their natural range of movement; your opponent doesn't. You will soon learn to use this advantage so that your scrummage ball is rarely threatened.

Figure 8.10 Ball put in from the left.

Misstep
Sometimes you are unable to strike because of pressure from the opposition.

Correction
Sink your hips a little more into the scrummage, and swivel your hips around slightly to face the mouth of the tunnel. Also, work to increase flexibility in your shoulders, lower back and hips.

As soon as you have mastered some of the hooking techniques, it is time to try them out against another front row. Although at first it may seem very uncomfortable to have someone else's bony shoulder resting across the back of your neck, you will soon become used to this and accept it as one of the pleasures of front-row play.

Line-Out Throw

To execute the line-out throw, hold the ball near the back point across the seams in both hands behind your head, with the ball pointing down the line of touch and your throwing hand slightly behind your other hand (figure 8.11a). Stand with your feet shoulder-width apart and square with the touch line. Look at a point above the jumper to where you will throw the ball. Arch your back ever so slightly to put power into your throw (figure 8.11b) and move both hands forward quickly, keeping your hands on the ball for as long as possible. Release the ball as your body weight moves forward and point all of your fingers along the trajectory of the ball, keeping your elbows as close as possible (figure 8.11c). Step onto the field as you release the ball to follow the action and support the new ball carrier.

Figure 8.11   Line-Out Throw

a

b

c

PREPARATION

1. Hold ball across seam near back point, pointing down line of touch
2. Hold ball behind head in both hands
3. Keep feet square and shoulder-width apart
4. Look above jumper to where you will throw

EXECUTION

1. Arch back slightly and move both hands forward to throw
2. Keep hands on ball as long as possible
3. Release ball as body weight moves forward

FOLLOW-THROUGH

1. Point all fingers along ball's trajectory
2. Keep elbows as close as possible
3. Step onto the field as you release ball
4. Follow action to support new ball carrier

Misstep

You throw inconsistently.

Correction

Practice is essential. Try throwing in one smooth movement from a starting point behind your head. This will help to prevent unnecessary ball movement in the throwing sequence. Holding the ball in two hands for as long as possible gives you more control over the accuracy of the throw.

A jumper may come forward or backwards to jump or may jump straight up and down. To help you win possession, you and the jumpers should establish a range of signals that indicate the type of jump to be used and where the ball is to be thrown to in each line-out. Everyone in the line-out unit plus the half backs must know and understand these signals. You may wish to practise individually with the jumpers, but as soon as possible, the props should join in so that they too can practise their line-out skills. Your jumpers must always stand away from you, the distance from the touch line they will be in the match, so that you can concentrate on accuracy.

To increase accuracy, take time alone to practise all your throws. Use the targets available to you. Mark out a series of lines on the ground at the same distance from you as the jumper would be in a line-out. For a low, flat throw, aim at either a goalpost or a line on a wall at the correct height.

For a lob throw, aim at a basketball or netball ring and try to drop the ball into the basket. Alternatively, you may have a coach who can hold a target up on a pole. The coach stands at a jumper's distance, calls out a signal for that place in the line-out and then holds up the target at the required height. If you hit the target regularly, you know that your accuracy is improving, and this will also show up in your completion stats during matches.

Prepare for the realities of the match and practise the skills you will use. Your lock may wish to catch or tap the ball down so that you can practise gathering untidy possessions. For example, the ball may ricochet out of the line-out and onto the ground nearby; if you don't get there first, then the opposition hooker might. Clearing up untidy balls is another of your major roles at the front of the line-out, and it must become instinctive, even in practice.

Hooker Drill 1.   *Hooker Accuracy at the Line-Out*

The practice area should contain a range of targets—for example, lines on a wall or basketball rings. Make sure that the targets are at various heights and distances so that you can practise all of your throws. You may have a coach who can make or borrow a marker shaped like a long lollipop. This will allow the coach to stand away from you at various distances and hold up the lollipop to simulate a jumper's hands moving up into the catching position. This allows you to practise not only for accuracy but also for the timing of your throw in relation to the height and speed of the jump.

To Increase Difficulty

- Make three throws; then follow with a sequence of other tasks—for example, sprint, tackle a tackle bag, grapple for the ball with an opponent, then return for another three throws.

To Decrease Difficulty

- Increase the size of the targets.

Success Check

- Stand the correct distance from the target.
- Have the ball in both hands above your head.
- Throw with your arms and upper body, and keep both hands on the ball as long as possible.
- Throw to the desired height at the required speed.

Score Your Success

Hit each target 9 or 10 times out of 10 = 10 points

Hit each target 7 or 8 times out of 10 = 5 points

Hit each target 5 or 6 times out of 10 = 1 point

Your score ___

Hooker Drill 2. *Throwing to the Jumpers*

Once you have the accuracy and your jumpers are confident, try out your throws in a full practice situation. It is essential that your opposition does not know your line-out signals. Start with opposition only against each jumper, and gradually progress to a fully opposed line-out. After each throw, try to score over your opponents' goal line. When you return to the line-out to restart the practice, keep moving it to different points up and down the touch line so that you also have to practise reforming the line. Practise throwing various distances and following the ball into the play to tidy up any possessions.

To Increase Difficulty

- Work through 10 line-outs, calling the signal early, and play through the sequence, reforming the line-outs without rest or pause.

- After each throw, follow with a sequence of activity—for example, catch and drive the ball to develop passing among the forwards; then return and throw again.

- With full opposition, work between two lines 10 metres apart. Both sets of forwards try to win the ball and score over the goal line.

To Decrease Difficulty

- Work for quality rather than quantity.
- Have the opposition stay very passive.

- Use a slightly smaller ball so that you can grip it better.
- With passive line-out opposition, work from a line of touch 10 metres from the goal line, win the ball and then try to score against an active defence.

Success Check

- Spread your fingers across the seams of the ball.
- Give the signal for the throw early. Don't be afraid to change the signal if it looks as though the opposition knows what you are going to throw.
- Keep both hands on the ball as long as possible.
- Follow the ball onto the field.
- Clean up balls that are knocked down near the front.
- React immediately to uncaught balls.

Score Your Success

7 to 10 accurate throws to the jumper = 5 points

10 out of 10 throws to the correct signalled position = 5 points

Your score ___

LOCK

The priorities of the two locks are to win the ball in the line-out and push in the scrum. Usually, locks are noted for their height, catching ability and power. If you are tall and strong, have good basketball skills and enjoy contact, you may be the ideal player for this position.

When you practise scrummaging, first experiment with your foot positioning to see which placement generates the most force and also gives excellent resistance to the opposition's drive. Remember, your primary role is to ensure the scrum remains stable so you must find foot positions that help you stay balanced. A scrummaging machine that measures force will help you compare the various forces that you can

exert. If you don't have a machine, bind up against two other players and ask them to tell you which foot position feels strongest against them.

These are the lock's main priorities:

In the Scrum

- Provide solid support for the front row.
- Exert forward power when required.
- Resist the opposition's shove.
- Show a safe scrummaging position at all times.
- Bind tightly to both the lock and prop throughout the scrummage.

In the Line-Out

- Win the ball when it is thrown to you as the jumper.
- Compete vigorously against your opponent.
- Resist any drive at the line-out, and contribute to any from your own team.

In the Loose

- Catch or control any kick-off that comes to you.
- Drive in dynamically at rucks and mauls with a safe body position.
- Rip out any available ball in rucks and mauls.
- Contribute to your team's tackle count.
- Understand and involve yourself in attack and defensive roles in all areas of the field and in all situations.
- Maintain a high work rate around the field

Scrum Position

There are a number of ways you can bind with the other lock in the second row, but the most frequently used is the bind across and down onto the outside hip at waist level so that you pull each other's inside hips close together. If you are playing on the left of the scrum, you should bind under the arm and around the body of the right-side lock. By binding in this way, you will create a little more space for your hooker because your right shoulder moves slightly backwards in the scrum. Your outside shoulder should fit neatly under the buttock of your prop, and your outside arm should reach as far round the outside of the prop's hip as possible. As you advance into senior age rugby, this bind will change to binding through the legs of the prop and around and onto his inner thigh near his hip. Different countries allow this bind at different ages, so you will need to check with the age group Laws in your country.

 Misstep

Any force you generate in the scrum never seems to be powerful enough to move it forward.

Correction

Check that you are bound tightly to your partner at lock and also to the prop. As the ball is put into the scrum, squeeze your arms, bend your legs, lower your knees and drive.

When you bind up with your teammates ready to go into the scrum, bind with your lock partner first and then squat down behind the front row and bind onto them. For immediate stability your feet should already be in a wide, stable position, one foot slightly ahead of the other and legs slightly bent at the knees. If you prefer to scrummage with both feet back, you may have to squat. Alternatively, with one foot up and one foot back, kneel down on the back knee. If you scrummage with both feet back and you find it uncomfortable to squat, go down on one knee; then, at the moment you make contact, slide your foot back into position.

When the referee gives you the signal to engage, extend your legs and stay strong while both front rows make firm contact. It is essential that you move your feet and legs as little as possible and that you maintain a safe scrummaging position: head up, back flat, shoulders above hips and feet back (figure 8.1, page 107).

As the front rows engage, lift your grounded knee and push your shoulders forward firmly against the prop's rear thigh. Lock into your safe scrummaging position and push or resist on command. No matter how the scrum moves, keep your weight balanced within your stance. As the ball leaves the scrum, break off your bind and join in the next piece of action as quickly as possible.

Pushing and Locking-Out Techniques in the Scrum

The pushing and locking-out techniques are similar:

• **Pushing:** Extend your legs until they are slightly bent at the knee. On a given signal by the leader of the forwards, extend your legs. If you are successful in moving your opponents backwards, take short, sharp steps forward and repeat the sequence.

• **Locking out:** Direct all your effort downwards into your hips and knees, lock the joints, but keep your shoulders above your hips at all times. This should stop you from going backwards. The only point that may slide backwards is your point of contact with the ground. If you have only three or four studs per boot in the ground, you may slide back more quickly than if all were in contact. To make the best contact with the ground, turn your heels inwards and downwards until they touch the ground. If you have to take any steps backwards, make them very short and brisk to try to regain a good stud hold.

Misstep
You have a tendency to slide backwards when the opposition drives.

Correction
Make firm stud contact with the ground. The more studs you have in the surface, the better. This might mean that you have to turn your heels inwards and downwards when the pressure comes on. Accept some of the force into your knees and hips, like a spring being compressed, and then lock these joints out against any more backward movement. Move your feet only if you feel that you are becoming unstable.

If your opponents are to put the ball into the scrummage, you may decide to go for an eight-player shove. In this case your hooker also takes up a pushing position, and you and your second-row partner will be able to put all of your weight through both of your shoulders. The force in your push comes from your legs, abdomen and lower back. An eight-player shove is most effective if all the players push on a given signal by the leader of the forwards. If the opposition goes backwards, take short, brisk steps forward to regain your scrummaging position as quickly as possible.

Jump at the Line-Out

One of the most important requirements of the lock is a powerful and strong body core. This helps not only with pushing and resisting in the scrum, but, most important, when being lifted in the line-out. A strong abdominal core will stabilise you in the air and also help the support players lift you and bring you back down safely.

For an effective jump at the line-out, begin with a wide, stable stance and your hands ready, palms facing the hooker (figure 8.12a). Some players prefer to have a narrower base so they can take a short, sharp step into the jump sequence. Always take up your starting position, even though the ball may be going to one of the other jumpers in your line-out. The leader of the forwards will call out a signal to determine which jumper gets the ball. If the ball is thrown to you, jump up and towards the line of touch, eyes on the ball at all times (figure 8.12b). As you jump, the hooker should throw the ball to the desired height, normally the highest point of your jump.

Figure 8.12 Jump at the Line-Out

a

b

PREPARATION

1. Wide, stable stance
2. Palms facing hooker

EXECUTION

1. Jump up and towards line of touch
2. Keep eyes on ball
3. Hooker throws ball at highest point of jump

c

FOLLOW-THROUGH

1. Catch ball
2. Bring ball to chest
3. Turn back to opponents' line
4. Support players secure your position
5. Release ball to support player or scrum half

Misstep

You have a tendency to flap at the ball in the line-out, which gives an uncontrolled ball to your scrum half.

Correction

Ask the hooker to throw slightly lower and more softly. This will give you the chance to jump at the ball and drive your hands towards it. If you time your jump as well, you should be able to reach the ball before your opponent has the chance to contest it.

As you catch, bring the ball down quickly to your chest and turn your back towards your opponents' line (figure 8.12c). By then your support players should have secured you and the ball, and you can release the ball to them or to the scrum half. The same technique is used if you are to tap down the ball. A tap is simply a gentle touch with one or both hands, pushing the ball down to the scrum half. Follow the ball from the line-out, or join in the resulting ruck or maul sequence.

Develop a range of jumps to beat your opponent. You will succeed only with clear and easily understood signals between you and the hooker. To practise all of your line-out skills, work with support players, one in front and one behind. Always jump in towards the line of touch, even when you have no opposition. Your support players can also practise their skills. As your line-out develops, you may begin to use different strategies to win the ball. Some may be more complicated, involving players switching up and down the line. However, none will succeed unless you and the other members of the unit have worked hard in practice with the hooker.

Misstep

During each match your opponents eventually read your signals or recognise how you intend to win the ball and begin to make it more difficult to gain possession.

Correction

Always practise a range of jumping techniques. This will keep your opponents guessing and should produce a better chance of winning a controlled ball.

It is a good idea to practise jumping against a tackle shield. Make sure the shield is held at your jump height so that you make shoulder contact with it. This will give you the confidence you need to jump against an opponent. Then you can take the tackle shield away, moving to passive opposition (your opponent jumps but does not try to go for the ball). Gradually progress to a competition for possession.

Lock Drill. *Winning the Ball*

This drill gives you a chance to practise jumping to win the ball at the line-out while working against opposition. You will need your hooker, two support players and a scrum half to give the ball to. Initially, practise jumping and being lifted against a player who is holding a tackle shield. As soon as possible, work against an unshielded player so that you become used to jumping for the ball and making shoulder-to-shoulder contact (figure 8.13). Make sure that you practise all of the jumps you are likely to use in a match and also the signals for each of these jumps. Movement in line-outs is essential for the jumpers, so practise moving. For example, move from near the back to the front to step into the space between the two props for the surprise lift.

To Increase Difficulty

- Allow increasingly active opposition as the proficiency of the line-out increases.

To Decrease Difficulty

- Slow down the introduction of and numbers in the active opposition.

Success Check

- Distribute your weight evenly on both feet to allow you to move quickly either forward or backwards and to also feint one way or the other prior to the jump.
- On signal, start your movement sequence, but remember to jump to the line of touch.

Figure 8.13   Shoulder-to-shoulder contact.

- Catch, tap with both hands or guide with one hand to win the ball and push it down into the scrum half's hands.

Score Your Success

Clean possession from 5 throws, using effective signals = 10 points

Your score ___

Front-Five Drill 1. *Front-Row Binding and Engaging*

Practise binding and then engaging against the scrummaging machine until you feel comfortable and are working together as a unit. Then scrummage against three other players. It is essential that the players opposite you are used to playing in this position and know all safety rules and correct techniques.

Practise engaging until you can remain immediately stable. Then practise nudging the other group slightly upwards and backwards in the scrum. Try to work together as a unit, timing your push together.

As you become more proficient, your opposition may apply a little more resistance so that you begin to develop some scrummaging strength as well as technique. If you feel the scrummage is unstable in any way, go back to the machine and determine the cause of instability with your coach.

To Increase Difficulty

- Work against a number of different front rows in sequence.

- Scatter front rows around a large area so that you have to run from scrum to scrum.
- Add in some wrestling for the ball or rucks and mauls to encourage your work rate.

To Decrease Difficulty

- Concentrate solely on technique.
- Concentrate on quality rather than quantity.

Success Check

- Keep your feet flat and slightly more than shoulder-width apart.
- Keep your head up, your chin off your chest and your back flat.

- Keep your shoulders always above your hips and your legs bent.
- Crouch, touch, pause, engage.

Score Your Success

10 stable scrums showing firm engagement, safe position and good technique = 10 points

8 or 9 stable scrums showing firm engagement, safe position and good technique = 5 points

6 or 7 stable scrums showing firm engagement, safe position and good technique = 1 point

Your score ___

Front-Five Drill 2. *Binding, Engaging, Pushing and Locking Out*

The addition of two locks to the front row will give you a front five. Work against a scrummaging machine so that you can practise pushing. Bind correctly and tightly before you go into the scrum. Locks should remember to put the majority of the push into the outside shoulder. The inside shoulder may have nothing to push against because the hooker may move independently of the props.

To lock out, practise pushing against the machine until your legs are almost straight, and then stay in that position without moving for 5 seconds. You can do this only if you have a modern scrummaging machine that has a number of strong elastic bands, which exert pressure back at you. If you do not have access to a machine, practise against five other players.

Follow up the scrummage with a series of activities to simulate subsequent play—for example, scrummage, sprint, tackle and handle, return to the scrum (figure 8.14).

To Increase Difficulty

- Add more people to the opposition defence or more force to the scrummaging machine.
- Move the defender closer to the tackle bag.
- Allow the defender to compete for the ball as soon as the tackle is made on the tackle bag.

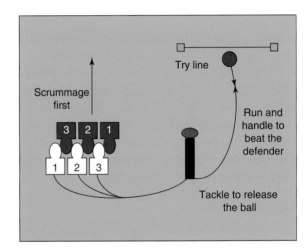

Figure 8.14 After the scrummage, tackle, sprint and handle, and return to the scrum.

To Decrease Difficulty

- Make the goal line much wider.
- Have the defender remain face down until the tackle has been made.
- Do not allow the defender to move forward from the designated start position.

Success Check

- Maintain a good scrummaging position.
- To push forward, squeeze your arms and grip, lower your knees and hips and straighten your legs.
- Take short, brisk steps to regain position if the opposition gives ground.
- To resist a shove, lock your hip and knee joints.
- Keep your heels in and down, if necessary, for the best possible stud contact with the ground.

Front-Five Drill 3. *Hooking Practice*

Initially, practise against a machine until your technique and timing improve. Practise the various ways of striking—you never know when you will need to use them. Work with the scrum half you normally play with so that you can become used to each other's signals.

While you are learning to hook, the opposition front row should concentrate on supporting you as a hooker, so you can practise your technique without the pressure of an opponent trying to win the ball.

Apply all safety measures in live scrummaging. Remember, always keep your shoulders above your hips. Avoid any mismatches in size, strength, weight or experience, especially prop against prop.

To Increase Difficulty

- Have someone drop a small object, such as a golf ball or coin, from directly above the strike area and out of your sight. Hook it as it hits the ground.
- Allow the opposition front row to be a little more active. For example, they nudge slightly as the ball is put in. Note that 3v3 can become very unstable if your opponents narrow their stance and try to push. The nudge should come from the thighs and buttocks and should travel forward no more than 15 centimetres.
- Allow the opposition hooker to strike as well. Props must maintain their wide stances to support both players.

To Decrease Difficulty

- Ask your scrum half to use a verbal signal to trigger the strike.
- Have the opponents remain passive, with no strike from the opposition hooker.

Success Check

- Use correct and tight binding at all times.
- Keep your shoulders parallel to the ground and above your hips.
- Position your hips and head slightly towards the mouth of the tunnel.
- Use the two most effective striking techniques.

Front-Five Drill 4. *Forwards Only Live Scrummaging*

Practise against another unit of front-five forwards who are of the same ability. Try to work with the scrum half who will be playing in the next game. You all have to be familiar with each other's styles of play and signals.

Decide whether you will be attacking or defending in the scrum. Line up, bind tightly and crouch. On the referee's or coach's signal, engage the opposition. Practise either pushing and hooking or locking-out techniques. Between attempts, break up and reform the scrum. Now is also the time to practise the all-player push. In this practice sequence, only five are in the scrum. The hooker can take up a pushing position to contribute to the drive, and the locks can shove through both shoulders.

Run a one-minute sequence that includes some of the skills you normally would perform in a game—scrummaging, running, tackling, rucking or mauling—then back to scrummaging. Repeat five times.

To Increase Difficulty

- Scrummage in five different positions on the field. Between scrums, run at pace while handling the ball.

- Scrummage in five different positions on the field. Between scrums, tackle a would-be set of attackers and wrestle for the ball or ruck or maul to regain it. Take up your defensive positions at either side of the ruck or maul situation.

- Alternate between pushing and locking.

To Decrease Difficulty

- Work for quality rather than quantity.

- Walk from one position to the next and concentrate solely on technique.

Success Check

- When going forward, sink your knees and hips and straighten your legs

- When resisting a shove, move your feet farther back and slightly wider, keep your knees and hips down, and lock your hips and knee joints.

- If you become unbalanced, quickly regain position.

Score Your Success

5 firm, stable contacts with safe body positions and effective scrummaging skills as attackers = 5 points

5 firm, stable contacts with safe body positions and effective scrummaging skills as defenders = 5 points

10 firm, stable contacts, then quick movement to the next action = 5 points

Your score ___

Front-Five Drill 5. *Live Scrummaging With the Back Row*

Stability in the scrummage occurs only if the first contact is firm and strong from both teams. Much of the stability comes from the width of your stance. If your stance is narrow, the scrum will become very unstable as soon as any push comes on. The stabilising forces for the two locks are the flankers and the number 8. The flankers help to steady the prop forward platform, and the number 8 binds the locks together.

Line up facing the opposition and crouch so that you can see where you will put your head. All players should look at the opposition. On the referee's or coach's signal, engage firmly, making sure that you do not recoil from the opposition and also stay balanced on making contact.

After each scrummage, play through a number of other sequences of action. For example, play a back-row move that goes to a ruck or maul, followed by further movement downfield until a stoppage occurs. Restart the game with another scrum and attack with the possession won until you score or the attack breaks down. Restart with another set piece.

Alternate between an attacking and a defensive scrum.

To Increase Difficulty

- Work against your opponents with very little rest between scrummages, but never until your strength begins to fail.
- Scrummage in 10 different positions on the field. Alternate between attack and defence. In attack, try to move the ball downfield using all your attacking skills and try to score. In defence, tackle a would-be set of attackers and wrestle for the ball or ruck or maul to regain it. Quickly take up your defensive positions at either side of the ruck or maul situation.

To Decrease Difficulty

- Work solely on technique, taking long rests between scrums.

Success Check

- Maintain a firm, wide stance.
- Keep your shoulders always above your hips and your feet back.
- Keep your head up and your chin off your chest, and look in to the space where you will put your head and shoulders.
- Maintain a firm binding with the player at the side of you and those in front.
- Avoid any sideways movement.

Score Your Success

10 firm, stable contacts with safe body positions and no backward or sideways movement = 5 points

10 firm, stable contacts, arriving first at the next action = 5 points

Your score ___

Front-Five Drill 6. *Practising Line-Out Skills*

Use the 5- and 15-metre lines on the field for practising throwing over the distances used in a match. So that you can practise playing away from the line-out, use four other players in defence. Defenders wear tackle suits and carry tackle shields. Place two defenders close to the line-out to act as a back-row defence and two others 10 metres back to simulate part of the midfield defence. The thrower and jumpers work together. The other props take their normal line-out positions except that one moves behind the middle jumper when the longer throw is practised. Props must react to the jumper's actions and provide support. The ball is fed to the scrum half, who runs either to the left or right and pops the ball back inside to a support runner. As a group you now have to attack the defence and try to score.

To Increase Difficulty

- Have the defenders stop using the tackle shields but keep the tackle suits on. They may be very vigorous and may grab but not tackle.
- Keep the practice channel narrow.
- Move some of the marker cones inwards so that the practice channel becomes gradually narrower as it nears the goal line.

To Decrease Difficulty

- Move some of the marker cones outwards so that the practice channel gradually widens as it nears the goal line.
- Decrease the number of defenders and retain the tackle shields.
- Before the throw, decide whether the jumper is to catch or tap.
- Have the scrum half signal her intentions much earlier.

Success Check

- As props, wedge the jumper as the ball is caught.
- As props, quickly close on the jumper when tapping down.
- Make good attacking decisions.
- Use running lines to create spaces in defence. Use offloads to keep the defence from slowing the ball down.
- Always turn the ball back inside towards the centre of the grid when space becomes tight near the edge of it.

Score Your Success

Score 8 to 10 times with no dropped passes = 10 points

Score 6 or 7 times with no dropped passes = 5 points

Score 4 or 5 times with no dropped passes = 1 point

Your score ___

Front-Five Drill 7.   *Game Sequences*

Practise line-outs as part of a game. This could be any type of game—for example, touch and pass, tag rugby, end ball or a practice match. The line-out starts the sequence of action each time. For example, substitute a line-out for a scrum when playing touch and pass. You might play a 10v10 game of touch rugby with backs playing against forwards. You can make up games from your own experience as long as some of the essential elements of rugby remain—pass backwards, release the ball after a tackle (this may be a two-handed touch at the waist), play line-outs when the ball goes off the side of the field, bring the ball back into play using a scrum after a technical infringement (e.g., knock-on, forward pass), free kick to simulate a set piece situation. If a back mishandles, restart the game with a line-out.

To Increase Difficulty

- Work against another group of forwards.
- Develop the opposition from relatively passive to fully active.

To Decrease Difficulty

- Do not allow the opposition to contest the ball.

Success Check

- The thrower and jumper have clear signals.
- Use correct foot positioning.
- Hold hands above your shoulders and spread your fingers.
- Jump inwards to land at the line of touch.
- Provide effective, stable and safe support for the jumpers.

Score Your Success

8 to 10 clean possessions out of 10 throws in a game = 10 points

6 or 7 clean possessions out of 10 throws in a game = 5 points

4 or 5 clean possessions out of 10 throws in a game = 1 point

Your score ___

SUCCESS SUMMARY OF THE FRONT FIVE

Success is measured by the number of possessions you win and protect in the game. Whether from the scrum, line-out or kick-off, your role in the front five is to win the ball so that others can use it. If you are also skilful enough to become part of the attacking sequences in the game, then so much the better. The best front-five players are also able to set up and continue running and handling sequences that lead to tries. As you practise the drills in this step, focus on perfecting your support and ball-winning skills and you will become a valuable asset to your team.

Throughout this step, you have moved from passive to active opposition in all of the positional skills required to play safely in the front five. There should be no compromise on safety. If you have scored at least 80 percent on each of the skills needed for playing in your position, you are ready to move on. If you have not scored at least 80 percent, go back and practise until your proficiency improves.

Prop Forward Drills

1. Prop Forward's Body Position in the Scrum   ___ out of 10

2. Prop Support of Receiver at Kick-Off   ___ out of 10

Hooker Drills

1. Hooker Accuracy at the Line-Out   ___ out of 10

2. Throwing to the Jumpers   ___ out of 10

Lock Drill

1. Winning the Ball   ___ out of 10

Front-Five Drills

1. Front-Row Binding and Engaging   ___ out of 10

2. Binding, Engaging, Pushing and Locking-Out   ___ out of 15

3. Hooking Practice   ___ out of 10

4. Forwards Only Live Scrummaging   ___ out of 15

5. Live Scrummaging With the Back Row   ___ out of 10

6. Practising Line-Out Skills   ___ out of 10

7. Game Sequences   ___ out of 10

Total   ___ out of 130

The Middle Five

The players who occupy the middle-five positions are the back row (blindside flanker, openside flanker and number 8) and the two half backs (scrum half and fly half) (table 9.1). These players are the primary users of the ball. They work hard to set up attacks for the rest of the team. They pin down the defence and create space for others. They are the main link players between the front-five and back-five players. They also are a major defensive unit and often are the players who make the first defensive tackles against an attack from a set piece.

FLANKERS AND NUMBER 8

The two flankers and number 8 make up the back row. Teams that have a good back row are normally very successful. Although the players work as a tight unit in attack and defence, the positions have slightly different skills. All the back-row players need speed and contact skills, especially in the tackle. The openside flanker also should possess a range of attacking skills, similar to those of the centres, to aid the continuity of the team.

Good back-row players often are interchangeable. This kind of flexibility within this small unit makes the best use of all three players. By interchanging, they can be most creative in attack and most destructive in defence. All back-row players need well-developed contact and continuity skills.

These are the main priorities of the flankers and number 8:

At the Scrum

- Make a contribution by pushing.
- Defend, support or initiate an attack.

- Number 8 controls the ball at the base of the scrum for the scrum half and, when necessary, initiates attacks from this position (figure 9.1).

Figure 9.1 Number 8 attacks from the base of the scrum.

Table 9.1 Middle-Five Positions

Position	Qualities and responsibilities			
	Individual	**Scrum**	**Line-out**	**Loose**
Back row: number 8, open and blindside flankers	Comfortable with and an expert in contact; good handling ability; good tackler; good communicator; fit enough to run at pace all through game; power runner as ball carrier	Pushes in every scrum Flanker on the left: provides first line of defence down their right side of scrum Flanker on the right: is second tackler after scrum half down their left side Both flankers: support any pick and drive by number 8 on his inside shoulder Number 8: covers inside shoulder of tackling flanker; initiates attacks in suitable attacking positions from base of scrum	Supports jumper in jump-and-catch sequence; quickly closes off any gaps; protects ball; sometimes cleans up loose balls; occasionally acts as forward, peeling around front of line-out; available as alternative jumper On opposition's throw: Drives through any gaps and tries to win back ball Openside flanker: When playing at tail, threatens first ball carriers in their attacking move Blindside flanker: Follows up and supports openside flanker on his inside shoulder, retrieves loose ball or tackles other ball carriers	Contributes to team's attack and defence sequences; stays on feet in contact; maintains good body position in rucks and mauls; drives dynamically into contact; is a scavenger when ball is on ground; moves quickly to support ball carrier in attack; tackles ball carrier in defence
Scrum half	Quick in thought and action with good vision; passes and kicks accurately and with precision; strong legs and shoulders; comfortable with contact against much bigger players; decisive; understands game; has pace, power and endurance to maintain high work rate throughout game; has sprinter's start and hits full speed quickly; must be one of the main communicators in the team	Passes cleanly off ground under pressure; kicks accurately over scrum; recognises attacking opportunities, particularly down right side; is major part of defensive screen around scrum	Catches ball cleanly when delivered at various speeds, heights and distances; passes accurately each way under pressure; kicks accurately over line-out; quickly covers field in defence and acts as sweeper; eyes and ears of defence	Tackles aggressively; performs all skills under pressure; creates space for others to use; reenters play quickly after contributing to attack or defence; recognises gaps quickly and has pace to go through them
Fly half	Quick in thought and action with good vision; tactically very aware of possibilities; passes accurately both ways under pressure; executes team's kicking game plan with precision; decisive; understands game; must be the main communicator in the team	Knows when to play flat or deep; can stop first defender with effective running line; takes part in defensive screen around scrum	Plays close to defence when needed; kicks accurately under pressure; can stop defence from drifting across field, thus holding attacking space out wide; threatens opposition; creates space for others	Constantly threatens opposition; handles and kicks with accuracy to left and right; quickly identifies weaknesses in opposition defence and takes advantage of them

Misstep
Any back-row moves are stifled near the scrum.

Correction
Run your moves wider out from the side of the scrum, perhaps using the scrum half or full back as the first-pass receiver. They will have more momentum because they will already be running when they receive the pass and therefore have a better chance of succeeding.

In the Line-Out

- A tall back-row forward can become an extra jumper in the line. Those who are a little shorter can become lifters for jumpers in various positions in the line.
- Back-row players provide strong, effective defence from the line-out, tackle any players who attack close or move across the field to bolster the defence close to the contact area.
- Back-row players move quickly to a position that allows them either to defend or support close-in or near the midfield.
- When required, a back-row player acts as a sweeper or support and peels off the end of the line-out to go forward.

In the Loose

- Approach rucks and mauls powerfully.
- Quickly and legally win any loose ball even if it means going to ground.
- Drive in dynamically with good body position at contact situations.
- Understand when to join rucks and mauls and when to stay out, as determined by attacking options and defensive requirements.
- Be strong on the ball at rucks and mauls, ripping it free when necessary.
- Support all attacks and act as the dynamo who fires up the rest of the team.
- Work with the other two in the mini-unit to top the team's tackle count.

Misstep
The opposition always seems to have a hand on the ball you carry into contact situations.

Correction
If you drive in with the ball leading with your right shoulder, the next player must come in left shoulder first and drive up and into your chest. This will shut off the ball from the opposition.

Your role as a back-row player is to make the best use of any ball you manage to scavenge in the game. You may win this ball in very close-contact situations or in the open field. Your choice of follow-up attack may be to maintain the continuity by passing to someone in a better position or to take on a defender who is blocking your team's progress up the field. Your decision is crucial to the continuity of the attack.

As a general rule, it is far better to pass the ball into the space at the side of a defender than to make contact. More often than not, passing guarantees continuity in attack, whereas contact does not, unless your players have particularly good continuity skills. For a review of footwork skills for avoiding contact, see step 2.

Misstep
You cannot produce the ball in contact situations.

Correction
Turn in to the tackle earlier than you would normally and keep the ball visible to your nearest support runner. This will prevent you from burying the ball into the defence and making it difficult to dig out.

Although you should try to avoid collisions as much as possible, you need to practise continuity in contact. No matter how good a player you are, at times the opposition will catch you with the ball. As the ball carrier, you have a range of options if you are about to make contact with an opponent. For a review of contact situations, see step 5.

Misstep
You release the ball slowly after a contact situation.

Correction
Pass before you make contact, preferably into a space. If you have to make contact, stay strong on a wide base, keep the ball visible to your support and push it backwards towards them as you make contact with the ground.

Misstep
Your attack lacks fluidity even though the ball is available.

Correction
Take the shortest route to the ball carrier: a straight line. Run at the nearer shoulder of any ball carrier, always expect a pass, but be ready to drive in to take the ball if the player makes contact with the opposition.

CAUTION Always wear protective equipment in both practice and match situations. Although not every drill in this section anticipates contact with a player, a piece of equipment or the ground, by its very nature rugby invites contact, sometimes by accident. It's better to be safe than sorry.

Back-Row Drill 1. *Pass or Contact*

In this drill you must decide whether to pass or go into contact. If you go into contact, you must decide how you will maintain the continuity of the attack. Do not prejudge what the defender may do. If you can, pass; if not, make the bump and in a split second follow up this action with the nearest support player. Be decisive, be strong and work briskly.

In a grid measuring 20 metres by 15 metres, play 5v5. The defenders spread out in the grid at various distances from the start point of the attack. The attacking team is trying to score by avoiding contact as much as possible. At times, however, you will run out of useful space, and your only alternative will be to go to contact in order to take away one or two players from the defence. Your next decision is vital: move the ball early or keep driving forward?

To Increase Difficulty

- Decrease the distance between the defenders.
- Narrow the grid towards the goal line.
- Allow defenders to reenter play towards the goal line after being passed.

To Decrease Difficulty

- Have the defenders stay in line and allow them to move side to side only.
- Widen the grid as it approaches the goal line.

Success Check

- Have a stable, wide base in contact.
- Keep the ball moving forward and visible to support players in contact.
- Keep your weight behind your leading foot at the point of contact.
- As a support player, have a good driving body position.

Score Your Success

5 scores with continuous forward movement and without losing possession = 10 points

4 scores with continuous forward movement and without losing possession = 5 points

3 scores with continuous forward movement and without losing possession = 1 point

Your score ___

132

Back-Row Drill 2.   *Working Through Contact*

Practise making contact while playing 2v1. Imagine there is no space to pass into and that you have to take a defender away from the area to give your support player a clear run upfield. Work in a narrow channel—5 metres by 10 metres will be sufficient—so that your support player has to stay close to you.

To Increase Difficulty

- Add one extra defender to the practice so that the ball carrier has the option to pass as well as run to beat the defence.
- Add more defenders down the channel for a continuous bump-and-pass sequence.

To Decrease Difficulty

- Allow the defenders to hold tackle shields.
- Add an extra attacker to support the first-pass receiver.

Success Check

- As you approach contact, lower your centre of gravity.
- Make a long, powerful last stride into contact with the ball visible to your partner.
- Drive low to high.
- Sometimes pivot on your front foot and either spin away from the contact or spin and pass.
- On a gut pass, push the ball up to your partner's lower chest.

Score Your Success

No dropped passes in 5 attempts = 10 points

1 dropped pass in 5 attempts = 5 points

2 dropped passes in 5 attempts = 1 point

Your score ___

Back-Row Drill 3.   *Running Lines*

Once you have practised running skills, try them in a game-like drill. To simulate a game, do not organise running lines or plan the contact area. Play spontaneously so that you can react accordingly. Play 5v3 in a channel 20 metres by 15 metres (figure 9.2) and play to score a try. You and a flank-forward partner begin the practice by bumping into a defender, driving the ball forward and then feeding the ball to the scrum half. This ball goes two passes out either left or right, and you follow as you would in the game.

The second-pass receiver runs at the defender and passes back inside to you very close to the defence. Your options depend on your distance from the defender and the closeness of your support. If you are a well-balanced runner with good handling skills, you may be able to catch and pass in a split second. If not, you may have to bump into the defender and find a way to keep the ball alive. Will you spin out of contact and pass? bump and pass? bump and drive through? bump, spin and drive? The decision is yours. Your priority is to keep the ball moving at pace through the channel.

To Increase Difficulty

- Allow defenders to be very active and try to legally slow down the ball.
- Allow the second-pass receiver to take the ball into contact or pass inside.
- Add two more defenders.
- Have the defence play at match intensity to prevent a score.

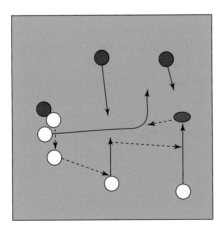

Figure 9.2   Running lines drill.

To Decrease Difficulty

- Declare which technique to practise and set up the contact situation accordingly.

Success Check

- Take decisive action at the point of contact.
- Keep a wide base in contact.
- Maintain good driving positions.
- Have your hands ready for all situations.

Back-Row Drill 4. *Pass and Contact Options*

Begin this practice as though you were the number 8, about to initiate an attack from the scrum. Your aim is to make as much use of the 5-metre offside line as possible and to get behind the back-row defence and score. When you pick up, run a wide arc to take you away from the nearside flanker. Once you are behind the defence, your options will open up. Your decision making has to be precise and accurate—pass or contact? Your support runners often can help you make that decision, as will the defence and the closeness of the goal line.

To set up a much faster attack 2 or 3 metres farther out, establish a signal that your scrum half can give to indicate that he is giving you responsibility for the ball so he can quickly run into the wider channel. For example, the scrum half may tap you on the hip and begin to run. As soon as you receive this signal, pick up the ball, drive close to the right side of the scrum, draw the left-hand defending flanker towards you and make a pass to the fast-overlapping scrum half.

One of the best places from which to play back-row attacks is the right side of the field, with a minimum of 15 metres between the scrum and the touch line. This will always allow you to have one extra player in the attack.

Use a full scrum plus a scrum half, a right winger and a full back (figure 9.3). Defend with the same number of forwards but no winger. The practice will help you fine-tune any attacks you may wish to use down the right-hand side of the scrum during a match.

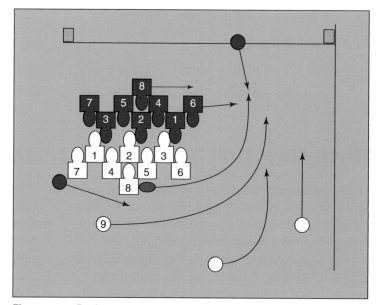

Figure 9.3 Back-row pass and contact options drill.

If the ball goes very quickly from the attacking scrum half to the full back or a winger, the role of number 8 is to try to run in directly behind the ball carrier. If the ball carrier angles the attacking run towards the posts, you may find that a switch pass will put you into space. Once you have passed the ball, you must follow it in fast support. On the other hand, if the ball carrier takes contact, all your other options—bumping, driving and rolling—will come into play.

To Increase Difficulty

- Add a left wing defender.
- Add an extra defender 10 metres behind the scrummage.

To Decrease Difficulty

- If you've added an extra defender, have that defender move farther away from the scrum.
- Make the back-row defenders start on their hands and knees.

Success Check

- Pass or carry the ball in quickly behind the back-row defence.
- Move the ball fast through the contact area.
- Have a wide, stable stance in contact.
- At contact, bump and roll to show the ball to your support players.

- If the ball carrier goes into contact, drive in quickly.
- Make an accurate pass to the overlapping player.
- Be decisive and quick at the point of contact.
- Keep your eyes open and look for attacking opportunities.

Score Your Success

5 scores out of 5 attempts = 10 points

4 scores out of 5 attempts = 5 points

3 scores out of 5 attempts = 1 point

Your score ___

Back-Row Drill 5. *Line-Out Deflection*

In the line-out, you may have a responsibility as a jumper to win the ball cleanly for a strike by the backs or a peeling sequence by the forwards. In either case your priority is to win a controlled ball using both hands and knock it gently down into a target area close by. From there it will be moved away quickly by the scrum half or driven around the corner of the line-out by a peeling forward.

You might, alternatively, catch the ball and drive forward with support from forwards on either side. This is done to tie in the opposition back row for a follow-up attack either close by or in the middle of the field.

To practise peeling at the line-out, the forward designated to catch the peel must join in the practice. Although traditionally a prop forward from the front of the line-out catches the peel, it is better to use either of the two locks, who are used to catching a ball in close-contact situations. Your props can follow up the play to protect the ball carrier in any contact situation. Make sure to stand the correct distance from the touch line when you practise your line-out sequences.

In this drill you have to choose one of three options. If you tap down to the scrum half, you must follow up the ensuing attack. If the opposition have good defensive jumpers and yours are well-marked, then a throw to the back with a peel around the back should make ground because the close defenders are involved in trying to cut off your line-out possession (figure 9.4). If you tap down for

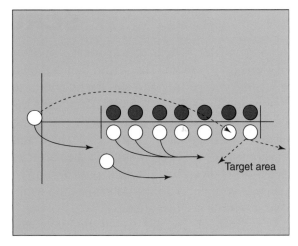

Figure 9.4 Throwing to the back and peeling around the back of the lineout.

a peel, you may be able to stand out from the next contact situation to receive the ball for a follow-up attack. If you catch and drive, you must keep the ball safe and strong until a teammate drives in to take it from your hands. Play towards a goal line and have five attempts at scoring using any form of attack described.

To Increase Difficulty

- Add more defenders and attackers to the practice, starting with a defending number 10.
- Have an equal number of defenders and attackers.

To Decrease Difficulty

- Have more attackers than defenders.
- Use tackle shields in the defence.

Success Check

- Move the ball quickly behind the defence.
- Use clear signals.
- Have your hands ready and above your shoulders, your inside foot forward and your weight distributed evenly on both feet.
- After looking at the opponents' formation, decide on your jump—forward, backwards or straight up—then signal and go for it.
- Jump high and towards the line of touch.

- When tapping, make sure the ball drops about 1 metre out of the line-out into the target area.
- When catching, spread your fingers and hold your hands close together. Pull the ball down quickly to your chest. Land in balance, bend your knees and sink your hips on a wide base to land.

Score Your Success

4 or 5 scores out of 5 attempts with accurate execution = 10 points

3 scores out of 5 attempts with accurate execution = 5 points

2 scores out of 5 attempts with accurate execution = 1 point

Your score ___

SCRUM HALF

The scrum half is one of the most important positions on the team. The scrum half is the link between the forwards and the backs and is the pivot around which the majority of attacks take place. In the position of scrum half, you will be called on throughout the game to make instant decisions in attack and defence. In the game you have three choices: will you kick, pass or run? The quality of your decision will determine the quality of your team's performance.

As scrum half, you are one of the major decision makers in the team: at line-out you may give the signal for the throw; at the scrum you may call the back-row moves; at rucks and mauls you may choose which side to attack. Because you must communicate these decisions, you should talk constantly to the forwards and backs.

You also are in the best place and may be the ideal player to act as pack leader for the team. Play with your head up, looking for weaknesses in the defence to be better able to decide whether your forwards should drive the ball through contact, release it or drive in contact so that a player with the ball can drive out from the maul to set up the next attack. You become the eyes and ears of the players in the pack.

To develop as a scrum half, practise passing from the ground to the left and right. A left-handed scrum half has an advantage because the vast majority of passes from the base of the

scrum are made with the left hand. This skill set becomes more important as you begin to play in adult rugby, because the Laws state that the opposition scrum half can follow you around and stand next to your team's number 8, thereby cutting off any right-handed pass.

These are the main priorities of the scrum half:

At the Scrum

- Pass accurately and quickly to both left and right without lift or back swing.
- Pivot around on your back foot to protect the pass (pivot pass).
- Pose a constant threat to the defence.
- Kick accurately with your right foot for position.
- Be the first tackler when the opponents use a back-row attack to their left side of the scrum.

At the Line-Out

- Pass accurately and quickly to the left and right, no matter how the ball arrives to you.
- Kick accurately with either foot for position.
- Contribute to the defence around the line-out.
- Be prepared to stand at the front of the line-out and help lift one of the forwards.

In the Loose

- Pass accurately and quickly to the left and right.
- Kick accurately.
- Pose a constant threat to the defence.
- Contribute to the defence around rucks and mauls.
- Act as the sweeper in defence and plug any holes that appear.

Passing Skills

As the scrum half, you must master a number of passes, especially from the base of the scrum. The ball receiver may be running at speed close by or fading away from the pass some 10 metres away. Decide quickly what force of pass is the best to use in any situation. The power in your pass is critical to the ball receiver's next action.

Your pass must be delivered so it gives the three-quarter line a range of options. If the pass is too hard, it may force them sideways; too soft, and it may check their forward movement by bringing them in range of the destroyers from the opponents' back row (figure 9.5). Many of these problems can be solved by developing a range of passes (figure 9.6)

1. A pass that spirals point first (figure 9.6) and covers a long distance so that your fly half can play around the edge of the back-row defence.

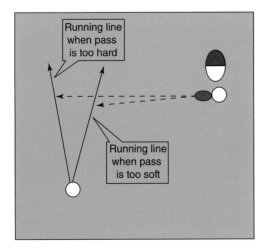

Figure 9.5 A pass that is too hard may force the ball carrier sideways. A pass that is too soft may bring the ball carrier back towards the opponents' back row.

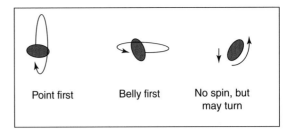

Figure 9.6 Passing variations.

2. A spiral pass that travels belly first. This arrives at the fly half over a shorter distance, does not fly as quickly and is much easier to control. This will allow the fly half to play closer to the back-row defence and put someone else around the edge of it.

3. Finally, passes that do not spin at all and are used to bring forwards or backs onto the ball at pace, often very close to the opposition. These passes are flicked or popped up using just the fingers, wrists and forearms and may turn gently end over end.

Passing From the Ground at the Scrum and at Ruck and Maul

The best way to describe the action for moving the ball quickly off the ground is a brushing motion. Try to imagine dust on the grass and just brush your hand across the surface of the grass to move the dust away with the tips of your fingers. Now make the brushing motion much longer and more vigorous so that your hand starts near your back foot and finishes up and beyond your opposite shoulder, pointing at your target. This is the passing movement.

You will find passing from the ground much easier if you take a wide stance with your legs slightly bent and your weight towards your back foot, with your other foot pointing in the direction of the intended pass. Practise the motion without the ball at first. As your arm moves through its arc, allow your weight to follow it so that it finishes over the other foot. This transfer of weight helps you put power into the pass. Pointing your front foot in the direction of the pass also helps you to shift your weight from the back to the front foot. Always start from a standing position, and make the imaginary pass in one movement. Stride in the direction of the pass, bend your knees, sink your hips, reach down, sweep away and point along the path of the ball.

Once this feels smooth, practise the pass sequence with the ball. Initially, you should use only one hand to move the ball away (figure 9.7). To pass to the left, use your right hand. Reach down with your passing hand behind the ball, spread your fingers wide near the back of the ball and sweep away to the receiver. Make sure

your hand follows through so that it points in the direction of the pass. (It may take you a number of attempts before you manage to make the ball fly off the ground.) Place the ball on the ground so that it is already pointing in the passing direction. To pass to your right, step in to the ball with your left foot first, and then plant and point your right foot towards the target receiver. To pass to the left, do everything as a mirror image.

a

b

Figure 9.7 One-handed sweep: *(a)* right hand behind the ball; *(b)* sweep the ball to the receiver with the right hand.

To make the ball spin, bring your hand up the side of the ball as you pass it. Practise more with your nondominant hand so that passes from either side are of the same quality.

After successfully sweeping the ball away with one hand, it is time to use both hands. Approach

the ball while keeping low to the ground. Watch the ball at all times, hands ready as a target. Step in to the ball quickly, pointing your leading foot at the receiver (figure 9.8*a*). Your rear hand sweeps the ball away in one movement while your front hand acts solely as a guide (figure 9.8*b*).

Misstep
Your pass has no power.

Correction
Pass the ball from your rear foot, sweeping it through a long arc and transferring your weight from your rear to front foot as you complete the pass.

Misstep
The pass wobbles rather than spirals.

Correction
Make sure that your hand is at right angles to the seam, and bring it up and over the top of the ball as you pass it. Spread the fingers of your rear hand and touch the ball lightly with the fingers of your front hand.

Figure 9.8   Passing From the Scrum

PREPARATION

1. Step into the ball quickly
2. Point leading foot at the receiver

a

EXECUTION

1. Rear hand sweeps ball away in one movement
2. Front hand guides only

b

FOLLOW-THROUGH

1. Finish low with hands pointing at receiver
2. Rejoin game immediately

c

Do not be tempted to put your guide hand fully on the ball. Begin by touching it only with the tip of your index finger and thumb (figure 9.9). This will prevent you from picking up the ball before you pass it. Finish low and follow through so that your hands point towards the receiver (figure 9.8c).

Figure 9.9 The guide hand touches the ball with the tip of the index finger and the thumb only.

When you wish to spin the ball point first, simply bring the fingers of your back hand from the rear base of the ball up the side to over the top of it as you move from your rear to leading foot. If you wish to spin the ball belly first, spread your fingers wide and put them down at right angles to the seam. As you sweep the ball to release it, the belly of the ball rather than the point will be heading towards the receiver. Again, simply bring the fingers of your back hand from the bottom of the ball up the side and over the top to make it spin.

As the scrum half, you must select a pass to suit the attack or defensive situation. The position of the receiver will decide the length of pass as you approach the ball. Passing too fast and hard or too soft and slow will be detrimental to the performance of your team. If a long pass is demanded, send out a fast, spinning, point-first pass. If a short pass is required, send out a belly-first pass. As soon as you feel confident, play against a defender. It is the receiver's decision whether to try to run outside or inside and then pass to an overlapping player. A spare player can roll the ball to you so that you can begin to practise under match-like conditions.

Sometimes as the scrum half you will have to deliver a very short, soft pass from the ground to a player running at pace. A spiral pass is not appropriate in this situation. You should develop a soft or flick pass that can travel from half a metre to 5 metres. This pass can be made from any point within your stance, and often it will be passed from outside your base. All the effort comes from the wrists and fingers. When you reach the distance limit of such a pass, you may also bring your forearms into play, which give some extra length to your pass. As you pick up the ball, keep your fingers spread wide around it and simply flick your wrists and fingers in the direction you wish the pass to travel. If your fingers are pointing downwards, flick them upwards; if your fingers are pointing directly forward, flick them sideways. Avoid spinning the ball for such a pass.

Kicking From the Scrum

The scrum half is an ideal player to kick the ball because the forwards often provide a shield against the opposition. Although being left-handed helps for passing, it's better to be right-footed for kicking because a kick over the top of the scrum can be effective only with the right foot. If you try to kick with your left, the opposition scrum half will be able to charge it down. Kicking from the base of the scrum is a simple skill, but players often have difficulty with it because they may take too many paces from picking up the ball to kicking.

To kick effectively, take up a position behind the ball at the base of the scrum. Place your right foot to the right and behind the ball and your left foot close to it. Make sure your weight is on this foot. Scoop up the ball in both hands (figure 9.10a). As you start your kick, transfer the ball to the palm of your right hand (figure 9.10b) and drop it onto your right foot. Watch the ball down onto your foot and kick high and through the ball (figure 9.10c). In simple words, the sequence is 'plant, scoop, kick'. In the early stages of learning this type of kick, you may need to add a step across with your left leg. Because this slows down the time it takes to make the clearance, go to the shorter sequence as soon as possible.

Misstep

You try to kick over the forwards but are constantly charged down.

Correction

Avoid taking any steps as you kick. Remember, plant, scoop and kick (figure 9.10).

Figure 9.10 | Kicking From the Scrum

PREPARATION

1. Wide stance; eyes on ball
2. Hands ready to scoop ball from scrum
3. Scoop ball up and away

a

EXECUTION

1. Transfer ball to palm
2. Kick up and through ball

b

FOLLOW-THROUGH

1. Foot follows through high
2. Watch ball as it flies
3. Chase ball to try to regain possession

c

Misstep
Your kick is inaccurate.

Correction
Watch your foot to the ball. Turn your body sideways to the target area, gradually altering this angle until you have the ball flying in the correct direction. You can then work on the height.

There are a number of reasons to kick the ball over a scrum:

- To clear the defensive area. Normally this kick should go long downfield and may even be aimed into touch.

- To clear the defensive area with a hope of regaining the ball. This kick would go long and high, down the 15-metre line with the nearest winger and flankers chasing to try to regather or catch the receiver in possession.

- To send a delicate chip over the close defence for your winger to run on to.

Sometimes you have to kick when close to the touch line, which will reduce your angle to the touch line. This will be the time to consider the kick and chase downfield, but remember that this should have a signal that all of the potential chasers should know and respond to, including the rest of the three-quarter line.

If you are kicking to put the ball into touch, place your kicking foot farther back than before. Pivot slightly on your kicking foot; then stride with your other foot to bring your hips more around to face the touch line. This will allow you to kick the ball at an angle towards the side of the field so that it reaches touch. Remember to take the ball on the far side of the number 8, away from the opposition scrum half so that you get time and space to kick.

You also will have opportunities to kick at the line-out and also at ruck and maul situations. In both cases the principles of kicking over the scrum still apply.

The only way your side will be able to regain possession is if the ball is kicked high enough for your players to arrive as it lands. It should travel far enough towards your opponents' goal line to clear any danger for your side. The distance you aim for depends entirely on the speed of those who are chasing. Also take into account the height

you can kick the ball. A ball that is in the air for a long time and goes forward the optimum distance gives more players the opportunity to arrive as it lands to contest possession.

You also will have opportunities to kick with your left foot, so practise equally with both feet. If you find that one foot is much weaker than the other, concentrate on improving your kicking on the weaker side.

If you have enough forwards in front of you to provide a shield against an opponent charging down your kick, it is far better to use the right foot near the left touch line and the left foot near the right touch line.

Sometimes you may not be the best person to kick to touch. If you are very close to the touch line, it may be better to give the ball to your fly half to widen the angle towards the touch line to create a better chance of achieving a greater distance. You must decide whether you have a good angle.

Running From the Scrum Half Position

Although as the scrum half you may be involved in an attack initiated by the back row, sometimes you may seize the opportunity to run with the ball. The ball may be delivered very quickly from good forward-driving play that releases you behind the defence. Or the blindside area may have few defenders, and you can see an opportunity to attack with other members of your team. In either case, you must explode into top speed within two or three strides to take the defence by surprise. At the same time, lower your centre of gravity so you can bounce off any would-be tacklers. At all times, try to carry the ball in both hands so that you can pass it away should you be confronted by a number of defenders. Bring the ball onto your forearm only when there is space ahead of you.

When you practise running from the attack point, try to imagine situations that may confront you. A tackler may come from the left or from the right. In either case, you should be able to swerve one way or the other. You may have to dart suddenly from an outside to an inside running line, so try to develop your sidestep (see step 2).

A simple way to practise your running lines is to put markers down where the defenders would be if you ran from behind the scrum. As soon as you have rehearsed the runs, replace the defender markers with players who try to tag you as you run.

Misstep
You never seem to make a clean break from the base of the scrum.

Correction
Practise without opposition: run your line around and swerve past a range of markers where the tacklers would be. Then add some of the tacklers, and practise your run to make sure that you have the correct line. Practise your running drills, especially those for explosive starts from standing.

You might now use some teammates as support runners. Your right winger and full back can be very potent attacking players from the scrum on the right-hand side of the field. Have them join you in your run, and play against two or three defenders.

Scrum Half Drill 1. *Spiralling the Pass*

You will need a selection of rugby balls and another player to catch your passes. Work together in an area big enough for you to send out a range of passes of various lengths.

Start away from the ball, and walk in to place your rear foot behind the ball. Stride sideways with the front foot and point it in the direction of the pass. Reach down and spread the fingers wide on your passing hand. Use only the index finger and thumb on your guiding hand. Bend at the knees and sink at the hips with your weight on your rear foot. Sweep the ball away in one smooth movement, transferring the weight from rear to front. Follow through the ball with your hands. Finish by pointing at the ball receiver.

For added accuracy, set up a pair of corner flags with cargo tape attached to form a square at the correct height for passing through (figure 9.11). Check this by going into your passing stance and lowering your centre of gravity as if you were getting ready to pass. If you can see your target through the centre of the square, then you are ready to begin. Place this half-way between you and your target player.

Figure 9.11 A square at the correct height.

To Increase Difficulty

- Make the target square smaller.
- Scatter 10 rugby balls in an area. Run to each ball and pass to a receiver.
- Have the receiver move about, requiring passes of various lengths and from various directions.

To Decrease Difficulty

- Talk through the action sequence and then do it.
- Place 10 balls 1 metre apart in a line. Walk up the row and pass to a partner who is following at a set distance.

Success Check

- Keep your rear foot behind the ball, and point your front foot in the direction of the pass.
- Spread your fingers wide.
- Use only the index finger and thumb of your guiding hand.
- Bend your knees, sink at your hips and keep your weight on your rear foot.
- Transfer your weight from rear to front.
- Sweep in one smooth movement.
- Follow through with your hands.

Score Your Success

5 accurate passes to the left = 5 points

5 accurate passes to the right = 5 points

Your score ___

Scrum Half Drill 2. *Controlling the Ball*

Practise passing skills in a grid about 15 metres square. One player rolls a ball at you, and another catches your pass. Control the ball and pass. Remember to keep your fingers spread and touch the ball with only the fingertips of your guide hand. Sweep the ball away from the ground without picking it up. Transfer your weight from your rear to your front foot as you pass. Point your front foot in the direction of the pass. Follow through with both hands to finish pointing at the receiver.

To increase accuracy and reflexes, build a short, wide tunnel of tackle shields and have a partner deliver or roll a ball through the tunnel (figure 9.12). The ball will suddenly emerge at your feet, and you have to gather it and pass, all in one movement.

To Increase Difficulty

- Have your partner follow the ball after rolling it along the ground.
- Have your partner select the direction in which to pass after rolling the ball.
- Have your partner try to knock the ball down as it is passed.
- Have your partner try to tackle you.
- Repeat all variations using the tunnel.

Figure 9.12 Delivering the ball through a tunnel of tackle shields.

To Decrease Difficulty

- Have your partner call the direction in which to pass before rolling the ball and select the type of pass.
- Have the target player stand still.

Success Check

- Bend at the knees and keep your centre of gravity low.
- Spread your fingers. Use only the fingertips of your guide hand to touch the ball.
- Sweep the ball away without picking it up.
- Transfer your weight from rear to front.
- Point your front foot in the direction of the pass.

- Follow through with both hands.
- On a pop pass, look for your target and flick the ball into the target's hands.

Score Your Success

5 smooth passes to the left = 5 points

5 smooth passes to the right = 5 points

Your score ___

Scrum Half Drill 3.   *Varying Passes*

Practise with two other players in a space wide enough for you to exchange passes of various lengths. One player acts as a feeder and calls out different signals for the type of pass you should send to the other player (e.g., 'Spiral-long'). Step in to the ball and deliver the required pass.

To Increase Difficulty

- One player selects the direction (left or right) in which to pass after the ball is rolled.
- The feeder follows the rolling ball.
- The feeder tries to knock the ball down as it is passed.

To Decrease Difficulty

- The feeder selects and shouts the direction in which to pass before rolling the ball.
- The feeder walks after the rolling ball and makes no effort to knock the ball down.

Success Check

- Have your fingers at right angles to the seam, spread wide.
- Use only the fingertips of your guide hand to touch ball.
- Step in with your rear foot and stride towards the receiver with your front foot.
- Sweep the ball smoothly.

Score Your Success

10 smooth, accurate passes = 10 points

8 or 9 smooth, accurate passes = 5 points

6 or 7 smooth, accurate passes = 1 point

Your score ___

Scrum Half Drill 4.   *Passing Options*

To practise your passing options, pass to pairs of players who decide the type of pass they wish to receive. The players line up behind you in two lines, line 1 and line 2. At no time are you allowed to look behind you. A number of balls are placed on the ground in front of you.

So that you and the receivers react quickly, your coach indicates who will run to receive the pass by calling out two numbers: the first number is the line and the second is the player in that line. For example, a call of '2, 1' indicates that the first player from line 2 should run to receive the pass, supported by the first player from line 1 (figure 9.13).

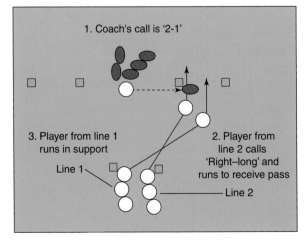

Figure 9.13 Scrum half passing options drill.

145

The nominated ball receiver will tell you the side (left or right) and the distance (close, middle or far) of the pass you should make. For example, the receiver may call 'Right, far' to indicate that he will appear to your right and will require a long, spiralling pass. Your role is to deliver the ball accurately to the receiver.

To Increase Difficulty

- Receivers call the direction and type of pass a little later.
- The coach delivers the ball to you as the signal is called.

To Decrease Difficulty

- The coach and receivers give signals very early.

Success Check

- Wait for the coach's signal.
- Do not reach for the ball until you know the passing direction.
- On spiral passes, sweep the ball smoothly.
- On flick passes, move the ball through your hands quickly.

Score Your Success

10 crisp, accurate passes of the correct type = 10 points

8 or 9 crisp, accurate passes of the correct type = 5 points

6 or 7 crisp, accurate passes of the correct type = 1 point

Your score ___

Scrum Half Drill 5. *Kicking Over Forwards*

Mark out a 5-metre square, about 25 metres away from the kicking area. Try to kick the ball high and land it in the square. Remember the correct kicking sequence: plant, scoop, kick.

To Increase Difficulty

- Place six balls in two groups of three that are 5 metres apart. Walk to one group and plant, scoop and kick. Then turn and repeat at the other group.
- Alternate kicking with your left and right foot.

To Decrease Difficulty

- Use six balls in a line 1 metre apart. Walk to each ball and kick.
- Make the target bigger.

Success Check

- Use a smooth step-kick sequence.
- Have a wide, low stance with your front foot planted firmly and your rear (kicking) foot in the ready position.
- Bend your knees, sink at your hips and scoop.
- Place your right hand along and underneath the seam.
- Swing your kicking foot, drop the ball and contact the seam along your bootlaces.
- Kick through the long axis of the ball.

Score Your Success

7 to 10 successful kicks = 10 points

5 or 6 successful kicks = 5 points

3 or 4 successful kicks = 1 point

Your score ___

Scrum Half Drill 6.   *Kicking for Position*

Set out a square target along a touch line. Do not set the target too far away at first. Master accuracy first; then try longer kicks.

To Increase Difficulty

- Have the coach call 'Left' or 'Right' to indicate the target touch line. (Note: You may need to alter your feet positions for the various touch lines.)

To Decrease Difficulty

- Practise five kicks to the right and then five to the left in your own time, trying to kick the ball anywhere across the touch line.

Success Check

- Have a wide, low stance with your front foot planted firmly and your rear (kicking) foot in the ready position.
- Bend your knees, sink at the hips and scoop.
- Place your right hand along and underneath the seam.
- Swing your kicking foot, drop the ball and contact the seam along your bootlaces.
- Kick through the long axis of the ball.

Score Your Success

7 out of 10 kicks through the square = 10 points

5 or 6 kicks through the square = 5 points

3 or 4 kicks through the square = 1 point

Your score ___

Scrum Half Drill 7.   *Running From the Scrum Half Position*

The role of the scrum half at the scrum is to threaten the defence, especially the back row. To do this, you must have explosive speed and vision. Practise in a narrow channel about 10 metres wide against a defender who is kneeling in the flanker position and an attacking number 8 who follows your attacking run. As soon as you pick up the ball and run, so too can the defender.

To Increase Difficulty

- Add a full back to make a defensive screen.
- Add more players to attack and defence as your skill level increases.

To Decrease Difficulty

- Make sure that you always have two more players than the defence.

Success Check

- Pick up the ball quickly.
- Stay low and be prepared to be tackled.
- Run at top speed, eyes open.
- Look for opportunities to pass to your number 8.

Score Your Success

7 to 10 attacks score = 10 points

5 or 6 attacks score = 5 points

3 or 4 attacks score = 1 point

Your score ___

FLY HALF

The fly half is perhaps the most crucial player in the whole team. Teams that are lucky enough to have a fly half with vision, skill and understanding are often highly successful and very difficult to beat. To be a really good fly half, you need to be a very calm, clear-thinking and skilful player. Your job is to find the best way to bring all of your attacking players into the game.

Throughout the game the opposition will be attempting to pressure you in the hope that you will kick the ball aimlessly either upfield or into touch. If you fall into such a trap, you end up giving the ball to your opponents. Sometimes you have to attack the opposition yourself to make some space for your back row or inside centre to drive in and support your strike at the defence.

The closer you can successfully play to the defence, the better. You must realise, however, that if you play close, the teammate two passes away may also be very close to the defence. If your pass is not accurate enough for such a style of play, your attacks will break down. To play successfully very close to the opposition, you must have excellent handling skills and be prepared to take on tacklers. This means that you sometimes must take some form of contact.

Misstep
The backs' moves are ineffective because the opponents are across the field awaiting the strike runner.

Correction
You are playing too far back from the defence, which allows them to drift across the field, or your initial running line is towards the opposite corner. Square up to attack parallel to the touch lines.

The alignment of the outer players (centres) must constantly change to accommodate what you, as the fly half, are trying to achieve in each attack. If they are too flat (not far enough behind you), they add no options to the attack. It is far better to have both of your centres run so that they can read the number on your back (figure 9.14). If your centres stay in good alignment, you will always have two passes available to you along the line, one to the inside centre and one to the outside centre. The patterns you and your centres play will constantly alter the width, depth and speed of your attacking runs. Remember, it is not where you are when you start your run that alters the shape of the defence, it is where you are in relation to the defence when you receive the ball. Close to the defence it is better to play a switch pass, whereas you should be farther away if you wish to play a loop.

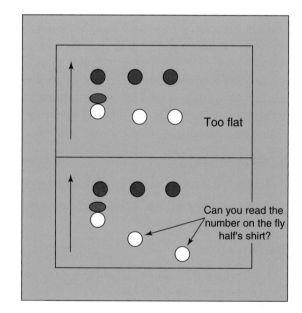

Figure 9.14 Centres shouldn't be too flat. They should be in good alignment, able to read the number on the fly half's shirt.

148

Misstep

The outside backs seem to overrun the play.

Correction

Start the outside backs a little deeper on the fly half. Can they read his shirt number? Time the runs from when the fly half sets up the pass.

These are the main priorities of the fly half:

At the Scrum

- You are the eyes and ears of the attack and defence. Keep looking forward and scanning for signs of weakness or threat. Loud communication is vital.

- Take up a position behind or to the side of the scrum that will allow you to execute all of your options.

- Be decisive and take quick actions to fix close defenders.

- Lead the defence onto the attacking line.

- Pass accurately to either side.

- Kick accurately with either foot in attack and defence.

At the Line-Out

- Communicate effectively with your forwards and attacking teammates.

- Follow the lead of the first forward defender onto the attacking line.

- Use the space between the two back lines to the best advantage of your team.

- Keep the opposing close defence guessing by being prepared to have a go at them.

- Kick accurately with either foot in attack and defence.

- Stand wide enough to execute all of your attacking options and then move onto your running lines quickly to influence the defence.

- Pass accurately to either side.

In the Loose

- You are the eyes and ears of the attack and defence. Keep looking forward and scanning for signs of weakness or threat. Loud communication is vital.

- Make quick and decisive decisions in response to attacking options and possibilities.

- Pose a constant threat to the defence.

- Contribute to the defence around rucks and mauls.

- Pass and kick accurately to either side.

Kicking Skills

It is not always possible or desirable to run with every ball you receive during the match. Sometimes you may have to kick the ball downfield. A number of types of kicks, including the up-and-under, grubber and chip, can be used as attacking ploys (figure 9.15). Kicks are used to gain ground, regather possession or set up position. See step 4 for instruction on how to kick effectively.

Misstep

Your kicks are inaccurate.

Correction

Keep your head down and concentrate on striking through the centre of the ball. Also, alter the angle of your hips to the target area to see if this helps.

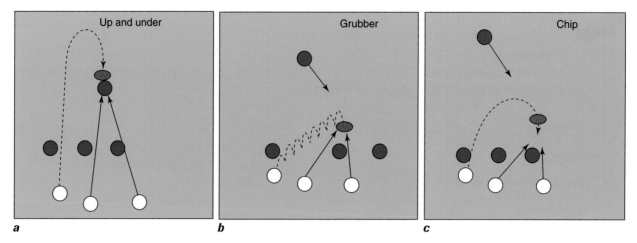

a   *b*   *c*

Figure 9.15 Kicking in attack: *(a)* up-and-under kick; *(b)* grubber kick; *(c)* chip kick.

Kicking as an attacking ploy should be viewed primarily as a last resort after you have tried all your other attacking ploys. It may, however, be used to put the defence in two minds. If they are coming up very quickly, you might chip the ball in behind them. The next time they move out of defence, they may slow down their advance, which gives you time and space to close in on them at speed.

To kick for possession, you need to kick the ball high enough and far enough forward for your players to arrive under the ball as it lands. Defenders and attackers will have to compete for the ball and so will have to jump to collect

it. The two main requirements for kicks for possession are kicking accurately (attaining the proper height and distance with your kick) and calling signals so that people know you are going to kick.

Your scrum half is likely to kick for possession to the right side of the field because it is an easy kick to make when the forwards are in front and can be used as a screen to prevent any charge down by the opposition. If you are also right-footed, it is better for you to kick from the left side of the field, which gives you a wider angle, especially when kicking down the 15-metre line or high and towards the posts.

Misstep

Your kicks go into touch very close to the kicking point.

Correction

To achieve the best distance, widen your angle if you can and kick left foot to right touch line and right foot to left touch line.

Any kicks that are to land between the 22-metre line and the goal line must be accurate. If they are not accurate, the ball can be marked by the defending player who catches the kick. Therefore, you need a number of chasers who aim to arrive as the ball lands to contest the kick and

prevent the mark. Often, it is better to kick high, so that the ball lands just outside the 22-metre area because the catcher has to follow up with a run, pass or kick back. Whichever of these actions follows the kick, your team has the opportunity to regain possession and counterattack.

One of the most devastating attacking kicks is the one that travels across field (figure 9.16). This type of kick is almost impossible to defend against. An accurate kick will put one of your attackers, probably your winger standing out wide, against one receiver who will need to turn and run back towards the goal line. Normally, this will create a blind spot for the defender that the chaser will run into. This gives the advantage to the attacker even though the ball still has to be chased and competed for. Even if the defensive winger has stayed back for this kind of kick, the advantage is still with the attacker because the defender will be standing still and the winger will be arriving at pace with the momentum to jump high and forcefully at the ball.

Regularly practise kicking against some form of defence. Most players can kick the ball without the pressure of a defender. Only good players can kick accurately when someone is bearing down on them with the intention of charging down the kick. As the fly half, you set the attacking tone of the team. You have to quickly assess the possibilities for attack, taking into account your

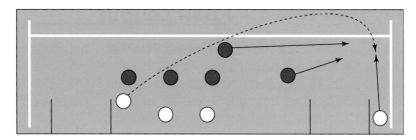

Figure 9.16 Kicking across the field.

position on the field, the quality of the possession, the closeness of the forwards and their ability to support the attack.

Passing Skills

As a fly half in a game, you may organise a move to try to disrupt the defence, especially from set pieces. At other times, you simply have to play without a plan. If the other backs, particularly the wingers and full back, understand their roles, they will run at gaps to attract defenders. Sometimes they will receive the ball from you if you notice that the gap has stayed open, and at other times they will act as decoys while you pass the ball across them to another attacker running into a gap. A good fly half can make an instant decision and send an accurate pass to a support player.

Misstep
The inside centre often drops the ball.

Correction
Make sure that you are not passing the ball too hard and directly at the player. Passes should be floated into a space in front of the receiver and to the target.

It is easy to deliver a pass without opposition, so you must work against a defender as soon as you feel capable. Your role in the game is to draw at least one defender towards you before you give the ball to your backs. Sometimes you may hold the ball for four or five strides; at other times you move the ball as soon as you receive it.

The distance from the defence at which you release the ball depends on the point along the tackle line you are trying to reach. For example, if your attack is trying to go around the defence, you may need to make a long pass to cut out one of the usual receivers. Make this pass back from the defence so that it creates time and space for

the outside players. If you are attacking close to the forwards, carry the ball fast at the defence and attempt to pass to someone running into a gap.

There must be constant communication among all players on a rugby field. Sometimes the people running at gaps will call for the ball, and you should be able to make the pass required to put that player into space. At other times, you may realise that the defence is already at a disadvantage, and you will have to communicate this to the players outside you before or as you receive the ball. Rugby is not a telepathic exercise—communication speeds up the attack so that the defence finds it difficult to cope.

Fly Half Drill 1. *Pass Length*

In this simple practice you receive the ball from the scrum half and have two support runners against one defender. One support runner runs as a centre, and the other runs from depth and appears in the gap between you and your centre partner (figure 9.17). You must make an instantaneous decision to catch and pop pass to the intruder in the line or to catch and pass slightly farther across to your centre partner.

Develop to working along two channels side by side. Use the first ball down one channel and then slow down after the first pass to allow your support players to regroup behind you as you go around the end and into the next channel to attack the next defender.

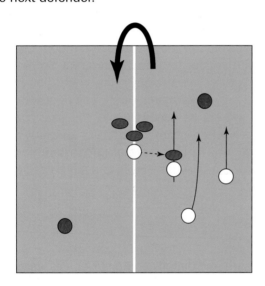

Figure 9.17   A support runner running from deep to the gap between the fly half and the centre.

Support players often will demand that you pass to them in specific ways. Simulate this by having your coach make the passing decision for you when you are the ball carrier.

In this practice the coach decides which of the two support runners will receive the ball and also the type of pass. No matter which pass you are to make, you must move the defender who is coming at you away from the direction of your intended pass. If you pass too early or drift away, the defender will run by you and tackle the next player with the ball.

To Increase Difficulty

- The coach calls the type of pass as you receive the ball.
- The coach decides which support player should receive the pass.
- The defender starts closer to the fly half.
- Add extra defenders and then more attackers until you build up to large-group games (10v8).

To Decrease Difficulty

- The defender starts farther away and directly ahead of you.
- The coach calls the type of pass before the scrum half delivers the ball to you.

Success Check

- Alter the defender's running line before you pass.
- On the pop pass, use very little arm movement and flick with your wrists and fingers.
- On a longer pass, push the ball across at chest height and use much longer arm movements.
- Run towards space behind the defender and aim to put a support runner into that area.
- Make accurate passes of correct power and length.

Score Your Success

10 accurate passes = 10 points

8 or 9 accurate passes = 5 points

6 or 7 accurate passes = 1 point

Your score ___

Fly Half Drill 2. *Beating the Defence*

The first defender running at you is only the first problem in a rather complicated equation. Rugby Union always presents a multilayered defence (figure 9.18).

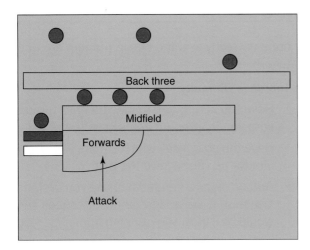

Figure 9.18 Multilayered defence challenging the attack.

If you go beyond the defence set up by the forwards, you have to beat your opposite number who is part of the midfield defence. If you break this line of defence, you have the back three to contend with. Putting a player into space is only the first step. As a fly half, you must understand where you will go next and what will happen should your plays be successful. If you pass the ball early, you are an ideal player to loop around behind the ball carrier and support in case you are required again in the attack. You then become one of the support players running from depth, and you may have other players in your team running alongside you.

Breaking down layers in the defence is difficult. Begin simply by playing 3v2 and develop to 4v3. When you get to this stage, begin to shape the defence to resemble different layers. For example, line up the three defenders as a triangle with two at the front and one behind. Can you penetrate or go around the first pair of defenders and then beat the last defender to score?

Your options are simple:

- Fix the defenders and put a runner around the outside edge (figure 9.19*a*).
- Widen the space between the defenders and put a runner coming from depth between them (figure 9.19*b*).
- Work hard for a 2v1 situation and put one of the other players around the edge (figure 9.19*c*).

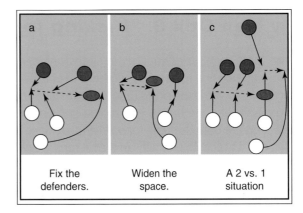

Figure 9.19 Options to beat the defence: *(a)* fix the defenders; *(b)* widen the space; *(c)* create a 2v1 situation.

As first-pass receiver, you must prevent the first defender from drifting across the field. Your running line and your subsequent actions should prevent the defender from being effective in the defence. It is then up to the other runners to go past the next defender and attack the last player in the channel.

You must practise to both the left and right, and you must work hard to get back in the game as soon as you have released the ball. You may be required farther upfield in a scoring position.

To Increase Difficulty

- When your coach decides that you are ready, play full tackles.
- Bring the rear defender a little closer to the front line of defence.

To Decrease Difficulty

- Slow down the practice to walking pace if necessary and have greater distances between the defenders.

Success Check

- Pull the defence out of shape.
- Draw the first defender towards you or use a dummy pass and attack the last defender.
- Pass quickly if the running line moves the defender away from the pass.
- Communicate with your support runners.

Fly Half Drill 3. *Kicking for Possession*

Mark out a number of squares to simulate kicking down a certain line (e.g., the 15-metre line) or kicking diagonally towards the posts (figure 9.20). Have your scrum half feed the ball to you so you can practise collecting the ball, stepping forward and kicking. Try to kick so that the ball remains in the air for a specific number of seconds. Go for height and accuracy first, and then progress to distance. Alternate among the squares until you can land the ball in them regularly. Gradually work farther away from the squares as your accuracy improves, and gradually add a number of defenders to put pressure on your kick.

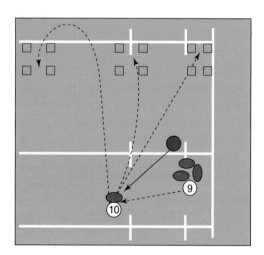

Figure 9.20   Fly half kicking for possession drill.

When you intend to kick the ball, signal to your scrum half as early as possible so she can pass it to you while you are stationary. Your scrum half should pass the ball to just in front of you so that you can walk forward, gather the ball, retain your balance and kick accurately.

Once you can kick accurately and long, it is time to begin working on diagonal kicks from the 15-metre line to the far touch line. Remember, this attacking kick is almost impossible to defend if it is done correctly and the chase runners are good catchers in the air.

To Increase Difficulty

- Have the scrum half follow the pass to pressure you by running across the line of vision.
- Have the coach call which square you should aim for as you receive the ball.
- Add an extra defender to chase you. Defenders should be at the same distances they would be if they were running from ruck, maul, line-out or scrum.
- Add two attacking centres to chase after the kick. The defence adds a player to act as full back.

To Decrease Difficulty

- Have the coach designate the square before the scrum half passes you the ball.
- After the pass, have the scrum half quickly walk up and touch you before you kick to provide a little time to set up the kick.
- Make the target areas much bigger.

Success Check

- Walk forward, gather the pass and kick.
- Make high, accurate kicks.
- Signal to the scrum half early.
- Do not kick while running.
- Sidestep, then kick if the defender is very close to you.

SUCCESS SUMMARY OF THE MIDDLE FIVE

The middle-five players in the team act as the link between those who provide the ball—the front five—and those who are put into positions to strike for the score—the back five. The back row and the half backs who make up the middle five are the ball users, pinning down the defence and creating space for others. They also play a major role on team defence. Because the middle five must possess good all-around skills, it's important to practise body and ball movement skills at match pace and intensity as often as possible. If you are playing in a middle-five position, have another player or a coach evaluate your skills.

The middle five are the dynamos for the whole team. If you play in one of these positions, you need to master the many skill sets of the playing positions close to yours. Before moving on, make sure you scored about 120 points or scored at least 80 percent in the drills for your own position.

Back-Row Drills

1. Pass or Contact   ___ out of 10

2. Working Through Contact   ___ out of 10

3. Running Lines   ___ out of 10

4. Pass and Contact Options   ___ out of 10

5. Line-Out Deflection   ___ out of 10

Scrum Half Drills

1. Spiralling the Pass   ___ out of 10

2. Controlling the Ball   ___ out of 10

3. Varying Passes   ___ out of 10

4. Passing Options   ___ out of 10

5. Kicking Over Forwards   ___ out of 10

6. Kicking for Position   ___ out of 10

7. Running From the Scrum Half Position   ___ out of 10

Fly Half Drills

1. Pass Length   ___ out of 10

2. Beating the Defence   ___ out of 10

3. Kicking for Possession   ___ out of 10

Total   ___ *out of 150*

The Back Five

The back five is composed of the centres, wingers and full back (table 10.1 on page 158). These players react to the attacking situations the rest of the team sets up for them. They follow up an initial attempt by others or are the main threat used to break down the defence and often become the players who score the tries.

CENTRES

The main role of the two centres is to create space for players overlapping on the outside. To do this, they must understand effective running lines and possess good handling and contact skills. Centres should be able to ride tackles and still make controlled passes. In addition, the most dangerous centres are fast and have good evasive skills. Many of the skills detailed in steps 1 to 7 are essentials for the centre.

Misstep
When under pressure from the opposition, you do not release the pass for fear of it being knocked down by a defender.

Correction
Turn in to the tackle earlier than you would normally, and keep the ball visible to your nearest support runner. This will prevent you from burying the ball into the defence and making it difficult to dig out.

Centres often carry the ball very close to the opposition, where the skills to cope with the defensive pressure are essential. Occasionally, they have to make contact with an opponent, so they should be fully prepared for collision situations. Good centres can ride attempted tackles or burst through them and offload the ball behind the defence or buy time for the support to arrive. Step 5 discusses contact skills in more detail.

If you have good peripheral vision and are skilful, you may make a good centre. The ability to take in visual information over a wide angle allows you to watch the ball as it works its way towards you and, at the same time, watch the defenders arriving to try to stop the attack.

Although you may have good natural peripheral vision, practice may help you extend your field of vision (see centre drill 1, page 161). To check your present field of vision, stand 5 metres from two corner flags that are 5 metres apart. Have someone gradually move these flags apart until each flag is at the edge of your vision. Measure

Table 10.1   Back-Five Positions

Position	Qualities and responsibilities		
	Individual	Set piece	Loose
Centres: inside and outside	Good all-around vision; very strong in shoulders and lower body to withstand high-speed impacts; good pace and power; well-developed handling skills; good vision and understanding of game; good communicator; strong, safe tackler	Understands when to close and when to maintain distance from opponents; misshapes defence and creates gaps; knows most effective defensive systems and how to apply them	Takes advantage of all opportunities provided by other players; creates opportunities for finishers; understands how to create space and stop defences; running and evasive skills constantly threaten defence; strong, safe tackles in defence prevent ball carrier from crossing tackle line
Wingers: left and right	Speed above all, plus power, aggression and understanding; strong in shoulders and lower body to withstand high-speed impacts; safe tackler; safe under the high ball, kicks well; understands and applies the back three system in defence	Looks for ball (especially the left winger) to hit gaps in defence or help centres create overlap attacks; catches attacking kicks; kicks accurately upfield for distance or touch	Scores when given any opportunity
Full back	Strong in shoulders and lower body; good pace and power; kicks well with either foot; safe under the high ball; understands and applies the back three system in defence	Marks and tackles any player who threatens to penetrate or overlap defence; safe and strong when defending against ball carriers and kicks	Threatens defence by joining attack out wide or through middle; looks for attacking opportunities; organises the defence from behind; marks and tackles opponents who break through tackle area; strong, safe tackler; accurate, safe fielding of kicks and returns to touch or downfield

the distance between the flags to determine your current field of vision. Regular measurement will tell you whether your training methods are also helping to extend your field of vision.

These are the main priorities of the centres:

At the Scrum

- Take up a position behind or to the side of the scrum that will allow you to execute all attacking options.
- Be decisive and take quick action to fix defenders.
- Pass accurately to either side.
- Kick accurately with either foot in attack and defence.
- The inside centre aligns with the fly half to make best use of his ability. If you both play flat, you need slick passing skills.
- The outside centre aligns with the inside centre to make best use of his skills.

At the Line-Out

- Keep the opposition's close defence guessing by being prepared to have a go at them.
- Kick accurately with either foot in attack and defence.
- Pass accurately to either side.
- The inside centre uses the space between the two back lines to the best advantage of the team.
- The inside centre runs decoys to create space for other players in the backs.
- The inside centre takes on the defence at times to prevent them from drifting out.
- The outside centre runs effective attacking lines and, when necessary, hits up into the defence to create a contact point for the forwards.

- When playing an out-to-in defence, the outside centre, along with the winger, may go for the hit on the ball carrier.

In the Loose

- Keep looking forward and scanning for mismatches or threats. Loud communication is vital.
- Make quick and decisive decisions in response to attacking options and possibilities.

- Play as close as possible to the defence to prevent them from drifting out.
- Pose a constant threat to the defence.
- Pass and kick accurately to either side.

Creating Space

As a centre creating space, look at the defence before you receive the ball and take up your usual alignment every time your team wins possession. Make your decisions early and stick to them.

Misstep

You are slow to decide what to do next and therefore you constantly waste good attacking opportunities.

Correction

Learn yours and your team's strengths and play to them. Understand your options and stick to your decisions.

Depending on the defence, catch the ball early or move wide to catch it late in its flight. The option you choose depends on the power of the incoming pass. If the gap is in front of you, move into it and then move the ball away from any covering defence. If the gap is in front of another player, deliver the ball to take best advantage of the space. Remember to support any pass to take best advantage of any opportunity.

Misstep

The player collecting your pass in the gap always seems to drop it.

Correction

Take the power out of the pass. Lob the ball into the space at the side of you. This will put the ball at eye level for the receiver, who can then accelerate on to the ball.

Although one of your main priorities as a centre is to make space around the edge of the defence, for your winger, you should also be able to create gaps in the opposition defence to allow a player arriving from depth to penetrate the opposition back line or for you to work the ball in behind their players.

Every time you line up at scrum or line-out, you and the other backs form a series of triangles. Figure 10.1 shows just a few of the possible triangles that the midfield backs and the back three can create. These shapes must be copied in practice, so that you become used to the various angles at which these players would enter your attacking line. Always start your support runners in the positions they would occupy during a match. These vary according to the attacking situation. The practices detailed in step 6 are ideal for these groups of three, and time should be created for each of the triangles to run together in training sessions.

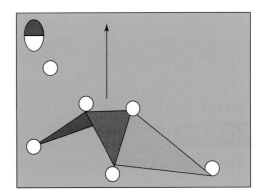

Figure 10.1 Attacking triangles created by the midfield backs and back three.

If you are the centre who is not carrying the ball, you can also help to widen or close the gap in front of the ball carrier. Remember, the defence reacts to the running lines of both players. If you wish to widen the gap, run so that the distance between you and your partner becomes wider as you near the defence. To narrow the gap, run closer together as you near the defence. At the same time, other players who are going to enter the attacking line should know what you are trying to achieve and should run to arrive between you and your partner if you are widening the gap, or to the outside of your partner if you are narrowing it to play an overlap move.

If your support players run in too flat a line, you will have only one passing option. Support players should run 2 or 3 metres back from you before you pass the ball, so that you can see all possible receivers and accurately deliver the ball to the player who is running in a gap.

 Misstep
You have difficulty making passes in heavily defended areas.

Correction
Always carry the ball in both hands so that you can take any opportunity to pass. Remember, your priority is to create space for others to exploit. Your running lines should misshape the defence. As soon as this happens, either pass to another player or attack the line yourself to take advantage of any misshape.

Riding the Tackle

When your team wins the ball, you will have the opportunity to attempt to score. You won't always have a clean run through a gap, and mostly, you will be faced with a tackler. If no one is in a better position to receive a pass, you will have to take on the defender and may need to resist the tackle.

To successfully ride the tackle, you need to make early decisions. Know where you are trying to go to and what will happen next. Try to work out the impact angles so that you can use your opponent's force to move you away from the tackle.

Hold the ball safely in both hands close to your chest. Keep low as you run, and look for the spaces ahead of you. Accelerate hard and try to avoid any tacklers. As the tackle comes in, lean over the top of the tackler, lower your body and move away by bumping into and bouncing off the tackler's shoulder. Keep the momentum of the attack going by either picking up your pace quickly or passing to a support player who is running at speed. (See step 5 for more on contact skills.)

 Misstep
Riding contact seems impossible. Each time you try it, you are brought down.

Correction
When you go into contact, keep your legs away from the tackler by leaning over and to the side of your front foot. Don't make contact unless you have no other alternative. Try a running line that will move the defender away from the intended tackle area, and then swerve or sidestep past the would-be tackler.

CAUTION Always wear protective equipment in both practice and match situations. Although not every drill in this section anticipates contact with a player, a piece of equipment or the ground, by its very nature rugby invites contact, sometimes by accident. It's better to be safe than sorry.

Centre Drill 1. *Developing All-Around Vision*

While you look at a partner, another player stands about 10 metres away to the side, just inside the widest angle of your sight. Continuously pass to and receive a pass from your partner, while the third player gives you visual signals by raising the left arm, right arm or both arms, which you must try to identify. Practise to both sides, and constantly check to see whether your field of vision is becoming wider.

To Increase Difficulty

- Move forward as you handle the ball, first walking, then jogging. The signaller moves as well.
- Have the person signal just before you catch and just after you pass the ball.

To Decrease Difficulty

- Have the signaller give only one signal during one length or run.
- Move the signaller well into your line of vision.

Success Check

- Concentrate on the ball.
- Keep your head still, but use your eyes.

Score Your Success

Correctly identify the signal 10 times out of 10 = 10 points

Correctly identify the signal 9 times out of 10 = 5 points

Correctly identify the signal 8 times out of 10 = 1 point

Your score ____

Centre Drill 2. *Passing Under Pressure*

You will pressure the defence only if you put yourself under pressure as well. To practise the pressure pass, have a defender try to knock the ball out of your hands as you make a pass. Set up a narrow channel approximately 10 metres wide and 15 metres long with three attackers and two defenders at the far end. As the first ball carrier, carry the ball close to the first defender before making the pass. The receiver has to catch and pass in a couple of strides before the second defender can knock down the ball.

Begin by practising without the defender. Try to catch and pass within one or two paces. As soon as you can do this, put the defenders in place. You should always feel pressure from the defender as you pass, so you must be close to your opponent before you pass.

To Increase Difficulty

- Have the defender move to the open side, into your blind spot.
- If your coach allows it, have the defender try to tackle you.
- Work down the channel, making passes first from the left and then from the right. Use more defenders.

To Decrease Difficulty

- Run a little slower so you have a little more time, and create a little more space between yourself and the defender.

Success Check

- Gradually increase your pace until you reach match speed.
- Reach to catch and push the ball across your chest.
- Work close to the defender.
- Do not rush the pass.
- Reduce your speed as the ball approaches to keep some space between you and the defender.

Score Your Success

10 out of 10 quick, accurate passes within two strides = 10 points

9 out of 10 quick, accurate passes within two strides = 5 points

8 out of 10 quick, accurate passes within two strides = 1 point

Your score ____

Centre Drill 3.   *Feeding a Player Running From Depth*

This drill allows you to practise skills that widen or narrow the gaps in the defence so that other players in your team, such as the wingers or full back, can take advantage of that attacking opportunity. Work with the fly half and your co-centre plus either a winger or full back. Practise in a channel 15 metres wide and about 20 metres long. Always involve two defenders, who are the focus of the attack. They stand as if they were opposing the attacking centres.

When the attackers launch the attack, a number of triangles are formed with the centres and one of the wingers or full back; one of these is shown in figure 10.2. The player at the rear point of the triangle normally penetrates the defence. The front two points (centres) have to widen or narrow the gap ahead to allow this to happen. One of the centres must carry the ball at the defender to fix the defence. Once this happens, the other attacking centre can run to affect the shape of the defence. The rear player runs at any gap and receives a pass from the ball carrier.

To Increase Difficulty

- Allow defenders to defend in a formation of their choice.
- Have the coach roll the ball into the channel for the fly half to pick up and then attack.

To Decrease Difficulty

- Two defenders follow and only shadow the centres or play grip tackle.

Success Check

- Use constant, reliable, accurate communication.
- Run quickly, but with control.
- Support runners run at gaps as they arrive.
- Pop soft passes into space.
- Support runners both present targets.

Score Your Success

10 out of 10 successful passing sequences = 10 points

9 out of 10 successful passing sequences = 5 points

8 out of 10 successful passing sequences = 1 point

Your score ___

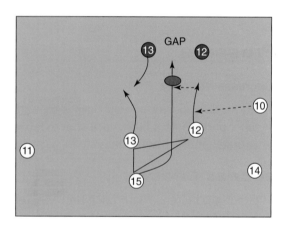

Figure 10.2   Feeding a player running from depth drill.

Centre Drill 4.   *Riding the Contact*

Make sure you have mastered the contact drills in step 5. In a match you should try to avoid contact as much as possible, but if you know that a tackler is about to collide with you, you may be able to use that force to your advantage. This drill allows you to practise riding contact. Play in a channel no wider than 10 metres so that it is difficult to avoid contact. The channel can be as long as you wish, depending on the number of tacklers available. Tacklers are spaced at 5-metre intervals and hold tackle shields. Be sure to wear any protective equipment you would wear for a game.

Pay attention to the tackler coming at you to anticipate the angle of the hit. Prepare to alter your own body angle or running line to bounce away from the edge of the tackle (figure 10.3).

When you start your run, try to check the defender (see step 2, Footwork) and then go around the tackle. You may be able to bump and spin or soak up the force of the hit. Try every trick you know to lessen the defender's power. Keep moving the ball forward as fast as you can.

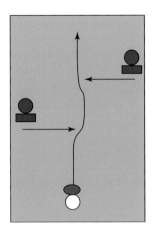

Figure 10.3 Riding the contact drill.

To Increase Difficulty

- Have two defenders approach at once, one from the left and one from the right, to simulate a multilayered defence.

To Decrease Difficulty

- Widen the channel to give the attacker a little more space.

Success Check

- Check the defender by running at the inside gap.
- As the defender commits to the tackle, move your feet away and towards the defender with your shoulder.
- Bump the defender firmly, bounce away and keep running.

Score Your Success

Run 5 lengths of the channel with little or no stoppage = 10 points

Your score ___

WINGERS

The main requirement for the winger is speed. When agility and strength are added to speed, you have the makings of a good player. You can increase your speed by using the running drills in step 2. You also have to learn to run at pace with control while moving your body quickly off a straight running line.

 Misstep
You can score within 22 metres of the goal line with ease, but never seem to score from farther out.

Correction
Work on your speed over a greater distance. Normally, you should sprint no farther than 40 metres, but occasional practice over a greater distance will not harm. Work on acceleration over short distances and then on holding the speed for as long as you can.

If your centres have done their job well, you should be running at pace each time you receive the ball. Pick up speed quickly and attack the space. At the same time, watch what the closest defenders are doing and constantly look for support. If you know that you are likely to be tackled, slow down to allow your support to catch up or run at an angle slightly away from the touch line so that your support is nearer to you.

 Misstep
You are given space on the outside but always want to step back inside to beat the defence.

Correction
Are you playing on the correct wing? Normally, left-handed or left-footed people should play on the left; and right-handed or right-footed people, on the right. If you are on the correct side, work on your running speed using sprinting drills and practise running on the outside with some of the drills in this step and in step 2.

Unless you have only a short distance to go to the goal line, first head towards the covering full back and then accelerate hard away towards the corner. This should check the defender's run so that you can more easily win the race for the goal line.

It is very unusual for wingers to have to beat only one player. Usually wingers first have to accelerate past their immediate opponent and then beat the last line of defence. Try to practise under such pressure. You also may need to acquire skills for beating tacklers, especially close to the corner flag.

Misstep

The one-on-one situation presents many problems for you, and you score fewer than half of the tries you should when faced with one defender.

Correction

Develop your sidestepping and swerving skills (see step 2). Work against a live defence and constantly alter your running line of approach until you find the one that pulls the defender out of position enough for you to score.

Misstep

You do not seem to be able to score the classic winger's try (a try scored at the corner with defenders left lying on the ground after vain attempts to stop the score).

Correction

Practise beating a defender on the outside near the corner flag and then diving in to score. Once successful, put two tackle bags half a metre apart at the corner and dive between the bags to score.

As you run with the ball over even a short distance, the defence in front of you can quickly change. You may sometimes appear in the back line, away from your normal position, to try to penetrate the defensive line. Here, too, the defence in front of you will change and present many different problems. Your role is to be a constant threat.

You also need to possess the defensive qualities normally associated with the full back (see next section). Modern back-three players are interchangeable, and many can play either winger or full back.

These are the main priorities of the wingers:

At the Scrum

- Take up a position that will allow you to execute all attacking options.
- The blindside winger looks for opportunities to make the extra man in the attacking three-quarter line act as a link, overlap player or penetrator.
- Play your part in the back three defence, and kick accurately with either foot.
- Pass and kick accurately to either side.

- Be decisive and loud under the high ball.
- Know your role in defence. Who takes the last man?

At the Line-Out

- Take up a position that will allow you to execute all attacking options.
- The blindside winger looks for opportunities to make the extra man in the attacking three-quarter line act as a link, overlap player or penetrator.
- The blindside winger plays his part in the pendulum defence and kicks accurately with either foot.
- When playing an out-to-in defence, the openside winger, along with the outside centre, may go for the hit on the ball carrier.
- Test your opposite number at every opportunity by attacking him with your skills.
- Pass accurately to either side.
- Be decisive and loud under the high ball.
- Know your role in defence. Who takes the last man?

In the Loose

- Keep looking forward and scanning for mismatches or threats. Loud communication is vital.
- Make quick and decisive decisions in response to attacking options and possibilities.

- Pose a constant threat to the defence.
- Pass and kick accurately to either side.
- Be decisive and loud under the high ball.
- Know your role in defence. Who takes the last man?

Winger Drill 1. *Beating the Last Line of Defence*

Defenders, especially those in the last line of defence, will be running to tackle you from various angles and directions. You will need a number of defenders to help you with this practice. Begin with touch tackles and gradually develop to full tackling once you have been regularly successful at beating the defence. As the physicality increases, both attackers and defenders must wear the full protective equipment normally used in a game. Play from the 10-metre line towards the goal line, between the 15-metre line and the touch line.

Each defender is numbered 1, 2 or 3 and stands by a marker (figure 10.4). The coach rolls the ball out in front of you into the channel, then calls a number (1, 2 or 3). The indicated player runs into the channel and tries to stop you from scoring on the goal line. Each time the defenders go back to their markers, they change their numbers so that you never know which player will come at you.

Rolling the ball along the ground prevents you from looking at the defenders. As soon as you pick up the ball, you have to make an instantaneous decision about how you will attack the goal line. In this practice, you will be able to use all of the running skills acquired in step 2.

To Increase Difficulty

- Decrease the distance between the defenders and the attacker.
- Have the coach roll the ball farther forward into the channel.

To Decrease Difficulty

- Widen the channel.
- Have the coach call the tackler's number before rolling the ball.

Success Check

- Create space with your pace or by choosing the appropriate running line.
- Dominate the defender; do not let the defender dominate you.
- Use a running line that keeps the defender near the 15-metre line before using the open space.

Score Your Success

5 tries from 5 attempts = 10 points

4 tries from 5 attempts = 5 points

3 tries from 5 attempts = 1 point

Your score ___

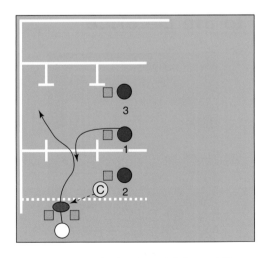

Figure 10.4 Beating the last line of defence drill.

Winger Drill 2. *Winning the Race for the Corner*

You must have confidence in your ability to beat a defender on the outside. This drill lets you practise with a defender who is always trying to push you out towards the touch line. If you add a change of direction, you can practise the running lines used by most wingers. Use a channel from the half-way line to the goal line and between the 15-metre line and the touch line.

The defender has the ball and passes it to you as a signal to start the race. Once you receive the ball, swerve around your markers (figure 10.5) and head for the corner. The defender's marker is placed so that the defensive pressure comes from slightly behind you as you run at the corner flag, to prevent you from dodging infield and to force you to accelerate hard to score in the corner.

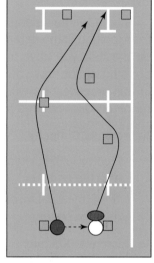

Figure 10.5 Winning the race for the corner drill.

Look at the defender only as the ball is delivered to you. Looking over your shoulder slows you down. Run through the first two markers quickly but in control; then accelerate hard towards the corner. Unless the defender is standing directly in front of you, concentrate only on winning the race to the goal line.

To Increase Difficulty

- Stand a tackle bag about 1 metre from the corner flag and on the goal line so that when you score, you can bump into the tackle bag just before you put the ball down.

To Decrease Difficulty

- Put the defender's marker a little farther out to give you an advantage.

Success Check

- Look at the defender as the ball is delivered.
- Run quickly but in control; then accelerate hard to score.
- Concentrate on winning the race to the goal line.

Score Your Success

10 scores out of 10 attempts = 10 points

9 scores out of 10 attempts = 5 points

8 scores out of 10 attempts = 1 point

Your score ___

Winger Drill 3. *Reacting Quickly to the Defence*

Mark out a 5-metre square 5 metres inside a rectangle that is 15 metres wide and 22 metres long (figure 10.6). Use four defenders. The front two carry tackle shields close to the internal square. The other two defend the goal line. At the start of this practice, turn your back to the square. The coach rolls the ball towards you and nominates one of the shield holders to enter the square. You have to turn around, pick up the ball, beat the first defender in the internal square and then attack the goal line. The coach calls one of the last two defenders into the rectangle for you to try to beat for the score.

Check the defender by attacking the space near the touch line; then head quickly for the space you have created. If the defender wrongly anticipates what you are going to do and creates a space, use it to your advantage.

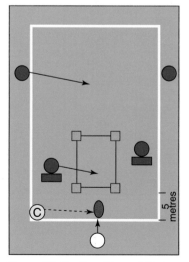

Figure 10.6 Reacting quickly to the defence drill.

To Increase Difficulty

- Move the line of secondary defenders closer to the shield holders.

To Decrease Difficulty

- Widen the channel.

Success Check

- Run quickly, but with control.
- Make contact with the first defender on your terms.

- Dominate the second defender with your speed and your choice of running line.
- Use defenders' decisions to your advantage.

Score Your Success

10 scores out of 10 attempts = 10 points

9 scores out of 10 attempts = 5 points

8 scores out of 10 attempts = 1 point

Your score ____

FULL BACK

A full back needs many qualities and skills. In this position, you have to be brave because most of the tackles you make will probably be at full speed and full stretch. You also have to catch, run at speed, kick and play like a centre when you enter the line. Safety in defence is a priority, particularly under a ball that has been kicked high. Learn to catch with both feet on the ground and, more important, while jumping. Learn to execute a variety of kicks (see step 4). You will have to perform these skills under extreme pressure with tacklers approaching from a number of different angles.

Misstep

You do not seem to be able to consistently catch the high ball.

Correction

Keep your eyes on the ball and turn sideways to the chasers. Point your fingers upwards, palms facing you and elbows together. Reach as the ball comes down and pull it to your chest as you sink down from the knees. Alternatively, jump to catch if your opponents are close (see step 4, figure 4.7, page 167).

Misstep

You always seem to be under pressure while you are waiting to catch the high ball.

Correction

Learn to jump and catch the ball (see step 4, figure 4.7, page 61). Watch the ball as it descends, and time your run to move close to and behind where it will land. At the right time, stride under the ball, form a triangle with your thumbs and index fingers and stretch your arms upwards so you can see the ball through the triangle. Jump up and into the trajectory of the ball as you lift your front knee to protect yourself. Once you are in the air, no one can tackle you. Catch the ball at full stretch.

When entering the attacking line to try to penetrate the defence, time your run to make best use of the attacking opportunity. The classic place for you to join the attack is outside the outside centre. Often, this pulls the opposing winger towards you, creating an overlap. Nothing can stop you from joining the attacking line outside the winger if you have the speed.

You might consider entering the attacking three-quarter line between the centres, between a centre and a wing or on the very outside. You also may act as a decoy runner or as an extra fly half to take the ball up the narrow side with your winger and centre in support.

Misstep

You always arrive late when called into the three-quarter line to create an overlap.

Correction

Make sure that your initial position for entering the line is not too far away for your pace. You may start in this position, but as soon as the defenders begin to watch the ball, move quickly a lot closer to where you intend to join the line.

Misstep

Your defence is constantly caught out when your opponents bring the full back into the three-quarter line as an extra attacker.

Correction

Choose one of the following systems of defence and stick to it: go up hard and then across so that each defender goes to tackle one player further out from usual; the full back takes the full back; a winger steps in for the full back; the defending full back takes the last player, normally the winger.

One of your main priorities is to make quick decisions. Will you pass, run or kick? Your team's strategy and tactics may make some of these decisions for you, but you should be prepared to make full use of any ball you get from the opposition from a kick or turnover.

Of all the positions in the team, the full back has the most potential for attacking the opposition, especially following a turnover or an aimless or misdirected kick. This type of attack is called a counterattack. As full back, your options are to run and pass, run and dummy pass or kick. First make a decision, and then angle your run to make best use of the potential attack area. If appropriate, take it upon yourself to attack a large space or pass to someone else in a better position or run at the forwards to check their advance and then pass to the space you have created (see step 11). You will have opportunities to use a dummy pass to send chasers the wrong way and also to kick either for touch if you are under pressure or downfield to chase.

Misstep

Counterattacks are ineffective because the defence is always there to stop them.

Correction

Learn the basic counterattack patterns. The underlying principle is that the ball has to move out into space as quickly as possible, but any covering players—including the pack of forwards—must first be taken away from the intended attack area.

The game played by the back five is usually at high speed with big collisions, and so mistakes can be a regular occurrence. The best teams cover these mistakes quickly and continue with their attacks.

These are the main priorities of the full back:

At the Set Piece

- Take up a position that will allow you to execute all attacking options.
- Look for opportunities to make the extra man in the attacking three-quarter line act as a link, overlap player or penetrator.

- Lead the defence of the back three and kick accurately with either foot.
- Try to stay in line with the ball as your opponents move it across the field.
- Pass accurately to either side.
- Be decisive and loud under the high ball.
- Know your role in defence. Who takes the last man?

In the Loose

- Keep looking forward and scanning for mismatches or threats. Loud communication is vital.

168

- Make quick and decisive decisions in response to attacking options and possibilities.
- Pose a constant threat to the defence.

- Pass and kick accurately to either side.
- Be decisive and loud under the high ball.
- Know your role in defence. Who takes the last man?

Full Back Drill 1. *Making Quick Decisions*

Work close to a touch line. A player outside the touch line feeds you the ball by throwing it high or rolling it along the ground. A defender then puts pressure on you as you collect the ball.

Judge the height of the ball and the closeness of the defender. If necessary, jump to catch the ball (see step 4, figure 4.7, page 61). If you have a little space between you and the defender, you may wish to use this time to kick the ball to touch. If farther away from the defender, you may choose to keep the ball on the field and kick for position. If there is little pressure, you may decide to run and counterattack with support. If you decide to run, try to widen the space near the touch line. Your support runner will have space to receive a pass. If your opponents kick the ball into touch and you have time and space, you may decide to take a quick throw-in (or receive one from your winger) and counterattack or kick back long downfield. Your decision will depend largely on the quality of the opponent's kick chase defence, the numbers of players in support of you and the shape of the defence across the field. Remember, as soon as the practice increases in physicality, it is time to wear full protective game equipment.

Although in a practice you can try various ways of beating the defence, in the game you would run only if you had sufficient support to sustain the attack.

Once you begin to make good decisions, add an extra defender and two more attackers to help you, one attacker running back from a centre position and the other from the wing. The nearer defender can put more pressure on you. If you are caught as you land after jumping and catching the ball, your two support players practise going in and stripping the ball from your arms. If the ball is thrown too deep for the defender to exert severe pressure, practise setting up a counter-attack move.

To Increase Difficulty

- Have the defender move closer.
- Move farther from the touch line.

To Decrease Difficulty

- Have the coach throw the ball to your advantage rather than the defender's.

Success Check

- Judge the height of the ball and the closeness of the defender.
- If kicking for touch, do so quickly.
- If kicking for position, use a high and accurate kick.
- If running with the ball, try to widen the space near the touch line.

Score Your Success

Complete 8 to 10 actions = 10 points

Complete 6 or 7 actions = 5 points

Complete 4 or 5 actions = 1 point

Your score ___

Full Back Drill 2. *Joining the Attack*

This practice helps you time your run into the line so that you are effective when attacking. Your first problem is to look at the three defenders and decide which of the gaps between them you will attack (figure 10.7). Call a signal early and indicate the gap you will run at. The ball carrier makes sure that you receive the ball as you hit that gap. The ball carrier must attack the tackle line (where the two sets of back lines would collide in a game; see step 11). You support that player with the intention of receiving a pass that will put you across the tackle line. Give a second signal to the ball carrier as you approach the line to indicate the type of pass you want. Attackers and defenders must wear protective equipment for this drill.

Once you have mastered the timing, add a defender behind the current defence. Time your run to take the pass as your teammates close in on the tackle line. If everything is timed correctly, you should run through the gap and be able to draw the back player towards you so that you can pass to the outside player to score.

To Increase Difficulty

• The defenders may switch the players they're defending, as they would in a game, so that sometimes a defender is directly in front of the attacking full back. The ball carrier must put the ball into the hands of a player running at a space.

To Decrease Difficulty

• The defenders shadow the front three attackers only, leaving the full back free to cross the tackle line.

Success Check

• Run with purpose and determination.
• Target defenders' inside shoulders.
• Support the attacking player.
• Signal the type of pass you want.

Score Your Success

8 to 10 scores out of 10 attacks = 10 points

7 scores out of 10 attacks = 5 points

6 scores out of 10 attacks = 1 point

Your score ____

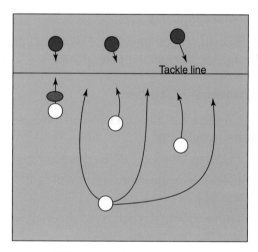

Figure 10.7   Which gap will you attack?

Full Back Drill 3. *Counterattacking With Wingers*

Counterattacking requires a mental attitude that must be practised. Classic counterattacks stem from possession gained from a badly aimed kick by the opposition, but you can counterattack from any situation. To practise basic counterattacking patterns, your coach should throw or kick the ball to your team in two ways.

The first throw for you to practise is straight upfield along the 15-metre line (figure 10.8a). The full back runs towards the nearest touch line and switch passes with the winger, who then joins with the other winger to attack down the opposite side of the field. The full back's running line leading up to the switch should take any defenders away from this attack area. (See Using Turnovers and Counterattacks in step 11.)

The second throw goes into the midfield. If the full back catches the ball while running at pace, the defenders from the opposite side of the field will probably be unable to reach the attack area, so the full back should head straight for the attack area with the openside winger as support (figure 10.8b).

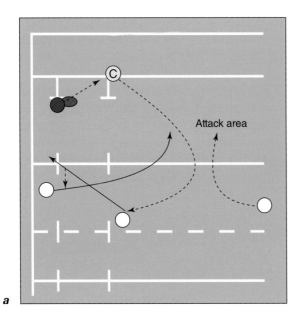
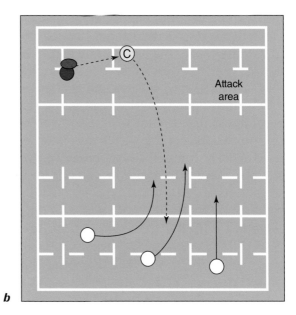

Figure 10.8 Counterattacking with wingers drill: *(a)* a pass straight upfield along the 15-metre line; *(b)* a pass into the midfield.

To Increase Difficulty

- Add another defender to chase the ball in the air.
- Move the defenders closer to the attacking full back.
- Start with 3v2 and gradually add attackers and defenders until you are practising with the middle and back five.

To Decrease Difficulty

- Allow the first defender to chase the attacking full back only, no other attacker.
- Instead of having only a one-player advantage, give the attacking side all of the back five.

Success Check

- Keep your eyes on the ball.
- Make your decision after catching.
- To switch pass, drag the defender away from the attack area. Don't forget that a dummy switch can be a useful attacking ploy in some of these situations as well.

Score Your Success

8 to 10 counterattacks enter the attack area = 5 points

Score at least 4 times = 5 points

Your score ___

SUCCESS SUMMARY OF THE BACK FIVE

The role of the back-five players is to take advantage of the space made for them by the other 10 players in the team. They must have good handling ability and speed allied with an awareness of space and an understanding of how to make the best use of it. The back five also may have to unlock the defence by attacking an area or an individual player, creating other attacking opportunities should they not score.

Each player should understand the concepts of creating space and be able to perform this skill under pressure. The role of the back five is to turn all opportunities into devastating and irresistible attacks, especially when the opposition turns over the ball in contact or by aimless kicking.

Safety in defence is also of paramount importance, and back-five players must understand their role in all of the ways of defending and have a desire to prevent the opposition from scoring by making aggressive tackles that stop the attack and give their team the opportunity to turn over the ball.

Because full backs, wingers and centres must be fully interchangeable in the game, each player should practise the skills associated with all of the positions of the back five. If your team attacks quickly from all situations and recycles fast balls, you will have no time to reform into a conventional attacking back line and you may find yourself at full back or out on the wing. It is your responsibility to make sure that your skills are up to a level to play in each position.

If you scored fewer than 70 points in this step, consider going back and practising your weak skill sets before moving to the next step, Team Attack, in which you will learn the relevance of gain and tackle lines and how to make best use of your attacking players and systems.

Centre Drills

1. Developing All-Around Vision — ___ out of 10
2. Passing Under Pressure — ___ out of 10
3. Feeding a Player Running From Depth — ___ out of 10
4. Riding the Contact — ___ out of 10

Winger Drills

1. Beating the Last Line of Defence — ___ out of 10
2. Winning the Race for the Corner — ___ out of 10
3. Reacting Quickly to the Defence — ___ out of 10

Full Back Drills

1. Making Quick Decisions — ___ out of 10
2. Joining the Attack — ___ out of 10
3. Counterattacking With Wingers — ___ out of 10

Total — ___ **out of 100**

Team Attack

How do you go forward to score but still pass the ball either laterally or backwards? Only Rugby Union and Rugby League have this problem to solve, yet both games create speed of movement forward with astonishing regularity, energy and excitement. The interaction between the ball carrier and the support players is of paramount importance to the effectiveness of any forward movement. Although some of this can be coached, the ability of the individual player ultimately decides the success or failure of the attack. To attain optimal performance, each player must understand the basic attack framework and put it into practice. Then, on the field, he must follow any agreed tactics and strategies or overrule them as the match or situation dictates.

ATTACKING GAIN AND TACKLE LINES

Rugby players use a number of imaginary lines across the field to play the game effectively. First are the lines dictated by the Laws—the offside lines—and these are different at the set pieces and in the loose. Those in open play are dependent on the point at which the ball comes into play or into your possession. Then there is the gain line, which is the line you have to cross to get the ball ahead of the other 14 players in your team.

Perhaps the most important line is the tackle line, which is the line drawn across the pitch that shows where the attack and the defence would clash if both lines of players ran at top speed towards each other. The angle and speed at which you run as attackers or defenders, and the depth of your attacking alignment, can reshape the tackle line.

The actions that take place at the tackle line often decide the outcome of the match. If the attackers dominate here and break through this line frequently, they are highly likely to win the match. On the other hand, if one team's defence is never busted by the attack, that team probably will win. As you can see from figure 11.1, the closer you attack initially from the scrum, the farther back the tackle line is and the more quickly you can cross the gain line.

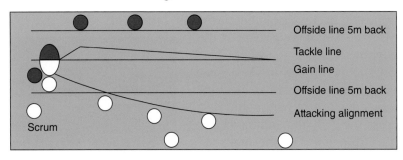

Figure 11.1 Imaginary lines used on the rugby field: offside line, tackle line and gain line.

From a Scrum

Although there are a number of ways of crossing the gain line from a scrum, here are three possibilities:

- The scrum half or number 8 picks up and runs to the right to attack the space at the side of the scrum and make as much ground as possible before releasing a quick ball for a follow-up attack at a retreating defence.

- A player from the right runs left and receives the ball to the rear left of the scrum (this is better done if the defending scrum half is standing by the rear foot of his scrum) to link with the winger and back-row forwards.

Any follow-up attack depends on forward movement, momentum, the speed of the ball, and so on, but you might be able to continue to hit the defence up that channel; fire quick, long passes to midfield to expose any gaps or to the far side of the field for an attack by the overlapping full back; or complete a pass to number 10 for a crossfield kick for the winger to catch or run onto on the far touch line.

- Two quick passes are made to the right to a midfield player on an angled run back at his number 10. If contact occurs, a quick ball is sent to overlapping players who are running right to attack a depleted and retreating defence.

Misstep

Your opponents always seem to have more defenders than you have attackers.

Correction

You probably are trying to play across and out wide too early. Hit the gain or tackle line hard and close to the scrum, and then either offload to a runner behind the defence or win the ball quickly and hit the defensive line hard again.

As you can see, one tactic can lead to a variety of follow-up attacks that every player should understand and have a role in. Organisation speeds up the movement by all players and gives your team a better chance of dominating the defence. If you can go forward in all you do, the immediate effect is to move the tackle line very close to the gain line so that you can, potentially, cross them at the same time. You will have as many players as possible behind the ball and, therefore, in play.

From a Line-Out

The line-out is the only time that the Laws say that opposing backs should be 20 metres apart. This distance becomes greater if the alignment of the attacking backs goes deeper. Therefore the deeper they stand, the greater distance they have to run before they can cross the gain line and the closer the tackle line is on the attackers' side of the gain line (figure 11.2). Work out what you think is the easiest and quickest place to cross both lines.

Many teams attack the area around the back of the line-out and try to cross the gain or tackle line there. When they succeed, they have 15 players behind the ball and the opposition has fewer players in defence. The ball has to be won quickly and then used against the depleted defence by making it difficult for the opposition players to get back in front of the ball.

As with the scrum, some teams set out to cross the tackle line as soon as they win the ball and peel around the back of the line-out or bring a midfield player or back-row forward back at an angle to hit the tackle line close to the rear of the line-out. A team that has very agile and quick backs who run

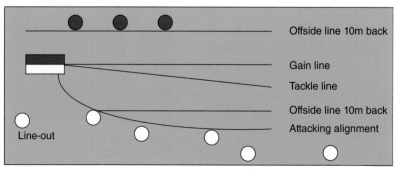

Figure 11.2 Line-out alignment, gain and tackle lines.

good patterns may have a series of moves designed to misshape the defence and then follow these with organised attacks depending on the reaction of the defence. Figure 11.3 shows a simple back's move that is easy to organise and run. What everyone needs to understand and plan for is what happens next if the attack is stopped or if the defence doesn't react as expected.

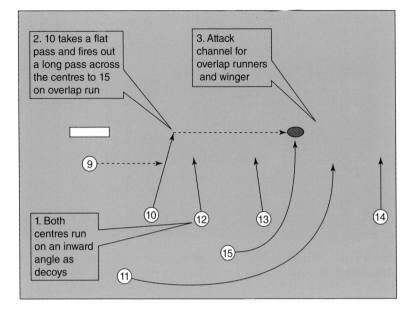

Figure 11.3 Miss two overlap ploy. Backs and winger run to attack the channel.

 Misstep

Your team never seems to be able to create an overlap situation following a line-out.

Correction

Use a full line-out so that both sets of forwards are together. Win the ball quickly near the back of the line-out and feed the number 10 playing flat. Number 10 runs at the opposition number 7 to check the up-and-out defence. As soon as this happens, move the ball out wide using centres as decoys and bring the back three into play in the space created.

The decision makers in the team must have the authority, knowledge and ability to change tactics or moves as the game progresses. If, for example, in the move shown in figure 11.3, one of the defenders runs on an out line to cover the full back and leaves a gap, the ball carrier should see that movement and take advantage of it by putting the ball into that gap with a pass to one of the decoy centres. Therefore, any decoy runner should expect the ball even though the general plan is to pass it to someone else.

Of course, there are other possibilities for using specific tactics against the opposition. You may know that the opposition's fly half is a poor tackler and so decide to attack the area just behind the inside centre's shoulder, the area covered by the number 10 in an up-and-out defence (figure 11.4). You can do this in many ways, but here are just two.

In figure 11.4a, the number 10 takes a flat pass and attacks the defending number 7, which will automatically trigger the defending number 10 onto an out run to cover the attacking inside centre (number 12). The ball is popped up to the blindside winger coming into the line outside the fly half and on to the covering number 10. Alternatively, once your attacking number 10 has fixed the defending number 7, the ball is given to the inside centre and the full back comes back inside to take a pass (figure 11.4b), once again on to the defending fly half. Such simple moves can be used all of the way down your three-quarter line if you know of a weak tackler, but remember to threaten the inside shoulder of the next player in line. This causes uncertainty in the defence because they, too, will know they have a weak defender and will hesitate to push out too quickly. This could lead to gaps or space elsewhere. All players must play with their heads up, see these faults in the defence, communicate to the rest of the attack and act on what they have seen.

The 2-metre rule means that the front of the line-out is one of the easiest places to cross the tackle line, especially if the player marking the 5-metre

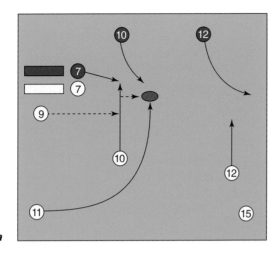
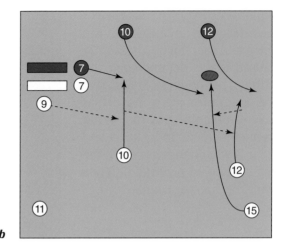

Figure 11.4 Attacking space behind the inside centre: *(a)* a flat pass to number 10, who pops the ball to the blindside winger; *(b)* a flat pass to number 10, who gives the ball to the inside centre.

area habitually watches the ball and wants to become involved in the line-out action rather than defending the area at the front. A quick throw to a line-out forward and back to the thrower or another player peeling up the 5-metre area is a good ploy to quickly put the ball ahead of the forwards and behind the defence. Once again, you must answer the question, What happens next? and have everyone understand what the possibilities are so that no matter what the decision is, everyone reacts positively to that action even though it might not achieve the best outcome.

Reducing the number of players in the line-out might release some of the big, ball-handling forwards to play down the centre of the pitch, mixing and matching with the centres. Either use them in the first wave of attacks or have them as a follow-up attack against the rest of the defence once the first attack is stopped. A simple pattern for attacking from a reduced line-out is to attack up the middle through the forwards (leave some of the line-out forwards near the touch line). If

stopped, go the same way first. If stopped again, hit back to link up with the hooker and back-row forward, who are running down the touch line against their wingers.

To be successful in attacking from the line-out, remember these principles:

- Win the ball quickly and fix the defence before moving the ball.

- If the forwards from each team are gathered together in a small area, win the ball quickly, move it away from them and make it difficult for them to defend.

- Use the space between the teams at the line-out. Close down the defenders quickly to fix them, and then play. The closer you can be to the defenders (and play comfortably), the more difficulty they will have covering any subsequent wide attacks.

- Your blindside winger and full back are essential contributors to successful attacks from line-outs.

 Misstep

The farther away from the line-out you play, the less influence your forwards have in the follow-up play.

Correction

Use a reduced line-out and stand your spare forwards in the gaps between your number 10 and the centres. Work out simple ploys for using these players as strike runners in midfield or as support runners to a wide attack.

At Ruck and Maul

At ruck and maul the tackle line is very close to the attacking team (figure 11.5). The easiest place to cross it is very close to the ruck or maul. Many teams work out a series of simple moves to disrupt the defensive formation in this area. These often include a number of quick, driving contact situations to build up momentum, suck in the close defence, drive the outside defence backwards and free up space for the attacking team to use.

Once this space is established, it is time for the attackers to spot the weaknesses in the defensive line. Often, these include mismatches such as a large forward defending against a speedy, agile and elusive back. Good teams have a signal for this situation so that the ball carrier farther down the attacking line knows to fire the ball quickly to the player in the mismatch zone. If your driving play sucks in the close defenders, other players in the defensive line have to move inwards to take their places, and spaces may begin to appear out wide (figure 11.6). However, the slower they move in, the more likely that gaps will appear in the centre of the field. Plus, the short-side defence may become more depleted, which will open up further attack possibilities down that side.

Experiment with alignment depth and recognise the strengths of the players and the units to form a team identity. Teams with powerful runners may test the defence by playing off a shallow alignment and using hard, direct running lines at individual defenders. The shallower you play, the less likely the defence will be to push too many defenders on out lines. At some stage you will create a 1v1 or 3v2 attacking situation.

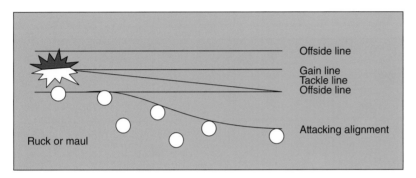

Figure 11.5 The tackle line is close to the attacking team at ruck and maul.

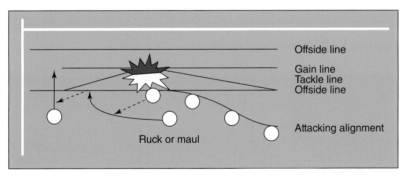

Figure 11.6 Space opening up wide or on the short side of the ruck or maul.

Misstep

Your team finds it almost impossible to break through the close-in defence around rucks and mauls.

Correction

The first thing you have to do is move the guard sideways so that you can put a player down the ensuing gap. In step 1 you learned a variety of passes such as the switch and loop, and this is the place to use those skills. Target the guard. Run as if you are going to try to make a break on his outside shoulder, and switch with a player going back down the channel at the side of the ruck or maul. You can also use this move one pass out from the ruck and maul.

If your team has very agile, quick backs with good hands, you may wish to play farther away from the defence and misshape it using attacking patterns and running lines. No matter which type of players are in the team, the intention remains the same—put a player into space with the best chance of scoring a try.

To create space for your team and overcome a defence, make tactical decisions to optimise the way you use the ball in your attempts to score. The three basic tactics to beat a defence (depending on the shape of the defence in front of you) are to pull the defence wide and penetrate it, pull it closer together and outflank it or pull it forward and kick the ball over it.

A wide and spaced defence gives you the opportunity to attempt to penetrate it by using a decoy runner to attract the attention of the defence away from the passer, who gives a short pass to the penetrating runner (figure 11.7). Close, instant support is required for the ball carrier, who needs to run strongly and have good ball-retention abilities.

If you are faced with a defence shaped like the one in figure 11.8, you could attempt to outflank it by having your close players on running lines that hold the defence away from the space. Your wider players can then target the space for the follow-up attack. Because you are deliberately playing close to the tackle line, you need good, quick, accurate handling to release a pass to a support player running at pace into the space.

When faced with a shallow, fast-approaching defence, as in figure 11.9, you may decide to kick into the space behind it. Your kick must be accurate, and your chasers must have a good chance of regaining possession. A wide variety of kicks—including the grubber, chip, crossfield, bomb and box—are at the disposal of all of the players in the backs. Your task is to use the most effective one at the right time and do it accurately so

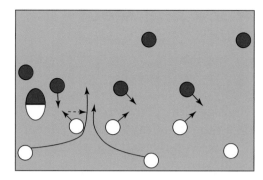

Figure 11.7 A short pass to a penetrating runner through a wide-spaced defence.

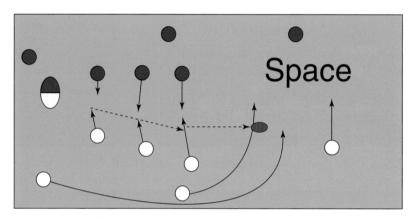

Figure 11.8 Outflanking the defence to create space wide.

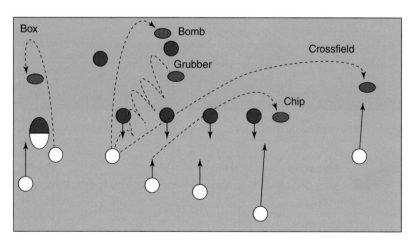

Figure 11.9 Kicking into the space behind a fast-approaching defence.

that the chasing player has the best opportunity to regather the ball. Remember, with the majority of kicks there is only a fifty-fifty chance of regathering the ball. Any inaccurate kick will give your opponents the ball. Unless you have accurate kickers, the better option may be to exert pressure by retaining the ball and controlling the pace of the game.

DEVELOPING PLAYING STRATEGIES

A playing strategy is simply a style of play. The best teams can change from one style to another, either during the game or from week to week, depending on whom they are playing. The ideal is to use a game strategy to start the match and then develop from there. If the strategy is working, keep doing it. On the other hand, if your opponents expected that strategy and know how to combat it, you will need to change.

No matter how you play on the day, about 80 percent of what you do will stay the same. The remaining 20 percent or so will be different—these are your weekly tactics. Your style is built on the players that are available to you—big, aggressive but slow forwards and average three-quarters will be better suited to some ways of playing than others. Likewise, very athletic and strong forwards plus fast and elusive backs will lend themselves to a different style.

Setting a style for your team begins with the players. First, examine the strengths and weaknesses of the each player, the mini-units, and so on. Once you have established these, decide on your style and go out and practise to that pattern. Here are some common ways of playing:

• **Touch line to touch line (figure 11.10a).** This is not simply firing the ball across the defence from one side of the pitch to the other while looking for a gap. It involves engaging the defence somewhere along its defensive line. After winning the ball, go the same way first until you reach the area close to the touch line. Once there, do the same on the way back across, still actively looking for space or gaps to attack and for overlap opportunities. The overriding rule of all tactics is choice. If you find that the strategy of going the same way after contact is not working, the main decision maker (probably the number 10) should decide whether to continue out to the touch line with the attack or hit back. Teams that can play this way are usually fast with excellent skills and high fitness levels.

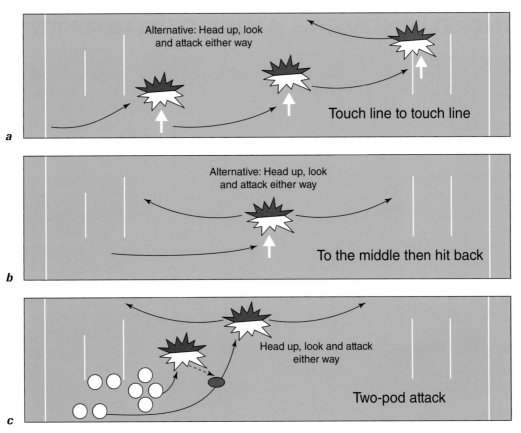

Figure 11.10 Three common strategies: *(a)* touch line to touch line; *(b)* middle and hit back; *(c)* two-pod system.

- **Middle and hit back (figure 11.10*b*).** This is a deliberate attempt to break the defence in the middle of the pitch and, if held, switch the ball back to where it was won and commit dedicated players against the remnants of their forwards. The main decision makers may decide to go the same way first in any attack, so be ready to run in support no matter what happens. The best teams take the ball to the middle of the pitch and attempt to break the defensive line. If held, they decide then which side to attack. Teams that play these tactics normally have good ball-handling forwards who are effective in the contact area but who may not be particularly quick around the field.

- **Two-pod system (figure 11.10*c*).** The forwards are divided into two interchangeable pods that work together immediately after a set piece. The backs may take the ball into contact in midfield and pass back to the forwards in the first pod, who hit and drive. When stopped, the scrum half feeds a runner from the second pod, usually on the far side of the contact area. This pod takes the ball forward at speed. Once stopped, the ball is won quickly and the remaining defence is attacked by the play makers. Teams that play in this way have good ball-handling forwards and others who are good in contact, but all are very mobile.

Your team also must develop a kicking strategy. A common kicking strategy is to kick the ball downfield out of your own half and trust your kick chase and defence. By rolling the ball into the corners, you will make your opponents kick to touch, or you may deliberately put the ball out if you have a dominant line-out. In this way you will be trying to make sure that the majority of the game is played in your opponents' half, preferably their 22-metre area. Your aim is to force your opponents to make mistakes by defending aggressively. This strategy can lead to many counterattack opportunities because your opponents normally will want to clear their half by using kicks as well.

Your team may be able to play any of these styles. If so, put all of them into practice at some stage in the season. The best style is the successful one.

USING TURNOVERS AND COUNTERATTACKS

Many tries, especially at the international level, are scored from turnovers. This is because the defence generally is out of position when the ball is given over. Most often, the ball carrier is turned or loses the ball in contact, or sends a wayward pass that is intercepted. Good teams look for these turnovers and know how to attack once they have the ball. Your reaction to a turnover depends on where you are on the pitch, what the score is, and various other factors. Plan for all scenarios in the game and practise your counterattacking routines. Generally speaking, if you win the ball unexpectedly from contact, the best thing to do is to make two quick passes away so that the ball carrier has time and space to look up and answer these questions:

- How close is the defence?
- Where is the space?
- Where is my support?
- How will we score?
- Should I run, pass or kick?

Another common way of receiving unexpected possession is from a kick downfield. Some basic principles from all kicks can be applied. The abiding one is, Don't be caught with the ball behind the majority of your teammates. Your essential role is to set up an attack that has a very good chance of clearing your half and open up the field for any follow-up attacks to give your team the best chance of scoring. If you are in any doubt, either kick back downfield as long as possible with a good chase, or kick into touch as far downfield as possible and then trust your defence.

Many of the most exciting attacks come when the ball is kicked to a wing or full back and is then run back at the chasing team from inside the 22-metre area. If this is team policy, all players must understand their roles in making such scoring attempts part of the attacking ploys available to the team. Any kick ahead may leave the kicking team exposed to some form of counterattack. Your task is to know how to make the most effective use of any ball that comes your way. Follow these basic counterattacking principles:

- If there is space out wide, use it (figure 11.11a). Otherwise, fix the chasing players, especially the forwards, by running the ball towards them (figure 11.11b).

- Switch the point of attack once the defence is fixed.

- Support, support, support at pace.

- Flood the attack area with players. Hit the space hard and keep going until you score or need to change the point of attack.

- Keep the pace high and don't allow the defence to rest or reset.

The final way of receiving unexpected possession is by being awarded a free kick or penalty. This can leave the opposition very exposed, especially if they have a large number of players near the ball or on the ground. Opponents near the mark of the penalty must immediately move 10 metres away and allow the ball carrier to run at least 5 metres. This effectively gives the ball carrier the opportunity to make ground into and possibly through any defensive structure and close to the opponents' goal line. A quickly taken tap penalty often leads to a try. For example, when a free kick is given at the scrum, the number 9 immediately throws the ball back to the number 8, who taps and runs from the base. This effectively takes out all the forwards from the defence and gives that player a free run into the three-quarter defence with close support from the back row, scrum half and inside backs.

Every team should have an acute awareness of what is possible from free kicks and penalties. Make it part of your team's overall strategy to take these quickly and support the ball carrier in numbers.

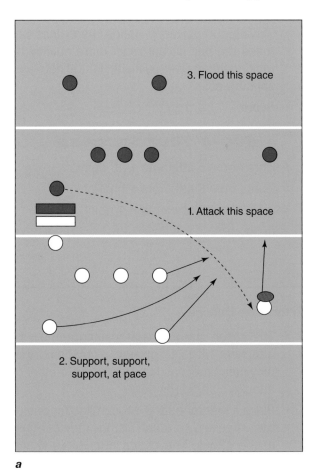

a

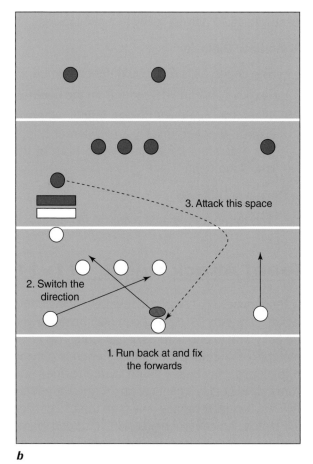

b

Figure 11.11 Counterattacking: *(a)* use the space out wide if it is available; *(b)* if no space out wide is available, run at the forwards to fix them in place.

CAUTION Always wear protective equipment in both practice and match situations. Although not every drill in this section anticipates contact with a player, a piece of equipment or the ground, by its very nature rugby invites contact, sometimes by accident. It's better to be safe than sorry.

Team Attack Drill 1. *Playing Against a Changing Defence*

Play 10v10 between the 15-metre lines and from half-way. The defence should wear tackle suits and any other protective equipment normally worn. Both teams line up with seven in the back line; the rest are forwards. The defensive seven are numbered from 1 to 7. A marker is placed at the side on the 15-metre line. The coach calls out three numbers as the ball comes into play. Those players have to touch the marker before they can join the defence. Players in the attacking team must assess the situation quickly and play against the defence in front of them. If the attack is slowed, it is likely that the defence will have reset with all 10 players ready to make tackles.

To Increase Difficulty

- The coach calls only two defence numbers.
- Remove only one defender from the defence.
- Place the marker 5 metres infield, where it can be touched quickly and where it brings the defenders back into play in front of the attacking team.

To Decrease Difficulty

- The numbers the coach calls don't play.

Success Check

- Look forward and communicate with all of your teammates.
- The defence will try to cover the spaces that are created. This will open spaces elsewhere, so don't automatically run to where you think the space is.
- Look at the movement in front of you; then quickly decide whether to pass, run, go into contact (do you really need to do this?) or kick.
- The support players in their running lines can make the ball carrier react more quickly by making themselves available for the defence-splitting pass.
- Score.

Score Your Success

5 scores from 5 attempts = 10 points

4 scores from 5 attempts = 5 points

3 scores from 5 attempts = 1 point

Your score ___

Team Attack Drill 2. *11v11*

Defenders wear full protective equipment including tackle suits. Any 11 players can play because you are not going to play scrums or line-outs. This gives each player the opportunity to experience playing in the loose. Play between the 15-metre lines and from half-way. Play a game of grip rugby. Defenders may not tackle; they may only grab the ball carrier. The coach can call when a 'tackle' has been made, at which point all those around the ball have to go to ground and play from there.

To Increase Difficulty

- The coach shouts for a specific number of attackers to go to ground. Sometimes that may mean that you have the same number of attackers and defenders.
- Place a marker near the touch line for one or two attackers to touch before they can join in the attack. The coach nominates which attacker(s) must touch the marker.
- Bring in full tackling.

182

To Decrease Difficulty

- Allow only a specific number of defenders to enter the 22-metre area.

Success Check

- Use any moves that you have learned and practised to break down the first defence. After that, attack the defence that is left standing.
- Keep your head up, scan the field and play.

- Once you see space, choose a running line that maintains that space for others to use.
- Communication is vital. Everyone contributes.
- Score.

Score Your Success

5 scores from 5 attempts = 10 points

4 scores from 5 attempts = 5 points

3 scores from 5 attempts = 1 point

Your score ___

Team Attack Drill 3. *Set Piece Practice*

Choose the moves that you wish to practise and then play 15v10. Use all of the pitch and try out each move in turn. Defenders are to play grip rugby, so full protective equipment should be worn. It is very unusual for strike moves to score every time, so you must continue playing if the move is stopped. What happens next? This stoppage could occur in the match, so be prepared to play on and strike again. In the blink of an eye, the first receiver needs to assess the support runners, the next attack direction and the speed of the ball from the breakdown and then determine who is available to receive the pass, if he needs to hit hard into contact, if there is space out wide, and so on. The important thing to remember is that not every decision is the best one, but if everyone reacts quickly to that decision, then the attack will continue and pressure will be maintained on the defence.

This is also a good practice in which to rehearse counterattacking. Your coach can either kick or throw in a second ball to give you the opportunity to run back at the defence. He may also give a free kick or penalty against your opponents at any set piece or loose play situation for you to use quickly.

To Increase Difficulty

- Use full-tackling defence.
- Use a second ball. As soon as the defence is broken, the coach throws in a second ball

behind the attack for them to retrieve and play with. The first ball is thrown to the coach.
- Allow the defence to contest the retrieval of the second ball. If they win it, they can play.

To Decrease Difficulty

- The coach controls the defence. Defenders can go forward only on the coach's signal.
- Play with fewer defenders.
- The coach gives plenty of warning prior to inserting the second ball and indicates where it will be thrown or kicked to.

Success Check

- Attack the defence that is left standing after the strike move.
- Keep your head up, scan the field and play.
- Communication is vital. Everyone contributes.
- The defence has no time to reset.

Score Your Success

5 scores from 5 attempts = 10 points

4 scores from 5 attempts = 5 points

3 scores from 5 attempts = 1 point

Your score ___

Team Attack Drill 4. *Playing From Rucks and Mauls*

Play 15v10 in one half of the field. The attackers have 15 players, and the defence must wear full protective equipment. The practice is full tackling. The coach introduces a second ball to the game at a suitable moment. To start the game, the coach rolls a ball towards the attacking forwards, who control it and begin to play.

In practice games like this, it is a good idea to give everyone a reference or starting point. The coach should decide whether this is a contact situation. When the ball comes into play, the attacking players react as they would in a match and try to score by beating the defence. If the ball becomes unplayable, the coach rolls a second ball in behind the attackers so they have to go back, regather and start again. The first ball should be given back to the coach immediately. He can use it again if the second ball becomes unplayable. This continuous practice can lead to an increase in fitness for the players. All Laws should be applied. The coach should award penalties or free kicks, if appropriate, and the teams should play on. For the sake of practice, the coach could award free kicks or penalties even if no offence was committed so that the teams can practise their decision making and reactions.

To Increase Difficulty

- Allow defenders to go for the second ball and try to retrieve it.
- When using a second ball, the coach throws the ball into a fifty-fifty situation so that both teams have a good chance of retrieving it.
- Play 15v15 while applying the same rules.

To Decrease Difficulty

- The defence does not contest possession when the second ball is rolled in.
- Play with fewer defenders.

Success Check

- Attack and misshape the defence constantly.
- Keep your head up, scan the field and play.
- Communication is vital. Everyone contributes.
- Score as efficiently and as often as possible.
- Show no mercy to the defenders.

Score Your Success

5 scores from 5 attempts = 10 points

4 scores from 5 attempts = 5 points

3 scores from 5 attempts = 1 point

Your score ___

Team Attack Drill 5. *Kicking to Score*

Play 15v10 with the same rules as team attack drill 4 except the scoring 'pass' must be a kick. Accuracy is vital, and scoring kicks should be made only if the kicker is as certain as possible of success. All kicks should be used, and they can be made from anywhere on the pitch.

It is possible to engineer situations in which certain kicks have a good chance of being regathered. For example, if you attack the middle of the field from a line-out and then hit back down the way from which you have just come, it is likely that your openside winger will be standing in acres of space, especially if, as a policy, you use the full width of the pitch from touch line to touch line. If your wingers are encouraged to play close to the touch lines, they will always have space for a crossfield kick.

To Increase Difficulty

- Narrow and shorten the playing area.
- Play 15v15.

To Decrease Difficulty

- Allow any kick to be used during the attack. It does not have to be the scoring 'pass'.
- Play with fewer defenders.

Success Check

- Misshape the defence to create a kicking opportunity.
- Communication is vital. Everyone contributes.
- Use the signals that you will use in the match to indicate which type of kick is required.

184

SUCCESS SUMMARY OF TEAM ATTACK

To attack successfully, you must remember some basic principles of play. First, you must go forward to meet the gain and tackle lines. You choose where to try to cross them. Once at the lines, you need support to carry on the momentum of the attack. Sometimes this will be in the form of driving play or of other players winning the ball back on the ground or being in a good position to receive a pass. This will give your team continuity in the attacking sequence and will put both mental and physical pressure on your opponents, leading to success in your attacking team play.

The drills in this step have been designed to develop your decision-making abilities. At some stage, every player will find himself with the ball in his hands or very close to the action. Your teammates rely on your quick and clear thinking to carry on the attack. To improve, you must learn from your experiences. The decision-making sequence is see, understand, decide, act and know. With good coaching and advice, you will learn from your mistakes and successes and adapt your future actions accordingly.

If you scored at least 35 out of 50 points on the drills in this step, you are ready to move on to step 12, Team Defence. If you scored fewer than 35 points, return to any drills that gave you problems and run through them again to improve your scores.

Team Attack Drills

1. Playing Against a Changing Defence	___ out of 10
2. 11v11	___ out of 10
3. Set Piece Practice	___ out of 10
4. Playing From Rucks and Mauls	___ out of 10
5. Kicking to Score	___ out of 10
Total	___ *out of 50*

Team Defence

Look at any final league table—Super 14, Tri Nations, Rugby World Cup, 6 Nations—and you will find that the winners almost always have the best defensive record, the lowest number of points scored against them. Most defensive coaches will tell you a simple fact—defence wins games.

The two basic kinds of defence are the one that goes up and out and the one that goes up and in. The up-and-out defence pushes the attack sideways and floods any outside space with defenders. It is the most used defence. The up-and-in defence hits and cuts off any passing movement before it reaches any space. Good teams vary their defence to keep their opponents guessing.

In earlier steps, you practised your individual tackling technique. More than any other game

unit, the strength of the defence is the sum of its individual parts. Like in a chain, a weak link will be discovered and exploited. It is very difficult to hide a poor defender, especially at the line-out or the scrum, but also in any general defensive line. Many teams have tried it, and most have failed. Even international teams have found that surrounding a poor defender with strong ones is still a recipe for defeat. The weak defender is attacked, drawing the stronger ones closer for protection and creating space elsewhere for follow-up attacks. The remedy is simple—practise, practise, practise tackling until each team member can tackle effectively. Then practise the team's defensive screen until you become successful at stopping any form of attack.

DEFENSIVE AIMS AND CHALLENGES

On defence, you must answer these three questions:

1. How can we win back possession?
2. How can we stop the invasion of our territory?
3. How can we stop the opposition from scoring?

The keys to defensive success are to be aggressive to achieve control of the game. Deny the opposition space to act and time to think by closing down the distance between you fast so that you tackle your opponents as far beyond

the gain line as possible. Go forward in the tackle and try to dislodge the ball. Quickly get back on your feet to contest possession. Pressure the ball carrier and legally try to stop or slow down any attempts to retain and recycle the ball in the tackle area. Reset your defensive line quickly to cover all possible follow-up attacks. Contest the ball at scrum, line-out, ruck and maul to make it difficult for the attackers to achieve good, controlled possession. Don't chase lost causes. If the attackers are winning the ball cleanly at the contact point, trust your defence and let the attackers have it. The more defenders you have on their feet, the better.

DEFENSIVE PRINCIPLES

Look at the defence as a set of layers, each one coming into play if the one in front is penetrated. At the set piece, the front line, mainly of the backs, is the most important line. The players in the next line, the back three, sweep across behind the backs, keeping pace with the ball. Their running line resembles the curve of an arc (figure 12.1). The closer their attack is to the set piece, the more their forwards can become involved in this first attempt to break down your defensive wall. Your forwards must set themselves in the defensive line as quickly after the set piece finishes as possible.

Once the ball has gone away from the set piece and you go into second phase, it is possible to further strengthen the layers of the defence. Start by sealing off a 5-metre channel on each side of a breakdown with a couple of heavy tackling guards whose role is to smash and prevent any attack down that channel. Have your scrum half (or a quick forward, if the scrum half is caught up) run in line with the ball but behind the front line as the sweeper. The role of the sweeper is to organise the defence just behind and around the breakdown, tackle any runner who breaks through and gather any short attacking kick that lands behind the front-line defence.

The front line must become an impenetrable and aggressive wall. Put your outside foot forward and be ready to run hard. Tell everyone around you who you are marking by pointing and shouting the player's name or number; communication in defence is vital. Move up together as a unit, in line and just slightly inside your opposite number. If your opposite number passes, drift hard after the ball but shout your intentions to the player outside you. Tackle any ball carrier who comes down your channel. A heavy tackle that goes forward is a bonus. Trust the person on your inside.

Those who stand guard on each side of the breakdown are important to the success of the defence. Look back to figure 11.5. The convergence of the gain and tackle lines is very close to the contact area. If a team can break through the defence in this area, it is likely to make significant yardage downfield because the rest of those in the defensive line will be out of position and unable to effectively and quickly cover a break.

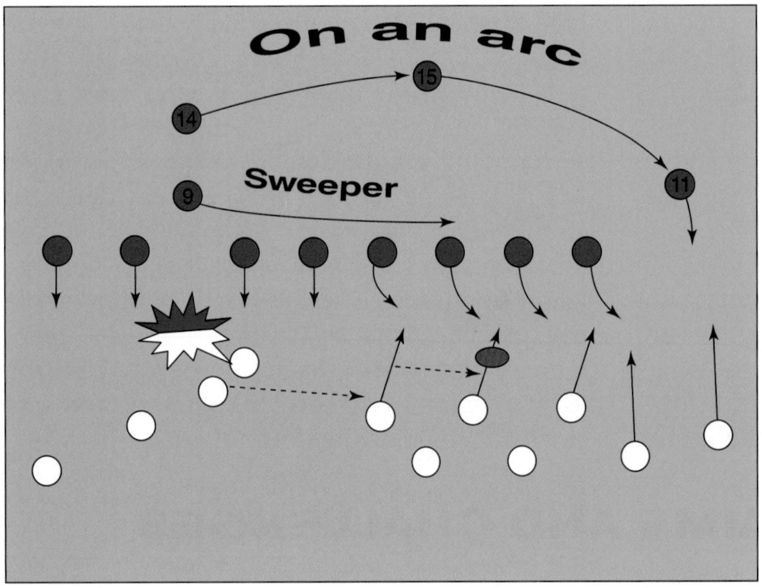

Figure 12.1 The running line of the back three resembles the swing of a pendulum.

Misstep
Your defence is constantly breached close to the ruck or maul.

Correction
Stop the guard and the bodyguard from moving sideways; they must go forward only. They cannot follow the ball out until it has completely cleared their area. At least two passes away, they run inside the C defender to protect his inside shoulder from an attack coming back down that channel.

Even the smallest space on either shoulder must become a no-go area (figure 12.2) because a break here will compromise the rest of the defence. It is essential that the opponents see this area as one they cannot break through and, consequently, do not attack there. Refer back to step 7 for detailed instructions on how to set the guards, bodyguards and C defenders.

The great danger in this area is that the guards move outwards, following the ball. If this happens, any attack worth its salt will flood into the space left behind them. Both guards on each side must go forward and fill the space. Only after the ball has left this zone can they push out and across. Nevertheless, they must be aware that some teams may bring a wider player back down this channel. The role of the guards after leaving their channel is to protect the inside shoulder of the defenders just ahead of them in the front defensive line.

The keys to success for the guard area in relation to the rest of the defensive front line are as follows:

- As you arrive at the breakdown, go far side first. Get guards in place quickly.

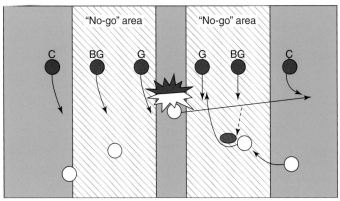

Figure 12.2 No-go areas.

- Match up the same number of defenders to attackers.

- If some attackers move from one side of the contact area to the other, react quickly but make sure the guards stay in place. Defenders from farther away need to move.

- Ideally, the bigger, slower forwards will gradually but urgently move inwards along the defensive line to be the guards.

- Defend with your head up, communicate loudly, point and move up as soon as you can.

TEAM DEFENCE AT THE SCRUM

Defence at the scrum to the left is slightly different than it is to the right. This is due to the scrum half being available to help on the right side but not the left (figure 12.3). The number 9 will be the first defender onto the opposing number 10 if the ball is moved to the defence's right. If the opposing number 9 runs to the defenders' left, the scrum half follows around and chases from behind in the knowledge that the left-side flanker would make the tackle.

A good way to start organising is to look at the pitch in 10-metre channels, starting from the scrum. The farther away your opponents move the ball, the less influence your back row can have. Their role, therefore, is to fill in on the inside shoulders of the backs and form the first line of defence if the opposition hits back against the flow.

In the first and second 10-metre channels, the back row, particularly the openside flanker and number 8, and the scrum half are fully involved in the front-line defence. The rest of the backs push up and then run outwards on to the next unmarked player. Assuming that the opposing number 10 is defended by the defending numbers 7 and 9, the attacking number 12 would be marked and chased down by the defending number 10, and so on down the line. If the opposition brings someone into the line—for example, its number 14 outside its number 10—then the defending number 10 makes the tackle on the would-be extra player (figure 12.4a). If the opponents' number 12 passes back inside to number 14, that player is taken by the defending number 9 or 7 (figure 12.4b). Remember, trust the player on your inside shoulder.

If the ball goes to the defence's left from a scrum, the scrum half either follows the ball

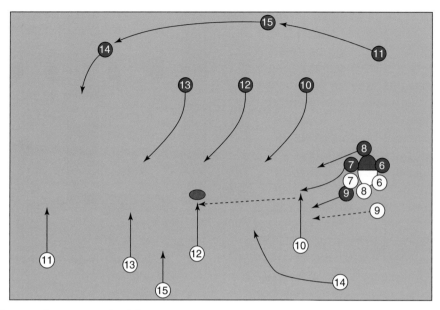

Figure 12.3 Defence at the scrum to the right.

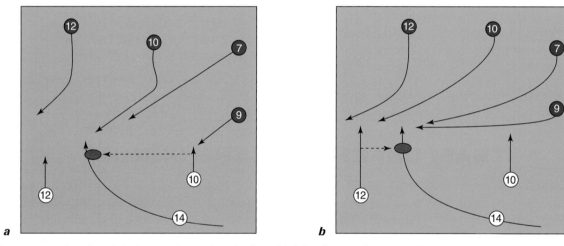

a   *b*

Figure 12.4 Attackers bringing number 14 into the line: *(a)* defending number 10 tackles number 14; *(b)* when number 12 passes inside to number 14, defending numbers 9 and 7 cover.

around, especially if the number 8 picks up and runs, or more likely comes to the back of the defensive scrum early and stays behind the offside line to be an extra defender (figure 12.5). However, on this side of the scrum the role would be of sweeper. If the attack moves the ball out wide, more than two defensive channels away, the winger steps up into the line and the full back takes out any overlapping player. Alternatively, the full back can step in and take the next to last player, and the winger can tackle the overlapping player. The success of this play depends on the physicality, pace and ability of each player.

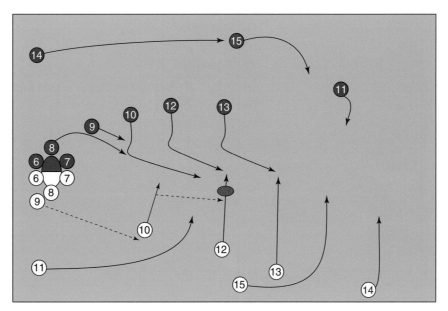

Figure 12.5 Defensive organisation when the ball goes left from the scrum.

Misstep

Your defence is vulnerable to overlap plays from the right-hand side of the scrum.

Correction

This likely happens because your opponents are using a number 8 pick-up and feed to the scrum half or bringing in a blindside winger to act as an extra player. First, consider bringing out your scrum half to stand at number 10 while everyone else stands out one player. Or bring your scrum half to the base of her own scrum behind the offside line on the open side. She takes the second player, leaving the number 8 to the flanker.

Scrums at centrefield require a mixture of both defences, and roles are strictly defined. First, the backs mark their opposite numbers and move with them before and when the ball emerges. If the ball moves away from the scrum, the principles previously discussed come into practice. However, the big danger to a defence is down the left side of the scrum because the opposition scrum half can pick and go that way in conjunction with the attacking back row. It is almost impossible to match their numbers without compromising the defence elsewhere. It is easy for the attack to make ground past the defensive back row if the attacking number 8 is quick off the mark and the attacking scrum is exerting pressure. Therefore, the defence is built on what will happen next. In principle, and if possible, the left flanker takes the ball carrier and the number 8 covers an inside or outside pass, although you could reverse these roles if you wish. If you have matched numbers to the left of the scrum,

hopefully you can take your opposite number in the tackle. The problem for the defence is the attacking number 9 and other attackers quickly arriving into this channel, resulting in more attackers than defenders (figure 12.6).

This is where the defending full back and scrum half play a vital role. In principle, number 15 covers the outside shoulder of the last defender and the scrum half sweeps across and behind to take anyone who penetrates. If you can slow down the attack at this point, other players from the scrum can quickly fill into the line and shuffle across to make a defensive line starting near the touch line. If you are close to your goal line, this is called a scramble defence. Everyone works frantically and urgently, in numbers, to prevent a score.

The out-to-in defence is difficult to learn and perform effectively. The first few defenders stand slightly wider than the player each is marking and go up and in quickly. Somewhere along the line, usually near the last attacker, is the target

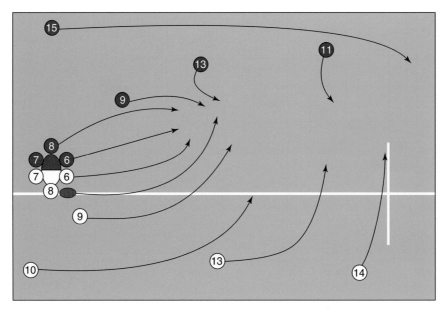

Figure 12.6 The attacking number 9 and other attackers overloading the short-side channel.

player who will make the telling pass, the pass to put another player in space. This could be the outside centre about to pass to an overlapping full back or a flanker on the hit back, standing out in space with a couple of players to the outside. Of course, it could also be a player on the end of the attacking line who has not realised that there is an extra defender out wide.

The defender opposite that player goes up more quickly than the rest and moves inwards hard to try to arrive with the ball (figure 12.7). This is effective if done well because the defenders are coming from out to in. Each defender is coming out of a blind spot because the attackers are watching the approaching ball.

The shock of taking a heavy tackle as the ball arrives and not seeing the tackler coming often is sufficient to make the attacking line go deeper, giving the defence more time and space to fill the field with defenders. The best teams are able to use both kinds of defence and choose the best formation based on the personnel in their team and also those in the opposition ranks.

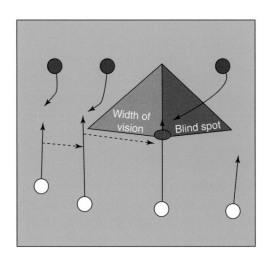

Figure 12.7 A defender moving up and in, trying to arrive with the ball and in the receiver's blind spot.

TEAM DEFENCE AT THE LINE-OUT

When organising your defence at the line-out, consider two attacking potentials: a forward's attack around or through and attacks away from the ball-winning area. As with most defensive organisation, you need to choose your tacklers carefully and make sure that they are in the correct place at the correct time. If your scrum half is a rugged and aggressive player who enjoys mixing with bigger players, you have an extra flanker type to become part of your close-in defence. Conversely, if your number 9 is a shy, retiring type but has a lovely pass and kick, then you may decide to reorganise your formations to move your scrum half into a more sheltered spot in the defence.

Defending a forward's attack is relatively simple, but you need to realise what your opponents are trying to do by attacking you at this point. First, they are trying to get big ball carriers behind your close defence and drag your organised defence sideways. Therefore, your line-out needs to neutralise this threat at the source. Consider these issues: How good is your line-out in comparison to theirs? How many have they committed to the line-out? Where are you on the field?

In principle, you need someone to defend any attack around the front of the line-out and then sweep up the line-out as the ball is won, and a player at the back of the line-out who is responsible for any attack there including flying out at the first receiver from the line-out to make sure that no attack back towards the forwards is attempted (figure 12.8). Normally, the scrum half and openside flanker are ideal candidates for these roles; but if you have a hooker who is quick and a good tackler, you may have him play these roles, moving your scrum half out of the firing line.

When the attacking team reduces the numbers of players in the line-out, the same two roles are allocated and the spare forwards go out into the first line of defence to mark any of their forwards who are standing there. However, if the attack reduces the numbers in the line-out to three or four, it is a good idea for the defence to leave a flanker at scrum half and the number 9 standing in the 5-metre channel at the front. The flanker's role is to defend the area around the back and then target the nearest ball receivers away from the line-out. The scrum half will sweep up the line-out to cover any attack coming through the middle. Once he is certain that no attack is coming through, he will either follow in behind the flanker and cover his inside shoulder or cover across and behind the first line of defence. It is essential that the flanker run the arc shown in figure 12.9 to prevent any hit backs from the attacking team. Your backs will become used to defending just ahead of these two players and feel safe in the knowledge that these players will cover any close attack that steps back inside.

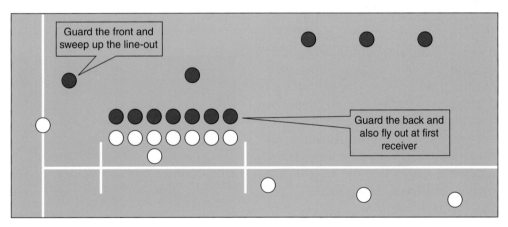

Figure 12.8 Defending the line-out.

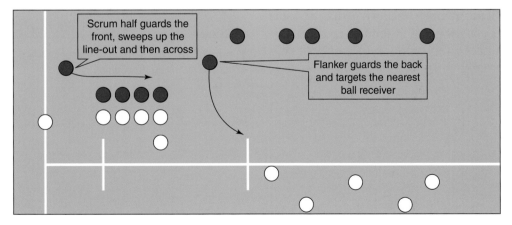

Figure 12.9 The player at the back of the line-out runs on an arc to prevent hit backs from attackers.

Misstep

Your defence is constantly being penetrated in midfield by the attack passing the ball back inside to a runner from deep.

Correction

In the in-to-out defence, communication is vital so the defence does not push out until the inside (first) defender feels she is in the correct position to cover the inside shoulder of the next player. At that moment, she can call for the push outwards. Everyone relays that call down the line so that the defence moves out as a unit and has no spaces for the inside pass to be effective.

As with all aspects of the game, there are no hard-and-fast rules, only Laws. Providing you stay within those Laws, each defence around the line-out can be altered to suit your team members and also the opposition.

The defence you use against an attack away from the line-out is very similar to the defence you use from the scrum. The main difference is that attack and defence lines are farther apart because the closest they can be at any one time, prior to the ball being thrown in, is 20 metres. This creates time for the defence to react to attacks. It is normal for the attack to try to tie down a defence as soon as possible after the ball has been delivered by having someone target a defender to attack. If the line-out was reduced in numbers, this may be done by one of the spare forwards running close to the shoulder of one of the centres, trying to cross the gain line near the line-out. Or if the line-out had seven forwards in, the backs could try to create an overlap or penetrating movement by executing a set move.

First, the defence has to stop the attack from going forward. It then has to make sure that the follow-up play has nowhere to go because all of the options are covered. The up-and-out defence is ideal for any moves from the line-out, especially if the leader of the defence (the fly half) has a couple of forwards covering from the inside. Often, this means the backs can mark an extra player out. Instead of marking the number 10 in the attack,

the defending number 10 moves out quickly to cover the opposing number 12 or any player coming into the line from behind (figure 12.10). If you can release two players from the line-out early, your players may be able to move another player farther out to stifle the attack.

Communication is vital, and the basic principle of trusting the player on your inside must be the mantra. Be aware of who is on your inside shoulder, and adjust your outward push accordingly. If you have the fastest player on the team there, you can push out as hard as possible. On the other hand, if a prop is standing there, you might need to slow down your outward movement.

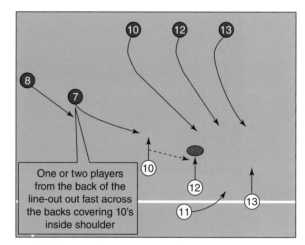

Figure 12.10 The defending number 10 moving quickly to cover the attacking number 12.

Misstep
In open play, the attacking team always seems to have a lot of space when moving the ball out wide and crosses the gain line most times.

Correction
Your line speed and outward movement are probably too slow to close down the attacking space. The C defender sets the speed and movement of the line. Everyone must listen for his call and the calls of the defender on the inside. Once the 'In' call is heard, then the whole line must act as a unit and go up and out in unison. Line speed is the key to success.

A simple attack pattern to defend is win the ball and attack up the middle. If you stop the attack, win the ball quickly and keep going the same way. When you run out of space, hit back into the open field. Once you move into the second phase of the attack, the open field defence comes into play (figures 12.1 and 12.2, pages 188 and 189). The two nearest defenders are responsible for going into any contact area to try to win back the ball if at all possible. There are dangers associated with this action, and all players must be aware of these. The two nearest players might be centres. Those players still in the defensive line have to be aware of who is standing opposite them in the attacking line and adjust their defensive positions accordingly. For example, you would want to avoid leaving a lock opposite a winger unless no other option was available.

If the ball has gone quickly from the line-out to the other side of the pitch, has been won fast and is on its way back, it is likely that the attackers are deliberately trying to target your slower forwards who are joining the defensive line at the far end of it. Some teams deliberately leave a quick player such as a flanker, hooker or winger out wide so that he can hit back and create mismatches with the defence. The biggest and slowest players in your team must move inwards along the defensive line as soon as possible so that they are not exposed or isolated with a lot of space about them.

When you are defending close to your goal line, the mentality and shape of your defence has to change. Your players need to mark their direct opposite numbers. As soon as your opponents win the ball, you have to fly up on them as fast as possible and immediately cut down the usable space. If they break through your line of defence, you have to rely on your scramble defence to cope with that breach.

KICK CHASE AND COUNTERATTACK

Kicking the ball downfield to relieve pressure or to try to gain ground is a frequent tactic, but your challenge is to prevent any effective counter-attack. By your defensive actions, you will try to make the opposition kick the ball back to you or to put it into touch for your line-out.

Although the pattern on the field after a kick may look chaotic, it is up to the kicking team to move quickly downfield with a well-organised chase, so that the ball-carrying team has no options in attack. As with the previous defences, all players have to understand this one so that they know their roles no matter where they are in the chasing line.

Attacking kicks downfield fall into three categories:

- Kicks to regather—box or bomb
- Kicks to gain ground—long down the middle or into either corner
- Kicks to score—high crossfield for the winger to chase, or bombs

In all cases, the kick chase principles are similar. The only difference is that in some chases, you may have at least one player running hard in front of the chasing line with a view to jumping to compete for the ball against the waiting defender. If the kick is too long, that player will chase to tackle or charge down any kicks from the catcher.

One of the most widely used kicks is the long downfield kick aimed at the posts so that any player who gathers the ball has a long distance to the touch line. The thinking behind this kick is simple:

- It clears the kicker's territory and may relieve some pressure.

- It lands a long way from the touch line so the ball carrier may not have such a long kick.

- It might result in an immediate kick back to counterattack with.

- The kicking team may apply sufficient pressure on the ball carrier to force a mistake.

The chasing group must consider a number of issues, including whether to commit everyone to the chase or to leave some back from the chase so that they have sufficient numbers to counterattack.

As with most situations in a fast-moving game, there are no hard-and-fast rules. Most teams always keep some players back for the counterattack opportunity. If the kick is part of an organised ploy, the chasers already will be in place prior to the kick and will have well-defined roles.

In principle, any kick chase must have a front line that stretches across the pitch and stays in line. If you have some bigger forwards mixed in with a number of faster backs, everyone must slow down to the speed of the slowest runner. Otherwise, the line will become disjointed and attacking opportunities will become evident to the ball carrier.

If the ball has been kicked towards a corner of the field away from the forwards, it is likely that the backs will chase unless the kick comes after a ruck or maul that has released some forwards for chasing duty in the middle of the kick chase line (figure 12.11). You cannot rely on the kicker to chase because the nearest defender may have completed the tackle just as the kick was made. When setting up the defence, always assume this has happened. The kicker's role is to stay back and receive any kick returns.

Forwards chase in the middle of the kick chase line. Players in the second line of defence apply the same principles as before—they run on an arc across the field (figure 12.12). If your wingers have both gone into the front line of defenders, a nominated player, normally one of the back row, becomes part of the second line. The scrum half sweeps across and behind and fills in when and wherever necessary.

Bombs over a set piece are attacking ploys, so you need to rehearse your kick chase in training. Normally, your two best catchers lead the chase, and the front-line defence tucks in behind them to gather any knockdowns or stop any counterattacks from the defence.

A number of simple principles apply to this kick chase:

- The first player to the catcher gets up in the air to try to catch the ball.

- The second chaser reacts to what happens.

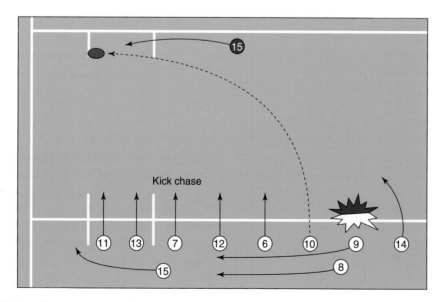

Figure 12.11 Kicking after a ruck or maul.

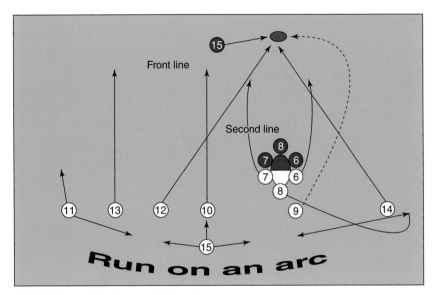

Figure 12.12 The second line running in a pendulum shape.

- The front line organises quickly with the flankers on the end of the line inside the number 10.

- The rest of the forwards make up the second line. Preferably, the locks are on either side of the props. They stay in line.

- Number 8 moves back to replace the blindside wing and to cover on the touch

line. He becomes part of the defence, if necessary.

- If one of the front-line players catches either the ball or the ball carrier in possession, the front five should be up to drive that defender backwards to contest the ball and try to force a turnover.

 Misstep
Your kick chase seems to be ineffective as a follow-up to a bomb down the middle.

Correction
Check that the kicks are not going too far and so giving the catcher too much time to either kick or run. If they are a good length, then make sure that you have the best jump and catchers to do the chasing. This may mean that it becomes a ploy rather than an off-the-cuff play. Remember, the role of the chasers at some kicks is to try to jump to catch the ball or at least deflect it back to support runners.

If the kick goes too far, it is up to the two front chasers to slow down and reset with the front line to create a solid defensive wall (figure 12.13). If one of the centres comes back into line, then number 7 can drop back and cover behind with number 9. This is so that you have cover and counterattack possibilities if the opponents' ball carrier manages to get a kick away. The front line must stay as a line and push up hard because, in this situation, field position is very important. The forwards who form the secondary chase line should fill in as quickly as possible behind the front line.

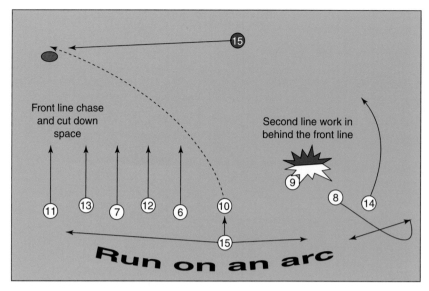

Figure 12.13 Creating a solid defensive wall when the kick goes too far.

CAUTION Always wear protective equipment in both practice and match situations. Although not every drill in this section anticipates contact with a player, a piece of equipment or the ground, by its very nature rugby invites contact, sometimes by accident. It's better to be safe than sorry.

Team Defence Drill 1. *Staying in Line*

Practise 11v11 across the pitch in one half, 10 metres apart. The nondefensive line carries tackle shields. The practice begins with every defender pointing to the player he is marking and telling the person next in line. As soon as the whole line is ready, the attackers jog forward and the defensive leader gives the signal for all the defenders to shout 'In' and move up quickly in line to make the hit. In this practice, the hit is to drive the shoulder up and into the rib area covered by the shield. As soon as the hit has been made, the defensive line moves backwards to the starting point but always looking at the attacking line. Use the opposite shoulder on alternate hits.

To Increase Difficulty

- One attacker from the attacking line wanders up and down and appears in a gap when the coach gives the signal to begin. Those in the threatened area have to decide who takes the extra player. Remember to trust the player on your inside shoulder. Always start inside the attacker's inside shoulder.

To Decrease Difficulty

- The extra attacker is given a specific area to run through.
- The defence has plenty of time to react by moving the lines 15 metres apart.

Success Check

- Create a solid wall of defenders.
- Everyone points at and communicates which player is to tackle which attacker.
- Move in line all at the same speed.
- Hits all happen at the same time.

Score Your Success

Complete 5 hits with the right shoulder = 5 points

Complete 5 hits with the left shoulder = 5 points

Everyone communicates and stays in line = 5 points

Your score ___

198

Team Defence Drill 2. *Up and Out*

Play 5v5. The players in the attacking line wear tackle suits and have a ball each. Lines begin 10 metres apart. The defensive line stands opposite the attackers and shouts to nominate its targets. The coach stands behind the defensive line and points either left or right. That is the signal for the attacking line to run up and out in that direction. The defensive team shouts 'In' and moves forward and out to meet and tackle the attacking line. In this practice, each player must make a full tackle on a player trying to break the line. The attacking team must watch and go in the correct direction the coach indicates. If the coach raises both arms, the attacking team should go straight forward with no deviation to either left or right. The coach must watch the tackles and make sure of correct techniques in small groups. Another group of players could be behind the coach ready to go as soon as the first group has completed the tackles.

To Increase Difficulty

- Defenders regain their feet as soon as possible and contest possession.
- One attacker moves out of the line to come into any gap. One defender acts as a sweeper

to take that player if a breakthrough occurs or to take the extra player at the end.

To Decrease Difficulty

- Use a walking pace until you learn the defensive running lines.
- Change from a full tackle to a hit and grab.

Success Check

- Create a solid wall of defenders.
- Everyone points at and communicates which player is to tackle which attacker.
- Move in line at the same speed and as a unit.
- Hits should happen at the same time, and all attackers should hit the ground.

Score Your Success

Complete 5 hits with the right shoulder = 5 points

Complete 5 hits with the left shoulder = 5 points

Everyone communicates and stays in line = 5 points

Your score ___

Team Defence Drill 3. *Open Field Defence*

Play 12v12 across the 22-metre area. Defenders should wear tackle suits. The coach starts the practice by rolling the ball to the attackers. The player collecting the ball must take a grab tackle and go to the ground along with two more players from the attacking team. Likewise, the defenders must commit three players to the 'contact area'. The defenders must quickly have their guards and bodyguards in place. The attackers have to attack to score. Communication with each other is a must. Also, the scrum half is nominated to act as a sweeper.

To Increase Difficulty

- One attacker behind the attacking line acts as a penetrating runner.
- Attackers make two quick attacks in the guard and bodyguard area.

To Decrease Difficulty

- Practise in a narrower area and slow down the attacks to give the defence time to reset.

Success Check

- Guards and bodyguards get in place quickly.
- Guards move correctly as the ball leaves the contact area.
- The in-to-out defence works smoothly with no obvious gaps.
- The scrum half acts as a sweeper.

Score Your Success

Successfully defend 10 out of 10 times = 10 points

Successfully defend 9 out of 10 times = 5 points

Successfully defend 8 out of 10 times = 1 point

Your score ___

Team Defence Drill 4.   *Up and In or Out to In*

Play 12v12 in one half of the pitch, defending a goal line. The coach uses two rugby balls to control the game. The coach makes sure the attackers are given a different ball to their best advantage at times that test the defence. Play from a contact situation as with the previous drill. The defence cannot contest the ball. As the attack closes in on the goal line, the defence should look for opportunities to signal an up-and-in defence to cut out the final telling pass.

To Increase Difficulty

- Play with an extra attacker.

To Decrease Difficulty

- Practise in a narrower area and slow down the attacks to give the defence time to reset.

Success Check

- Guards and bodyguards get in place quickly.
- Guards move correctly as the ball leaves the contact area.
- The defence moves up and out quickly to close down space.
- Communication is effective.

Score Your Success

Successfully defend 10 out of 10 times = 10 points

Successfully defend 9 out of 10 times = 5 points

Successfully defend 8 out of 10 times = 1 point

Every out-to-in defence is successful = 5 points

Your score ___

Team Defence Drill 5.   *Team Defence Practice*

Play 15v15. Defenders wear tackle suits. The coach uses a second ball to test the defence. Start from various set pieces and test the defence. Practise at match speed with full tackling; this is the only way to test the defence. The coach engineers situations to test the defence. The second ball can be thrown to the defenders as though it has been turned over, and it should be kicked downfield to test their kick chase. Every aspect of the defence should be tested including close defence at contact, scrums and the back of line-outs.

To Increase Difficulty

- Put one of the defenders off the pitch for 5 minutes to simulate being in the sin bin.

To Decrease Difficulty

- Reduce the number of attackers to 13.

Success Check

- The defence is tight, close and successful.
- Various defences are used when required—in to out, out to in, scramble and rush.
- Communication is effective at all times.

Score Your Success

No tries scored against the defence in 5 minutes = 10 points

Your score ___

SUCCESS SUMMARY OF TEAM DEFENCE

When considering the success of your defence, look at the four principles of team play and decide if you managed to stop your opponents from being successful in each category. Did you stop them from going forward, tackle any support runners quickly, break up their continuity and exert more pressure on them than they did on you?

Remember, even when you do not have the ball, you can attack the opposition through vigorous and aggressive actions. If you are successful in all of these categories, then you will likely win the game.

Although team defence is a unit action, your individual contribution is vital to its success. You should now understand your role in whatever defence your team uses during any part of a match. If you have been unable to contribute successfully as an individual in any of the drills, then you may need to go back into this step and work more on those areas that are below standard. Make sure you score at least 50 points before moving on. In defence it is true to say that the strength of the pack is the wolf, and the strength of the wolf is the pack!

Team Defence Drills

1.	Staying in Line	___ out of 15
2.	Up and Out	___ out of 15
3.	Open Field Defence	___ out of 10
4.	Up and In or Out to In	___ out of 15
5.	Team Defence Practice	___ out of 10
Total		___ *out of 65*

Strategies and Tactics

Imagine what it must have felt like to be William Webb Ellis, who in 1823 picked up a ball and ran forward with it during an informal game of football at Rugby School in England. William Webb Ellis's instinctive action created the game of Rugby Union for you to enjoy. If you have the pace, technique, skill and determination to evade all the defenders who are intent on stopping you, you can go forward at full speed in control of the ball and the game for up to 100 metres. Few other games permit such uninterrupted forward motion.

Usually, however, you will need help from teammates to keep the ball going forward towards your opponents' goal line. Rugby is unique in that to go forward, you have to pass the ball backwards. Passing the ball in this way sometimes creates a situation of diminishing returns because many of your players can end up in front of the ball and therefore out of the game (for example, when the backs pass the ball down the line from a line-out or scrum). As a result, many teams choose to kick the ball to gain ground and go forward. An inaccurate kick gives away possession, and without the ball, you lose control of the game.

Let's think about the game in a little more detail. The better you understand the game, the better your decision-making and playing abilities will be.

AIMS AND CHALLENGES

Your prime aim is to score more points than the opposition by carrying the ball over the goal line to score a try and by kicking conversions, drop goals and penalty goals. In attack, you and your team need to answer three questions:

1. How can we keep possession?
2. How can we invade the opposition's territory, cross the tackle line and get behind the gain line and prepare to score?
3. How can we score?

In defence, you and your team need to answer these three questions:

1. How can we win back possession?
2. How can we stop the invasion of our territory?
3. How can we stop the opposition from scoring?

The ball carrier controls the game, deciding when and where to pass, kick or run. As a team, you will be involved in contests for possession at kick-offs, scrums, line-outs, rucks and mauls, and when fielding kicked balls. It is vital that you all master the techniques and skills necessary for winning possession of the ball. Having won the ball, aim to keep the ball until you ultimately score by mastering your continuity and contact skills. When you have control of the ball, your opponents have no way to score. So be careful to kick purposefully and accurately.

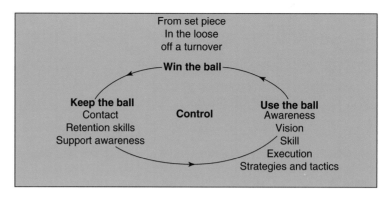

Figure 13.1 Controlling the game.

By having the ability to *win* and *keep* the ball, you establish control for your team and create the opportunity to best *use* the ball (figure 13.1). Do you penetrate (run through), outflank (run around) or kick over the opposition? Base these crucial decisions on the shape of the defence in front of you, your position on the field and the closeness and number of support players available. Try to play to your strengths and probe and exploit the opposition's weaknesses. Of course, you have to consider other factors, such as the weather, ground conditions, the referee and the state of play (How long to go? Does your team need to score? Does your team need to hang on to the lead?).

Remember, keeping the ball does not necessarily put pressure on your opponents, unless you can use it to go forward, beyond the contact point. In general, forwards often are the ball winners, and backs are the ball users. However, once players have left the set piece starting point, the numbers on their shirts should mean nothing. All players need to have the skills necessary for playing, including running, handling, ball winning and tackling. In the game, the nearest player to a tackled player should go in to help retain or win the ball. This means that any player may be required to play first receiver at the next contact point. If your handling ability is not up to this, then it is your responsibility to make sure you improve using the drills in step 1.

The principles discussed in the next section are fundamental and universal to each team playing the game.

PRINCIPLES OF PLAY

Controlling the game can be achieved only if you understand and implement the four principles of play: going forward, supporting, maintaining continuity and exerting pressure.

Going Forward

The keys to success in going forward are as follows:

- The attack goes forward towards the goal line and parallel to the touch lines rather than across the field.

- The ball carrier gets in front of the rest of the team as soon as possible after winning the ball.

- The ball carrier crosses the gain line or goes beyond the tackle line at the earliest opportunity to break the first line of defence to enable teammates to run at a retreating defence.

- The attacking team attempts to misshape the defence to create attacking space in which play makers can create situations that allow penetrators and support runners to go forward at speed.

- Score.

These keys to success can be achieved in various ways. For example, the forwards could retain possession and keep driving forward, sucking in the opposition, and then deliver the ball to the backs to run at retreating defenders. A quickly executed number 8 pick-up at the base of the scrum is one way of getting a ball carrier over the gain line quickly, as is a line-out peel and drive.

204

Backs will attempt to go forward with purpose by accurate passing and skilful running and evasion or by kicking over the defence and chasing. Many follow-up attacks or counterattacks are a mixture of forwards and backs interchanging positions and roles. Everyone needs to be able to carry the ball forward and, when necessary, pass to a support runner who is better placed to carry on the attack.

Supporting

In any rugby game you may handle the ball fewer than five times. So what are you expected to do for the rest of the game? When you are not handling the ball, you play a supporting role in either defence or attack to maximise the use of possession for your team. You need to be fit enough to run for most of the game. Good support is not accidental; it follows a deliberate pattern. By developing a good communication system in the team, you will know where and when to run in support of whatever team ploy is being executed in a particular area of the field.

If you are within 10 metres of the ball carrier, you should know what is happening and be ready to act and react. If you are within 5 metres of the ball, you are involved in the action and can influence the outcome by being available for support and giving the ball carrier more options. If you are within 1 metre of the ball carrier, you must already have made your decision and be directly involved in the action. The ball carrier and support runners have their own keys to success in support, as noted in the following lists.

Ball Carrier

- You are unlikely to beat all the defenders, so you must assess how far to go, where the support is and how and when to use it.

- You need support on both sides to maximise your choices and make defence difficult. Make sure that at least one of your support runners runs parallel to the touch lines to keep the ball going forward if you pass it. Demand that other support runners run at different angles or alter the distances between you to act as decoys.

Support Runners

- Keep your depth directly behind the ball carrier so you can decide at the last moment which space is best to attack: left, right or straight ahead. Perfect timing of your run is vital to add momentum to the attack.

- Be prepared to run positively in support all game. You won't always receive the ball, but you can be an important decoy. If at first you don't receive the ball, try again. Ultimately, you will.

Good support play is vital when your team is contesting possession and is in close physical contact. For example, line-out jumpers need to be supported in the air for safety reasons. Supporters need to hold up teammates in rucks and mauls so that they stay on their feet and keep driving forward.

Maintaining Continuity

Your aim is to maintain controlled continuity and control of the ball until your team scores. Attempt to sustain your attack despite the efforts of the defenders to halt it. The ball carrier will try to time the pass to a support runner so that both avoid contact and the receiver can carry the ball forward into space. You may need to use contact techniques to protect and recycle possession (use the ball again) during temporary stoppages to your forward movement (rucks or mauls).

A typical passage of continuous play might follow this pattern: Attack first against an organised, formal defence from a line-out or scrum ball. If stopped or slowed, recycle the ball quickly from the contact area. Launch a second attack into space and at a more disorganised defence. If halted again, recycle the ball under control quickly and attack again through the gaps of a now scattered defence. The key to success is an early, usable ball, allied to quick thinking, adaptable ball carriers and good organisation.

Attempt to keep the ball alive and move it around quickly, constantly changing the focus of attack and weakening the defence so someone is out of position or you create a mismatch. For example, one of your speedy, agile backs works against one of the opposition's big, cumbersome forwards. You might be able to create a situation in which your attackers outnumber defenders and you have adequate space in which to move forward and attack around the outside of the struggling defence. Your success will be based on how quickly you recognise the shape of the defence and on the quality of your decisions.

Good continuity requires ball-handling, contact and retention skills to keep the ball under control in tackle situations, quick decision making, well-timed support skills by close- and wide-running players and head-up vision and awareness.

Exerting Pressure

If you can exert sustained pressure on your opponents in attack and defence, you will force them to make mistakes from which you can score points. Attempt to deny your opponents space in which to play and time to think and act. If your team can get a ball carrier over the gain line and in behind the opposition's defence, can support quickly in numbers and can establish controlled continuity, your opponents will have difficulty dealing with the pressure this causes.

These are the keys to successful pressure *in attack:*

- Test the defence and then attack any weaknesses.

- Keep possession.

- Produce and use the ball quickly.

- Eliminate mistakes in your own performance as an individual and as a team.

- Keep the ball alive and constantly change your focus and point of attack.

- Use decoy runners to keep the defence guessing. Who might the next ball carrier be?

- Play at a pace that puts everyone under pressure to keep up with the play. If your scrum half is fit but also shattered during the game, then your intensity is good.

- Control the space between you and the opposition in both attack and defence.

- Put the ball behind the opposition by getting over the gain line and chasing kicks well to maintain possession.

- Misshape the defence and try to create mismatches or quickly attack the spaces being poorly covered by a disorganised or scattered defence.

These are the keys to successful pressure *in defence:*

- Deny the opposition space to act and time to think by quickly closing down the space between you to force errors by the ball carrier.

- Tackle your opponents as far behind their gain line as possible. Attempt to drive your opponents backwards in the tackle and dislodge the ball to reclaim possession.

- Attack the ball carrier. Disrupt and halt the opposition's attempts to retain and recycle the ball in the contact area.

- Organise your defence to cover all possible attacking tactics by resetting quickly.

- Attack your opposition at scrums, line-outs, restarts, rucks and mauls to make it difficult for them to win a good, controlled ball.

- Be hungry to reclaim the ball and hunt for it in numbers.

- Reset your defence fast and keep as many players on their feet as possible.

- Do not chase lost causes. If your opponents are winning the ball, let them have it. Trust your defensive system.

One of the best ways to exert pressure on your opponents is to score and be in the lead as game time passes by. When a team is only one score ahead or behind, the game is not won. You have to build a score in any way possible. The points need to keep mounting so that you go from one score ahead to two and then three. Once you are three scores ahead, you could almost say that the game is yours because the mentality of your opponents will change. They will start to really chase the game and may resort to extreme risk taking, which is to your team's advantage. Building a score can be easily incorporated into your strategy, but it must be part of the whole team training and practice. England won the 2003 Rugby World Cup because all of the team members knew how to work the ball into an area for the drop at goal by Jonny Wilkinson. They had practised this drop goal routine over and over again.

You can improve your mindset when chasing the game if you realise that it takes only 20 seconds to score. Even if you are 4 points down in the last minute of play, you still have time to work the ball from anywhere on the field into a try-scoring position, providing everyone buys into the strategy and works at his role in the team effort. This has to become part of your practice set. At some stage in training, you should work on going from various areas of the pitch, trying to score against a team in full match conditions.

DECISION MAKING AND BALL USAGE

As you play the game, you need to respond to the constantly changing situations that confront you. You will find yourself adapting to the actions and reactions of your own team and the opposition. Because game factors change very quickly, your ability to cope depends largely on your understanding of the situations you and your teammates face. Moreover, you need to understand each other and read the game in the same way to be effective. You will face various challenges in attack, when you have the ball, and in defence, when you don't.

By looking forward and scanning the positioning of the opposition and your teammates, you will better understand the possible options and outcomes. Decide what course of action to take; then act on your decision. All this must happen in an instant. Your ability and understanding of the game will be put to the test. You need two levels of understanding. First, you must understand the game well enough to decide on your action. Then, as a result of your action, you should know your involvement and the outcome to assess how well you understood in the first place.

In Attack

As the ball carrier or a player involved in the attack, you should ask yourself a number of questions: What is my role in the attack? How will we keep possession? How and where will we cross the gain and tackle lines? How will we score? In this way you will become used to the decision-making sequence of *see, understand, decide* and *act*. Figure 13.2 shows the many sequences a player goes through in understanding how to attack effectively. The level of your understanding will determine your decision-making ability.

If your action worked, you can store it in your repertoire of responses and try it again next time. If you misunderstood the situation and your subsequent action failed, think again, change and adapt accordingly. Your decision-making cycle then becomes *see, understand, decide, act* and *know*.

In Defence

In defence your role is simple—deny the opposition space and forward movement and make each contact area a contest whenever possible. By understanding and knowing how your team best defends and by understanding the attacking possibilities that your defensive shapes will allow your opponents, you will know how to prevent a score.

There are three basic tactics to beat a defence, chosen in response to the shape of that defence: pull it wide and penetrate it, pull it close together and outflank it or pull it forward and kick the ball over it.

As in attack, you need to begin by asking a number of simple questions (figure 13.3): What is my role? How will we win back the ball? How will we stop them from crossing the gain and tackle lines? How will we prevent a score?

Most defensive systems do not change from week to week. Teams play up-and-out or out-to-in or a combination of both. Therefore, the decision making that happens on the field of play is largely about making the defensive line as efficient as possible in response to the attack it is up against. For example, you can avoid mismatches with faster attackers by keeping your slower and bigger players away from defending large areas of space. If you have a poor tackler, move him away from the potential attack area. If you are playing a kicking team that will give you counterattack opportunities, you can keep an extra player back with the full back.

By making good decisions and by ensuring that everyone in the defence reacts to them, you can often make the attack revert to a particular tactic,

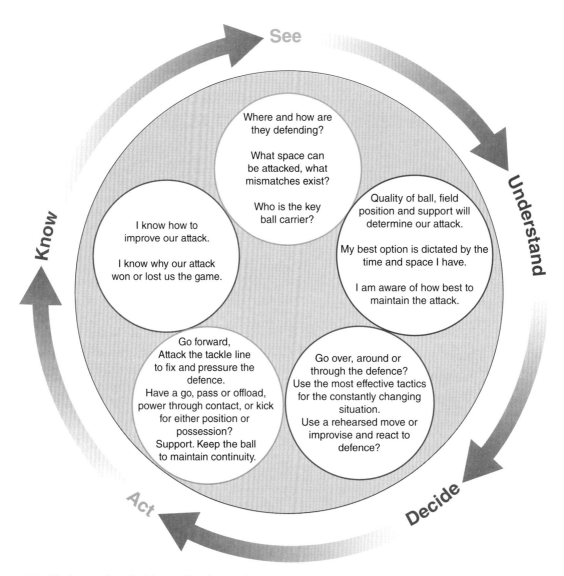

Figure 13.2 Understanding decision making in attack.

which is what you are trying to achieve. Stopping them from crossing gain and tackle lines, contesting every piece of possession, winning most collisions, counterattacking at every opportunity, for example, will put extreme pressure on their main decision makers. This often will lead to your opponents running out of options, which makes the role of your defence that much easier.

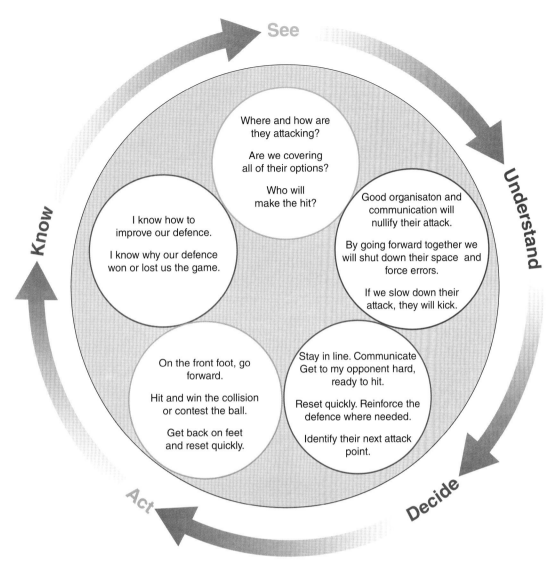

See

Where and how are they attacking?

Are we covering all of their options?

Who will make the hit?

Understand

Good organisaton and communication will nullify their attack.

By going forward together we will shut down their space and force errors.

If we slow down their attack, they will kick.

Know

I know how to improve our defence.

I know why our defence won or lost us the game.

On the front foot, go forward.

Hit and win the collision or contest the ball.

Get back on feet and reset quickly.

Stay in line. Communicate Get to my opponent hard, ready to hit.

Reset quickly. Reinforce the defence where needed.

Identify their next attack point.

Act

Decide

Figure 13.3 Understanding decision making in defence.

TACTICAL DEVELOPMENT

All the support running in a match should have a purpose. Your team needs to devise a plan so that everyone knows what the team may attempt in various positions and areas on the pitch. A full-sized pitch is approximately 100 metres long from goal line to goal line and approximately 70 metres wide from touch line to touch line. Playing the game successfully is like solving a jigsaw puzzle: piece bits together until you finally have the full picture and know how to score a try. Play in one part of the pitch, move the ball, then start again. Develop a pattern in the way you use and create space for each other. A scrum or a line-out brings 16 to 18 players close together, leaving a lot of space on either side for the remaining 12 to 14 players to attack and defend.

To help you create a framework for your team, divide the field into zones and create an overall view of how you might play in each area (figure 13.4).

Do not be stifled by your plan, but be confident about adapting, improvising and playing to what you see in front of you. If you are in your own 22-metre area and have space in front of you, have a go! Some of the best tries are scored from 70 metres or more because the opposition does not expect the ball carrier to run with the ball. If your opponents think they have you under pressure near your own goal line, they often lose the intensity of their concentration for a moment, relaxing and leaving gaps in the defence. Look to maximise your strengths and exploit the opposition's weaknesses, which may mean adapting your plan before and during the game. If you fight pressure with pressure, the opposition will never be able to drop its guard and its weaknesses eventually will become apparent.

To move the ball forward and score, you need to think and act much more quickly than the opposition. All your teammates need to communicate with each other at stoppages and as the game is in motion to ensure that you get more players near the ball, keep it and remain in control of the game.

In addition to a plan of action for various zones up the length of the pitch, it's a good idea to have a similar understanding of what may happen in channels going up the pitch. With a map of the field like the one in figure 13.5, you can communicate precisely where you intend to move the ball and get an idea of who can support the ball and where most of your players can support the ball. Create a grid reference system by combining the zones of figure 13.4 with the channels of figure 13.5. After winning the ball at a line-out in zone 3, channel A, you could indicate that you wish to move the ball by passing quickly by hand to zone 2, channel D.

If you have a scrum in zone 2, channel D, and decide to move the ball down the blind or narrow side in this 17- to 18-metre-wide channel, you can quickly have 12 players in support of the ball: the back row, right winger, scrum half, fly half, inside centre and front five. The defence will not have that number because you have the element of surprise. If you quickly cross the tackle line, your opponents will struggle to reset on their side of the offside line.

If you win the ball in channel A and move it to channel B, you could get eight support players involved quickly to keep the ball moving forward. If you aim to attack in channel C, six support players would be readily available, and in channel D you could probably get four players in good support positions. But how will the opposition react? If all your players know what is likely to happen, hopefully they will arrive first, act quickly, keep the defence guessing and target any opposition weakness.

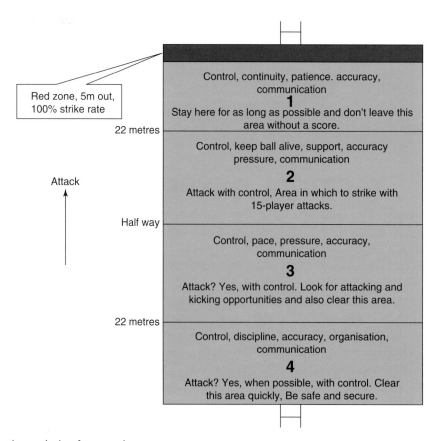

Figure 13.4 Creating a playing framework.

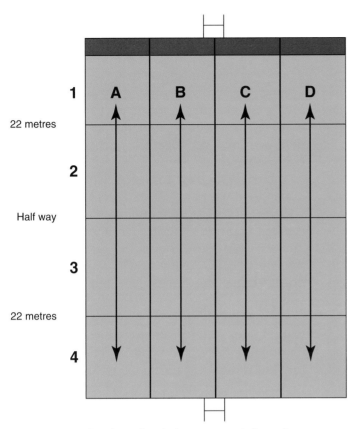

Figure 13.5 Identifying the playing zones and channels.

No matter how your team plays, it is essential to have good communication from all players. Before you go down in a scrum or arrive at a line-out, everyone should know what you intend to do with the ball. For example, you may move the ball quickly from channel A to channel B, where your centre and flanker intend to link up and recycle and reuse the ball. It might be that you can then attack the blind side you created back in channel A, having moved the defence across into channel B with your first play. This might allow some of your fast and agile backs to run against their rather slower-moving forwards.

If you are attacking in the red zone, especially if you have a scrum, then you must score. Because the opposition defensive line is on the goal line, the attackers have a vast advantage over the defenders. The defence will try to rush out as fast as possible to smash into any attacker, so be prepared for it. Here a little diagonal chip or grubber is very effective, as is a pick-up from number 8 and a drive for the line followed by the bigger forwards running onto early ball, a ball delivered while the team is still going forward.

If you are the defence, your role is to cover all options: who will be there for the kick, how you will stop the drive, whether you will simply go hard on a man-to-man defence and hit any ball carrier hard or use the out-to-in defence. These decisions are made primarily on the training ground but are refined as the game unfolds.

To help in the early stages of development, you may need to orchestrate the attacking options around the field in the form of moves that you plan and rehearse in training. These are just starting points for your attacking sequence, and you should know what will happen next if the move is stopped or slowed by the defence. An overview of how the defence might react and an understanding of the implications of that for a follow-up attack are essential for you to achieve effective attacking patterns. The predictability of some teams will allow you and your coaches to plan particular moves to play against their defensive patterns. You can practise these moves by having the rest of your squad act as your forthcoming opponents. The essential requirement is to develop the follow-up attack so that your opponents are never able to regather their composure or reset their defence.

As your team develops this understanding, you will be better able to put strategies and tactics together to break down the defence. Once you have developed this attacking framework, your team will have a comprehensive understanding of the game and will be able to play confidently.

SUCCESS SUMMARY OF STRATEGIES AND TACTICS

By understanding the game and practising your techniques, you will become a skilful and intelligent performer who can fit easily into any pattern and also deal with unpredictable situations during a game.

In your attempts to go forward up the pitch, you will need to overcome the challenge of having to play a lateral game, in which you pass the ball sideways or backwards in order to go forward. Some of the starting points of the game are dictated and predictable, such as scrums, line-outs and restarts. Your challenge is to be unpredictable and spontaneous and to understand what best to do between these set pieces.

At each point during the game, you and your teammates will make choices about what to do next. At set pieces such as scrums, you will be aware of the various tactical possibilities and make a choice before the action starts and then during the action. Each new decision is in the hands of the player with the ball, and you must react to the new decision and change your actions accordingly. Scan and assess the possibilities around you and recognise gaps and spaces to attack. For example, if the defence in front of you is spread, then you could penetrate it. When the defence is bunched together, you could move the ball wide and outflank it.

You will not go forward effectively unless you understand gain and tackle line principles. You will not have support unless the players without the ball appreciate running in lines of support. You will not achieve continuity until you manage the contact area well. You will not put pressure on the opposition unless you put pressure on yourself.

Maybe one day, like William Webb Ellis, you will do something instinctive in the game that no one else has done before and take the game forward with a new technique or idea for others to attempt to imitate and understand. There is always something new to understand and learn. Keep enjoying your rugby and 'Think even when you blink'.

Glossary

advantage—When the nonoffending team, following an infringement, takes the opportunity to develop play and gains some of its opponent's territory (a tactical advantage) or scores.

agility—The ability to move quickly from one position to another—for example, moving from the ground to your feet or nimbly changing your direction of running.

attack—The action of the team in possession of the ball that is trying to score.

back five—Players who wear numbers 11 to 15. They are five of the players generally known as the backs (together with the scrum half and fly half).

back row—Players who normally wear numbers 6 to 8 (the two flankers and number 8) whose role is to destroy the opposition's attacks and create opportunities in attack for their own team.

back three—Players who normally wear numbers 11, 14 and 15 and whose role is to defend against kicks, initiate any possible counterattacks and act as strike runners in support of the midfield attack.

backs (also known as three-quarters)—The players who normally wear numbers 9 to 15 and play outside the scrummage and line-out.

ball carrier—The person carrying the ball.

bind—To wrap arms around other players and grip tightly. Players normally bind in scrummages, rucks, mauls and line-outs.

blind side—The narrow side of the field between the touch line and the set piece, ruck or maul; usually the area with the fewest defenders.

body composition—The relative proportions of muscle, bone, fat and other vital parts in the body.

box kick—A punt, normally by either the scrum half or fly half, that flies high over and beyond a scrummage or line-out for teammates to chase.

breakdown—The moment when a sequence of activity (passing, running in attack, etc.) stops as a result of the actions of the defence or the inability of the attack to maintain continuity.

centre—The player who makes space for the winger.

channel—A narrow practice area or a relatively narrow strip of pitch running up and down the playing field.

chip kick—A kick that floats just over and behind a close opponent for either the kicker or a teammate to catch.

contact area—The generic name for points at which tackles, attempted tackles, rucks and mauls occur.

continuity—Maintaining possession through a series of phases of play.

conversion—A kick at goal after a try has been scored.

dead ball—A ball becomes dead when the referee blows the whistle to indicate a stoppage of play or when an attempt to convert a try is unsuccessful.

defence—The actions of the team without the ball, which is trying to prevent the opposition from scoring.

drift defence—The action of defenders who, having gone forward to tackle their opposite player, then move across after the ball has been passed to assist with or make a tackle on the next player.

drive—To bind together and push opponents back; to run powerfully in a close group towards the opponents' goal line. An action normally associated with forwards.

drop goal—A drop kick that crosses over the crossbar and between the goalposts to score 3 points.

drop kick—A kick in which the kicker drops the ball point first and kicks it as it makes contact with the ground.

drop-out—A drop kick awarded to the defending team that may be taken anywhere along or behind the 22-metre line once the ball has been made dead by the defence in the in-goal area.

dummy pass—A way of fooling the defence by setting up to pass, going through the passing movement but retaining the ball.

fair catch (mark)—A defender makes a fair catch (mark) when, in the 22-metre or in-goal area, he cleanly catches the ball directly from an opponent's kick (other than kick-off) and at the same time calls 'Mark!' A fair catch may be made even though the ball on its way touches a goalpost or crossbar.

field of play—The area between the goal lines and touch lines. The lines are not part of the field of play. See also *playing area*.

first 5/8th—The Southern Hemisphere name for the fly half.

flanker—The player who wears number 6 or 7 and acts as a link and continuity player between the backs and forwards in attack and defence.

flexibility—Increased joint mobility that helps to prevent injury. Flexibility is improved by stretching the muscles and connective tissue around a joint.

fly half—A key decision maker in the team who wears number 10. This player is the key tactician who receives possession from the forwards via the scrum half.

forward pass—A pass that travels towards the opponents' goal line and results in a scrummage or counterattacking opportunity for the opponents.

forwards—The players who normally wear numbers 1 to 8 and take part in scrummages and line-outs.

foul play—Any action by a player that is contrary to the letter of the Laws and spirit of the game, including obstruction, unfair play, misconduct, dangerous play, unsporting behaviour, retaliation and repeated infringements.

free kick—A kick awarded for a fair catch or to the non-offending team as stated in the Laws of the game. A goal may not be scored from the free kick. Also, a penalty awarded for technical infringements at scrum and line-out.

front five—Players who wear numbers 1 to 5 and occupy the front row and the middle two positions of the second row in the scrummage.

front row—Players who wear the numbers 1, 2 or 3 and make direct contact with the opposition at each scrummage.

full back—The player who normally wears number 15, is usually the last line of defence and is used as a penetrative runner in attack.

gain line—An imaginary line between the two teams designating the line that the attacking players would need to reach for the ball to be ahead of the forwards.

grab tackle—The action of using two hands to grab the ball carrier by the shirt to simulate a full tackle; normally used in practice or during drills.

grubber kick—A kick that is deliberately struck so that it rolls along the ground.

gut pass—A pass that does not leave the passer's hands until the ball is pushed up and into the receiver's midriff; normally used by forwards in close-contact situations.

half backs—The collective name for the scrum half and fly half.

head guard—A padded hat worn as protection during a match or training session.

hooker—The player who normally wears number 2, whose roles usually include throwing the ball into the line-out and hooking the ball back in the scrummages.

ice bath—A bath filled with ice and water that players sit in for a short period of time following vigorous exercise, to aid recovery.

impact bench—The players on the substitutes' bench who might be able to change the nature of the attack or defence to the team's advantage more so than those players on the field.

infield—The position away from the touch line and towards the centre of the field.

infringement—An action that violates the Laws of the game.

in-goal—The area between the goal line and the dead-ball line and between the touch-in-goal lines. It includes the goal line but not the others.

inside—The direction or place from which the ball has just been passed away from the forwards.

inside centre—The centre playing next to the fly half; player usually wears the number 12.

inside pass—A pass back in the direction it has just come from.

inside shoulder—The shoulder nearer to the ball as it is coming along the line.

International Rugby Board (IRB)—The association of national Rugby Football Unions, whose role is to promote, foster and extend the game and to alter and develop the Laws of the game.

kick—A kick is made by striking the ball with any part of the foot (except the heel) or leg from toe to knee, including the knee.

kick-off—A drop kick taken at or from behind the centre of the half-way line to start the half and by the defending team after the opposing side has scored.

knock-on (throw forward)—A knock-on occurs when the ball travels in the direction of the opponents' dead-ball line after a player loses possession of it; a player strikes or propels it with the hand or arm; or it strikes a player's hand or arm and touches the ground or another player before it is recovered by the player.

lay-off pass—A soft pass into the space created by the ball carrier.

line of touch—The imaginary line at right angles to the touch line at the place where the ball is thrown in from touch.

line-out—A formation of at least two players from each team lined up in single lines, parallel to the line of touch (i.e., at right angles to the touch line) in readiness for the ball to be thrown in between them after the ball has gone into touch.

lock—A player who usually wears number 4 or 5, plays in the middle row of the scrummage and jumps for the ball in the line-out and in kick-off situations.

loop pass—A pass that puts the receiver into a space in the defence. The receiver has normally just passed the ball and run around and behind the ball carrier to receive the return loop pass.

loose forwards (loosies)—A Southern Hemisphere name for the back row.

loose head prop—The player who wears number 1, packs on the left-hand side of the front row and supports the jumper in the jump-and-catch sequence in the line-out and at kick-offs.

mark—The place where a free kick or penalty is awarded. See also *fair catch (mark)*.

maul—A formation, which can take place only in the field of play, of one or more players from each team on their feet and in physical contact closing around the player who is in possession of the ball.

middle five—The half backs and back-row forwards.

midfield—The fly half and two centres, or the middle of the playing field.

miss pass—A lateral pass that deliberately misses one or more support players to reach a player more appropriately positioned to make best use of the ball.

no side—The end of the match.

number 8—The player who wears number 8, normally packs down in the third row of the scrum and is usually the extra jumper at the rear of the line-out.

offload—A pass made immediately after contact or in contact with an opponent or opponents; a pass often made with one hand that is used to keep the pace of the game high or to put a support runner through the defensive line at that point of contact.

offside—In general play, when a player is in front of the ball after it has last been played by another player of the same team; from a set piece or ruck or maul, when a player remains or advances in front of the offside line or the hindmost feet; and at line-out if a player advances within 10 metres of the line of touch before the line-out is ended.

onside—Means a player is in the game and not liable to penalty for offside.

out of play—When the ball has gone into touch or touch-in-goal or has touched or crossed the dead-ball line.

out-to-in defence—The movement of a defence as it first moves forward as the opponents win the ball and then laterally inwards as the ball is passed, trying to arrive at the same time as the ball at some point in the attacking line.

outside centre—The centre who normally wears number 13 and always plays next to the winger on either side of the field.

overlap—An attacking sequence that normally results in attackers outnumbering the defenders and leads to an attack around the defence.

pass—The movement of the ball from one player's hands to another's.

peel—The act of collecting the ball from the back of a line-out and driving around the end towards the midfield; normally done by the forwards.

penalty kick—A kick awarded to the nonoffending team as stated in the Laws of the game. A player may take a kick at goal from a penalty kick.

pitch—Another term used to describe the playing area or playing field.

place kick—Kicking the ball from the ground after it has been placed there for that purpose.

playing area—The field of play and the in-goal areas. The lines are not part of the playing area. (See figure 1 in *The Sport of Rugby*, page xv)

pop pass—A soft, floated pass that flies slightly upwards into space in front of the receiver.

possession—When a team or player has the ball under control.

principles of play—The general strategy of how to play the game: going forward, supporting, maintaining continuity and exerting pressure.

punt—A kick in which the player deliberately drops the ball and strikes it before it touches the ground.

put-in—The act of the scrum half putting the ball into the scrummage conforming to the Laws of the game.

receiver—The next player to catch the ball.

recycle—Maintain and use possession after making contact with the opposition.

referee—The official who keeps the time and score and applies the Laws during a match.

replacement—A player who takes the field as a temporary substitute for another player, usually due to a blood injury for which the replaced player needs to receive medical attention.

roll—Planting the foot firmly at the point of contact and then pivoting around this point to spin out of the contact area.

ruck—A formation, which can take place only in the field of play, of one or more players from each team on their feet and in physical contact closing around the ball on the ground among them.

running line—The direction a player runs in either attack or defence.

screen pass—A pass that uses the passer's body as a screen to prevent the defence from seeing the pass being made; normally used by forwards in contact situations; very similar to the gut pass.

scrum half—The player who wears number 9 and acts as the link between the forwards and backs.

scrummage (scrum)—A formation, which can take place only in the field of play, of eight players from each team closing up in readiness to allow the ball to be put on the ground among them. It is used to restart the game after an infringement.

second 5/8th—The Southern Hemisphere name for the inside centre.

second row—Players who wear numbers 4, 5, 6 and 7 and form the second line of players in the scrummage behind the front row.

set piece—A general term used to describe a scrum or line-out formation.

sidestep—A sudden change of forward direction by the ball carrier to run past a defender.

sin bin—A small area at the side of the field of play in which a player serves a 10-minute suspension from the match. Any player receiving a yellow card from the referee serves this temporary suspension.

spin pass—A pass that spirals as it flies; normally used by scrum halves but may also be used by other players, for speed, distance and accuracy.

sprigs—The Southern Hemisphere name for studs.

strategy—The playing plan a team adopts to make best use of its strengths and the opposition's weaknesses.

strike runners—Players who run into space and attempt to score.

studs—Alloy or rubber attachments to the soles of boots to assist grip. Studs must conform to the regulations contained in the Laws of the game.

substitute—A player who takes the place of another player either for tactical reasons or because of an injury that prevents the replaced player from continuing on the field.

sweeper—The player behind the first or second line of defence who runs across the pitch in line with the ball and whose role is to tackle any penetrating ball carrier.

swerve—A running line that takes the ball carrier towards a defender and then arcs quickly away from an attempted tackle.

switch pass—A pass that hides the ball from the opposition and changes the direction of the attack.

tackle—When a player carrying the ball in the field of play is held by one or more opponents so that, while held, the player is brought to the ground or the ball comes into contact with the ground.

tackle line—An imaginary line between the two teams drawn along the points at which the attack and defence would meet if they all ran towards each other.

tackle suit—A padded garment used in practice to help protect the player during contact training.

tactics—The way a team plays during a match taking into account the influence of the weather, opponents, the referee and other factors that might influence play.

tag rugby—A noncontact form of rugby that replaces the tackle with the removal of a ribbon from the ball carrier.

three-quarter line—The formation and alignment of the backs.

three-quarters—See *backs*.

throw forward—See *knock-on (throw forward)*.

throw-in—Throwing the ball into the line-out from touch.

tight-head prop—The player who wears number 3, packs on the right-hand side of the front row and supports the jumper in the jump-and-catch sequence in the line-out and at kick-offs.

touch—The state of the ball when, while not being carried by a player, it touches a touch line or the ground, a person or an object on or beyond the touch line, or when a player who is carrying it touches a touch line or the ground beyond it. At this point, the ball is out of play.

touch-in-goal line—The extension of the touch line from a corner flag to the dead-ball line.

touch line—The line that defines the side of the field of play and runs the length of the field from corner flag to corner flag.

touch rugby—A noncontact form of rugby that replaces the tackle with a two-handed touch.

try (touchdown)—The grounding of the ball in the defending team's in-goal area by a player of the opposing team who is holding the ball in hands or arms, who is exerting downward pressure on the ball with hands or arms while it is on the ground, or who falls on the ball so that it is anywhere under the front of the body between the waist and neck, inclusive.

union—The controlling body under whose jurisdiction the match is played.

up-and-in defence—The movement of a defence as it first moves up (forward) as the opponents win the ball and then in (laterally) as the ball is passed, trying to arrive at the same time as the ball at some point in the attacking line; also known as out-to-in defence.

up-and-out defence—The movement of a defence as it first moves up (forward) as the opponents win the ball and then out (laterally) as the ball is passed.

winger—The player who normally wears either number 11 (left wing) or number 14 (right wing), is normally on the end of the three-quarter line and is usually one of the fastest players on the team.

wipers kick—A kick that travels diagonally from one side of the playing field to the other, crossing over and behind the opponents' defence to land behind the far winger and roll towards the corner.

zone defence—A form of defence in which a player defends an area on the field and tackles any ball carrier who runs into that space.

About the Authors

Tony Biscombe was already a very experienced rugby teacher and coach of 25 years when he joined the Rugby Football Union (RFU) as a development officer for the North of England in 1989. In this role, he travelled extensively, taking on a variety of coaching assignments for the RFU.

In 1997 he was recruited by Sir Clive Woodward to the England Management Team as the technical support manager, where he provided video analysis and statistical support to the coaches and players on the England squad. In 2005 he had the same role with the British and Irish Lions in New Zealand.

His career with England spanned 10 years, 123 Internationals and 3 Rugby World Cups. In 2003 he was part of the back-room staff of the England team that won the Rugby World Cup in Australia. The defeat by South Africa in the Cup final of 2007 was his last game, and he retired from his role on December 31 of the same year. He lives in Leeds with his wife, Larraine, and close to his grown-up children, James and Zoe, and granddaughter Robyn.

Peter Drewett is a former director of rugby and head coach for the Exeter Chiefs. He is an RFU senior coach and was the England U21 manager, winning the Six Nations Grand Slam in 2004 and 2006. He has played and coached rugby at various club, county, divisional and international levels.

With Tony Biscombe, Drewett developed the *Supercoach* CD-ROM, a rugby teaching and coaching aid and the first software package of its kind. The product has been praised for its content and design. He also developed the Tag Rugby resources and introduced the non-contact version of rugby in the early 1990s with Nick Leonard.

Peter was previously an exercise and sport science lecturer at the University of Exeter. He lives in Sidmouth, England, with his partner Jenny and has four children, Tom, Olly, Megan and Richie. In his spare time he enjoys exercising to stay fit and healthy.

STEPS TO SUCCESS SPORTS SERIES

The *Steps to Success Sports Series* is the most extensively researched and carefully developed set of books ever published for teaching and learning sports skills.

Each of the books offers a complete progression of skills, concepts and strategies that are carefully sequenced to optimize learning for students, teaching for sport-specific instructors and instructional program design techniques for future teachers.

The *Steps to Success Sports Series* includes:

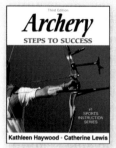
Archery — Third Edition — STEPS TO SUCCESS
Kathleen Haywood • Catherine Lewis

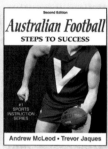
Australian Football — Second Edition — STEPS TO SUCCESS
Andrew McLeod • Trevor Jaques

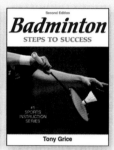
Badminton — Second Edition — STEPS TO SUCCESS
Tony Grice

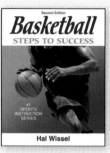
Basketball — Second Edition — STEPS TO SUCCESS
Hal Wissel

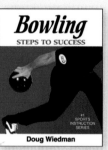
Bowling — STEPS TO SUCCESS
Doug Wiedman

FENCING — Steps to Success
ELAINE CHERIS

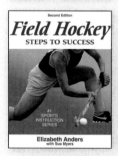
Field Hockey — Second Edition — STEPS TO SUCCESS
Elizabeth Anders with Sue Myers

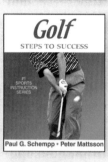
Golf — STEPS TO SUCCESS
Paul G. Schempp • Peter Mattsson

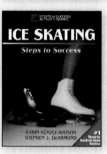
ICE SKATING — Steps to Success
KARIN KÜNZLE-WATSON • STEPHEN J. DeARMOND

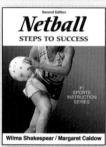
Netball — Second Edition — STEPS TO SUCCESS
Wilma Shakespear / Margaret Caldow

Racquetball — STEPS TO SUCCESS
Dennis Fisher

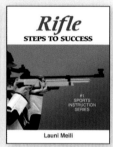
Rifle — STEPS TO SUCCESS
Launi Meili

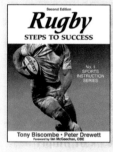
Rugby — Second Edition — STEPS TO SUCCESS
Tony Biscombe • Peter Drewett — Foreword by Ian McGeechan, OBE

Self-Defense — STEPS TO SURVIVAL
Katy Mattingly

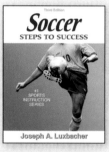
Soccer — Third Edition — STEPS TO SUCCESS
Joseph A. Luxbacher

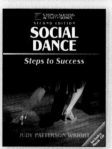
SOCIAL DANCE — SECOND EDITION — Steps to Success
JUDY PATTERSON WRIGHT

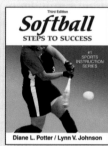
Softball — Third Edition — STEPS TO SUCCESS
Diane L. Potter / Lynn V. Johnson

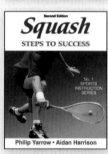
Squash — Second Edition — STEPS TO SUCCESS
Philip Yarrow • Aidan Harrison

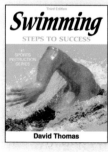
Swimming — Third Edition — STEPS TO SUCCESS
David Thomas

Table Tennis — STEPS TO SUCCESS
Richard McAfee

TEAM HANDBALL — Steps to Success
REITA E. CLANTON • MARY PHYL DWIGHT

Tennis — Third Edition — STEPS TO SUCCESS
Jim Brown

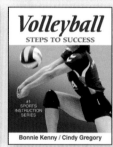
Volleyball — STEPS TO SUCCESS
Bonnie Kenny / Cindy Gregory

Weight Training — Third Edition — STEPS TO SUCCESS
Thomas R. Baechle • Roger W. Earle

To place your order, U.S. customers call
TOLL FREE 1-800-747-4457
In Canada call 1-800-465-7301
In Australia call 08 8372 0999
In Europe call +44 (0) 113 255 5665
In New Zealand call 0800 222 062
or visit **www.HumanKinetics.com**

HUMAN KINETICS
The Premier Publisher for Sports & Fitness
P.O. Box 5076, Champaign, IL 61825-5076